AF378769

Growing Public

Social Spending and Economic Growth
Since the Eighteenth Century

Growing Public examines the question of whether social policies that redistribute income impose constraints on economic growth. Taxes and transfers have been debated for centuries, but only now can we get a clear view of the whole evolution of social spending. What kept prospering nations from using taxes for social programs until the end of the nineteenth century? Why did taxes and spending then grow so much, and what are the prospects for social spending in this century? Why did North America become a leader in public education in some ways and not others? Lindert finds answers in the economic history and logic of political voice, population aging, and income growth. Contrary to traditional beliefs, the net national costs of government social programs are virtually zero. This book not only shows that no Darwinian mechanism has punished the welfare states, but uses history to explain why this surprising result makes sense. Contrary to the intuition of many economists and the ideology of many politicians, social spending has contributed to, rather than inhibited, economic growth.

Peter H. Lindert is a Distinguished Professor of Economics at the University of California, Davis, and a Research Associate of the National Bureau of Economic Research. His writings have touched on a wide range of economic and historical topics relating to Europe, the United States, China, Indonesia, and the global economy. His textbooks in international economics have been translated into eight other languages.

Growing Public

Social Spending and Economic Growth Since the Eighteenth Century

Volume 2
Further Evidence

PETER H. LINDERT

University of California, Davis

CAMBRIDGE
UNIVERSITY PRESS

CAMBRIDGE UNIVERSITY PRESS
Cambridge, New York, Melbourne, Madrid, Cape Town, Singapore, São Paulo

Cambridge University Press
32 Avenue of the Americas, New York, NY 10013-2473, USA

www.cambridge.org
Information on this title: www.cambridge.org/9780521821759

© Peter H. Lindert 2004

This publication is in copyright. Subject to statutory exception
and to the provisions of relevant collective licensing agreements,
no reproduction of any part may take place without
the written permission of Cambridge University Press.

First published 2004
Reprinted 2005, 2007

Printed in the United States of America

A catalog record for this publication is available from the British Library.

Library of Congress Cataloging in Publication Data

Lindert, Peter H.
Growing public : social spending and economic growth since the eighteenth century /
Peter H. Lindert.
p. cm.
Includes bibliographical references and index.
ISBN 0-521-82175-4
1. Government spending policy – History – Case studies.   2. Income distribution – History –
Case studies.   3. Transfer payments – History – Case studies.   4. Welfare economics –
History – Case studies.   I. Title.
HJ2005.L565   2004
339.5′22 – dc22   2003061672

ISBN   978-0-521-82175-9 hardback

Cambridge University Press has no responsibility for
the persistence or accuracy of URLs for external or
third-party Internet Web sites referred to in this publication
and does not guarantee that any content on such
Web sites is, or will remain, accurate or appropriate.

Contents

APPENDICES

Preface to Volume 2

ix

This volume covers most of the range of ideas and issues in the two-volume set, but readers will also want to consult Volume 1, which is written for a wide nonspecialist audience. Here is a condensed outline of the contents to Volume 1:

PART ONE: OVERVIEW

1. Patterns and Puzzles

2. Findings

PART TWO: THE RISE OF SOCIAL SPENDING

3. Poor Relief before 1880

4. Interpreting the Puzzles of Early Poor Relief

5. The Rise of Mass Public Schooling before 1914

6. Public Schooling in the Twentieth Century: What Happened to U.S. Leadership?

7. Explaining the Rise of Social Transfers since 1880

PART THREE: PROSPECTS FOR SOCIAL TRANSFERS

PART FOUR: WHAT EFFECTS ON ECONOMIC GROWTH?

Bibliography for Volume 1

For readers wishing to dig deeper into the evidence of these two volumes, the main underlying data sets are available online at either (http://www.cup.org/ 0521821754) or the author's home page (http://www.econ.ucdavis.edu/ faculty/fzlinder).

Permissions for Both Volumes

Portions of Chapters 7 (Volume 1) and 16 (Volume 2) first appeared, in different form, in Peter H. Lindert, "The Rise of Social Spending, 1880– 1930." *Explorations in Economic History* 31, 1 (January 1994): 1–37.

Portions of Chapters 7 (Volume 1) and 17 (Volume 2) first appeared, in different form, in Peter H. Lindert, "What Limits Social Spending?" *Explorations in Economic History* 33, 1 (January 1996): 1–34.

A portion of Chapter 13 of Volume 2 first appeared, in different form, in Lorenzo Kristov, Peter Lindert, and Robert McClelland, "Pressure Groups and Redistribution." *Journal of Public Economics* 48, 2 (June 1992): 135– 163.

PART FIVE

THE UNDERLYING FRAMEWORK

13

A Minimal Theory of Social Transfers

"Well, OK, that may work in the real world, but does it work in theory?"

— Attributed to an economist

To explain both the causes and the consequences of social spending, it helps to have a coherent framework, one that reveals the logical links between the host of points being made. Without a unifying theoretical approach, the numerous conclusions this book has reached may seem ad hoc and eclectic. Readers will be better served, and perhaps better persuaded, if the ideas are all part of a single logic, with a minimum of qualifications. Fortunately a unifying framework does fit the book's conclusions, and this chapter sketches it.

The approach offered here violates a particular scientific procedural code. According to one orthodox code, one is supposed to get a set of theoretical assumptions and work out their predictions, before testing the predictions empirically. This book travels the path in reverse. Induction comes first, and logical deduction comes last. I am definitely guilty of reverse engineering from the historical facts back to a set of model predictions and only then to the assumptions of the model. This chapter tries to optimize its theoretical design in a particular way, minimizing some combination of the falsehood and the complexity of the assumptions that deliver predictions that fit the facts. The quest, then, is for the simplest plausible set of assumptions that predict most of the book's main empirical conclusions.

FROM THE BOTTOM UP

To model the political process that taxes some groups and transfers to others, one must make a basic initial choice of between two modeling strategies. One strategy builds a model in which private pressure groups battle against each other by throwing resources into the political process. This approach

3

proceeds from the bottom up, replacing the optimizing incumbents and candidates at the top with a political marketplace that mechanically awards the fruits to the pressure group that lobbied more effectively from below. An example is the median-voter approach, where the game is played at ground level and the political process is no more than a scoreboard. The other choice builds from the top down, carefully modeling the self-interest of one or a few at the political summit. Such top-down modeling replaces self-interested pressure groups at the bottom with mechanical reaction functions that deliver votes, money, and power to those at the top in response to their carefully modeled behavior.

The case against a bottom-up theory and in favor of a top-down theory has been well put by Mancur Olson:[1]

the metaphor of voluntary and mutually advantageous bargains and the transactions costs that limit them [as in the Becker pressure-group model] is not enough by itself and is not even the natural starting point for a theory of government and politics.

To understand governments and the good and bad things they do – and the horrible anarchies that emerge in their absence – there can be no substitute for a theory of power . . . . We must understand not only the gains from voluntary exchange but also the logic of coercion and force.

The two approaches have their respective advantages. The top-down approach better models autocracies, as in the more recent works of Mancur Olson. It is also preferable for explaining particular political outcomes that hinged on small-group bargaining among agents at the top, with a host of issues bundled together. The bottom-up approach better fits more competitive political settings driven by swings in the public mood or in the self-interest of pressure groups, as in Mancur Olson's earlier work and in Gary Becker's treatment of redistributive fights with deadweight cost consequences.[2]

The bottom-up approach tends to have more appeal for anyone seeking to chart how historic changes in broad groups' self-interests affect taxes and social spending. The appeal is especially strong for a study of democracies in the Organization for Economic Cooperation and Development (OECD). Accordingly, I follow the bottom-up approach in the belief that it offers more useful predictions with less stringent assumptions. The optimizing behavior of autocrats, bureaucrats, and other incumbents can still be incorporated as long as they are just another set of pressure groups in a highly competitive political marketplace.

Choosing to dwell on pressure-group competition has its costs, of course. The greater the unilateral power of incumbents, the less appropriate is the framework chosen here. The model will have nothing to say about social spending in socialist dictatorships. It will also ignore many electoral and governmental institutions, such as the difference between presidential versus parliamentary systems. It even ignores political parties. At its worst, the pressure group model pretends that it does not matter who is in office, since incumbents are modeled as precariously perching on a political balance beam held in place by the balance of pressure group powers. I am not entirely comfortable with the implication that it does not matter to taxes and transfers whether George W. Bush or Albert Gore won the 2000 presidential election. Yet one has to simplify to some extent, and all predictions have an error term.

THE BASIC MODEL OF REDISTRIBUTIVE FIGHTS

The Becker model of pressure-group competition is impressively frugal. Becker managed to reach plausible and testable conclusions about economic growth and government budgets just by assuming competition among self-interested groups. It can be extended to generate a richer harvest of predictions that fit the facts by thinking further about group concerns and, in the sections to follow, about the distribution of political voice.[3]

Assume that a government transfers income between two groups of economic agents, with possible side costs, in response to political pressure groups. The ultimate size of the transfer depends on the pressures exerted by the competing pressure groups. The pressures can take various forms – voting to remove or reelect incumbents, campaign contributions, violent revolt, or bribes. The key attributes of the pressure are that it costs resources and will affect the redistribution.

Let $G > 0$ be the real value of a proposed transfer from N_T taxpayers, the T group, to N_S subsidized individuals, the S group. To simplify, assume that the transfers are equally shared within each group, so that everyone in S receives G/N_S and everyone in T pays G/N_T. In addition to the direct effects, deadweight costs or benefits can alter how the effects of the transfer are distributed between the two groups. Let us focus on the case of net deadweight costs, D_S and D_T, rather than net benefits. Each member of the subsidized group must bear costs $D_S(G)/N$ as a subtraction from its gain of G/N_S, and each member of the taxed group must bear the combined cost $(G + D_T)/N_T$. The deadweight costs are increasing and accelerating functions of the amounts transferred: $D'_S(G)$, $D'_T(G) > 0$, and also $D''_S(G)$, $D''_T(G) > 0$.

The two pressure groups that fight over the transfer are not necessarily the same as the subsidized and taxed groups. In political life it is rarely the case that all people simply "vote their pocketbooks," as Becker implied. Introducing this generalizing distinction into the simpler Becker model buys a lot. We can directly model group sympathies, and we can pave the way for predictions about the whole range of cases in which the taxed or subsidized group has no political voice. There are nine possible groups, as designated by Table 13.1. Anticipating the direct and deadweight effects of a proposed tax and transfer, agents form two opposing pressure groups: the F group, of size N_F, in favor of the proposal, and the A group, of size N_A, against it. The familiar vote-your-pocketbook models would admit only groups SF and TA. We admit all nine groups, however, so that each group can involve

TABLE 13.1. *Nine Population Groups Defined by Affected-Group Status and Political Pressure-Group Membership*

| | Affected-Group Status | | |
Political Camp	To be Subsidized (S)	Neither Taxed Nor Subsidized (U)	To be Taxed (T)
Actively in favor (F)	group SF	group UF	group TF
Inactive (I)	group SI	group UI	group TI
Actively against (A)	group SA	group UA	group TA

a mix of persons to be subsidized, taxed, or unaffected, even though we will certainly imagine a correlation between the F and S group memberships and between the A's and the T's. The two opposing groups apply pressures on the government, pressures that we imagine to be increasing functions of the time and money they spend on the political fight. Let E_F and E_A be their expenditures of resources in the struggle. The size of the redistribution $G = G(E_F, E_A)$ responds to the opposing pressures with diminishing returns to each side's pressure, so that $\partial G/\partial E_F = G_F > 0$, $\partial^2 G/\partial E_F^2 = G_{FF} < 0$, $G_A < 0$, and $G_{AA} > 0$. The groups' aggregate expenditures (E_F, E_A) determine the value of the transfer G, which in turn determines the values of D_S and D_T, and the net effects on the S and T group members.

Each individual within an active group cares about her own consumption Y_i and also about the per capita gain or loss to individuals in the affected S and T groups. Hence the ith individual's utility function U_i incorporates all three elements:

$$U_i = a_i(Y_i)Y_i + b_i[G - D_S(G)]/N_S + c_i[-G - D_T(G)]/N_T, \qquad (1)$$

where a_i, b_i, and c_i are the caring coefficients. They express, respectively, her rate of caring about her own consumption, the effects of the transfers on the average member of the subsidized group, and the effects on the average taxpayer.

Agent i maximizes U_i with respect to her individual expenditures e_{iF} and e_{iA}, subject to the constraint that prefisc income $W_i \geq Y_i + e_{iF} + e_{iA}$, and given the known expenditure functions of the opposing camp. A theorem by Peter Ordeshook ensures the existence of a Nash equilibrium in pure strategies, since this N-person noncooperative game meets the criteria for a concave game in normal form.[4] For the moment we set aside free-riding within the individual's own camp, though this later becomes a factor tilting the predictions toward stronger dependence of lobbying success on affected-group size.

The marginal benefits of a dollar or hour spent on lobbying equal the amount of individual consumption given up. That is, the first-order optimization conditions imply these conditions for an interior solution:

$$[b_i (1 - D'_S)/N_S - c_i (1 + D'_T)/N_T] \times G_F = a_i \qquad (2a)$$

for one who fights in favor of the transfer, and

$$[c_i (1 + D'_T)/N_T - b_i (1 - D'_S)/N_S] \times G_A = a_i \qquad (2b)$$

for one who fights against it.[5]

With large numbers of participants, as in a typical national fight over taxes and transfers, the individual behavior just sketched aggregates up to overall behavior with the same parameters and similar comparative statics. The e_{iF}s and e_{iA}s implied by the interior solutions in Equations (2a) and (2b) become aggregate E_{iF}s and E_{iA}s. The functional forms would not carry through, but under plausible assumptions the partial derivatives keep the same signs.[6]

Several key implications of the model are already implicit in the individual behavior, before aggregating to form total lobbying expenditures for the two sides of the fight. The individual's first-order conditions for her commitment to one or the other group shape the success of that group and the size of the transfer. Note that the marginal effectiveness of one's contributions to the political fight drop off as one contributes more and more ($G_{FF} < 0$ for those in favor, and $G_{AA} > 0$ for those against). It is also likely that the unit consumption cost a_i rises as extra contributions to the cause drive down one's own consumption (Y_i). Shifting any parameter of Equation (2a) or (2b) can make these marginal benefits and marginal costs fail to intersect at a positive level of contributions, so that the individual drops out of the redistributive fight.

Figure 13.1 illustrates. In the baseline case shown with solid lines, the individual joins the fight and contributes a positive e_{iF} (for someone in favor, or e_{iA} for an opponent) at point F's equilibrium between the extra benefits from contributing to the cause and the extra cost in terms of personal consumption. The marginal benefits curve is assumed to slope downward as a function of the amount contributed because the marginal effectiveness, G_F or G_A, should decline with the amount contributed.

Shifts in conditions can make people abandon the cause and contribute nothing but costless lip service. First consider the alternative case of a higher marginal value of one's own consumption (a_i), the upper dashed line. In this case, the curves fail to intersect in the positive range and the individual becomes passive. Such a rise in preference for one's own consumption can come from poverty. One has to stay alive in the short run, and the poor have a higher marginal utility of income devoted to consumption. Already we have a useful common-sense implication of the pressure-group framework: Poverty makes people drop out of political struggles. In a rich country, the poor stand on the sidelines more and vote less, as noted empirically in Chapters 7 and 15 through 17. The rich, by contrast, contribute more heavily, if only because

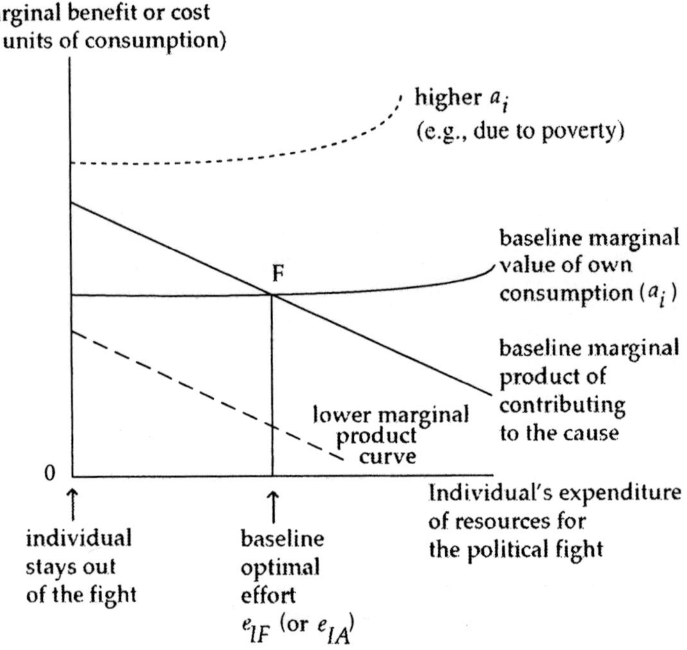

FIGURE 13.1. An individual's incentives to join a fight over redistribution.

they can better afford to sacrifice consumption. In poorer countries, elites have greater sway because fewer and fewer people can fight in the political arena. It stands to reason that the poor would be closer to joining the F group for fights over progressive redistributions from rich to poor and would be closer to joining the A group against regressive redistributions from poor to rich. Here is our first testable and plausible implication of the model:

Poverty makes the poor drop out of political fights, so that redistributions are less progressive and/or more regressive in poorer countries or countries with greater income inequality.[7]

This prediction, backed by the historical empirics of Chapters 7 and 15 through 17, helps to explain the Robin Hood paradox posed back in Chapter 1. It contradicts the common belief that greater income inequality would empower Robin Hood and others intent on soaking the rich. A main reason why greater inequality fails to tax the rich more is that the inequality discourages the poor from joining the fight for progressive redistributions.

On the other side of the equation, whatever pulls down the marginal productivity of contributing time and consumption to the political fight can again cause drop-outs, as with the dashed lower marginal product curve in Figure 13.1. This possibility gives a rich set of implications relating to the parameters on the benefits side of the equation.

The benefits of joining the fight could be shifted by changes in the deadweight costs of extra redistribution (D'_S and D'_T). This is a key point repeatedly stressed by Gary Becker. Raising the deadweight costs to be borne by the subsidized group will give the proponents (the F group) less will to fight and will cut their expenditures on the struggle. Raising the deadweight costs to be borne by the taxed group (the T group) strengthens their will to fight against the proposed redistribution. Becker thus conjures up an invisible hand of politics that can even convert pressure groups into efficiency watchdogs. By extension, if there are two or more designs for achieving the same redistribution, the more costly design will sooner or later draw greater fire in a competitive political arena. The deadweight cost effect fits a prediction already made by Becker and Mulligan.[8] It also fits the historical reforms noted in Chapters 10–12, and the budget stakes principle of Chapter 12. Under that principle, the higher the government budget already is, the greater the marginal cost of choosing the wrong design for any further change in tax and transfer rates. The budget stakes principle fits the present model because the higher the budget, the higher are D'_S and D'_T. The deadweight cost effect thus implies another plausible prediction of the pressure group model:

More costly redistributions have an inherent disadvantage in a competitive political arena.

Other parameters shaping the marginal benefits of contributing to the redistributive cause also deliver predictions that can fit, and seem to fit, historical experience. Consider the effect of the size of the affected groups, illustrated with the size of the subsidized group S. If you tend to favor helping this group with a transfer payment, how would the size of the S group affect your political contributions of time and money and your vote? If your concern for the group relates to the amount the transfer delivers *per recipient*, as assumed here, then the higher the group size, the less you will be inclined to contribute. If you really want to see them have more resources per person, spreading the same transfer (G) over a bigger N_S group offers less to each, pulling down the marginal benefit curve in Figure 13.1. You might give less or might drop out. The same would apply among the group fighting to defend taxpayers: The more taxpayers the proposal would burden, other things equal, the less a given transfer G burdens each one of them. Larger group sizes cause more dropouts. As Mancur Olson made clear, a larger group has a greater free-rider problem.[9] Therefore,

The larger is an affected group, the lower its per capita stake in the fight and the weaker its lobbying would be. That is, a larger subsidized group would receive less per recipient, other things equal. A larger taxed group may pay a larger total tax, but bear less of it per taxpayer.

Note that this weak-multitudes prediction about lobbies concerns transfers and taxes *per member of the affected group* and not the size of the transfer itself. The model allows, as intuition allows, a larger group to end up with either more or less in the absolute amount taxed and transferred. Against the negative effect on contributions per member of the caring group (group F or group A) must be set the possible effect of the size of the partisan group. Raising the N_S population over which a subsidy is to be spread may raise sympathies for the group as a whole, raising N_F or lowering N_A or both. Similarly, raising the N_T population that would share the tax may raise sympathies for the taxpayer group as a whole, raising N_A or lowering N_F or both. Thus there are two offsetting effects on the total amount taxed and transferred: The dilution of the tax/transfer per member of the affected group versus the extra lobbying resources from having more members who will take to the streets, contribute money, or vote for the cause.

The safest assumption is that the effects on contributions per member of the affected group still go in the direction implied by Equations (2a) and (2b), even though the total tax and transfer could be either raised or lowered. All that is necessary to give the per-member result predicted here is that the direct dilution of the benefits and the likely free-riding among members of the partisan group would outweigh the rise in the size of that partisan group in the determination of aggregate contributions per member of the affected group.

As an empirical illustration, Chapter 8 and Appendices D and E used recent historical experience to find that the higher the share of the population that was over the age of sixty-five, the lower their public retirement benefits *per elderly person*. This is despite Chapter 8's related prediction that the aging of the population would have only a slight (positive) effect on the total burden on taxpayers. Similarly, Chapter 15 and the same appendices also found that a larger school-age cohort meant less public schooling *per child*, other things equal. It did not find that having more children in the school-age cohort would reduce total public school expenditures, however.

The weak-multitudes pattern does not hold uniformly in fact, and a model should be prepared to explain exceptions. If we extrapolate the size effect back down to the smallest lobby, one person, then the model has an obvious problem. If greater numbers mean weakness in all comparisons, then you or I as individuals should be stronger lobbies than the farmers, the National Rifle Association, or the American Association of Retired Persons. Clearly the model must be modified somehow to allow for weakness at the bottom of the size range of affected groups. One way or another, the model should allow for a minimum scale, below which a new lobby cannot win redistributive fights in the political arena.

Some real-world cases of small groups with powerful lobbies might seem to support the basic pressure group model's prediction of a weak multitudes effect, but in fact call for adding something to it. Consider the fact that declining sectors reap greater and greater transfers from the rest of society as they dwindle in size. Agriculture is the extreme case, garnering huge subsidies throughout the OECD even as the number of farmers approaches zero. Just extrapolating to their smaller size using the basic theory probably gets the right result for the wrong reason. Mancur Olson has tried to explain agriculture's lobbying power in terms of the organizational free-rider problem: Small groups of producers organize better than larger groups of producers. This may capture part of the phenomenon of declining sector power. Another part of the explanation for agriculture is the bias in political representation in favor of small and declining places. In many countries, including the United States, the laws of representation give any 100,000 persons fewer elected representatives the larger, and more expanding, the political unit they live in. In all likelihood, however, one should emphasize the fixed-cost effect in lobbying, advanced by Richard Baldwin and Frederick Robert-Nicoud. Lobbying is a dynamic process, unlike the static model sketched here. Once a group has made large initial fixed investments in bending government, the marginal cost of keeping the redistributive gains is low. Its organization is efficient, and the law of the land is stacked in its favor. The fixed cost argument gives strength to declining sectors, who got organized in the past and now have the law, and captive government bureaucracies, on their side.[10]

A further implication of the basic model is that the most subsidized groups would probably be those that are small in population, but have many sympathizers outside the affected population, and draw on tax revenues spread over the whole of society. That generous outcome seems well illustrated by policies toward military veterans, the disabled, and the elderly ("you'll be older too"). It even includes those bafflingly generous subsidies to small farm populations from sympathetic outsiders, most of whom would never want to live on a farm themselves.

WHO CARES ABOUT WHOM?

It is one thing to say that in general people care what happens to others and another to make testable predictions from that vague generality. Putting the caring coefficients b_i and c_i to use requires a theory specifying who cares about whom. The pattern that makes the most sense empirically is "that could be me." You care more about the well-being of someone else, the greater the chance that you, someone in your family, or your whole family could end up in their state. The chance of ending up like them depends on many things, including their sharing your religion, living where you live, sharing your race and ethnicity, and having attended the same school. It also depends on the economic environment, which might or might not make you become like them. The that-could-be-me hypothesis says you will give more charity and political contributions to support people, the greater the probability that you could become like them. On the charity front, for example, in the year 2000 American individuals and institutions gave most heavily within their own religious units and to educational institutions (mainly colleges), less than 10 percent to human service, and less than 2 percent to people outside the country.[11]

If it is true, the tendency to self-project, or self-insure, would mean that a particular design of social transfers is more likely to be backed politically by persons with a high subjective chance of becoming a recipient of such transfers. On the tax side, it would mean that redistributive proposals are more opposed by those who see themselves more likely to be taxed than to be subsidized by the proposal. The caring coefficients could be driven by such self-projection.

Both the assumption about people's preferences and the implications for policy seem well supported empirically. The self-projection pattern is unmistakable. Some of the patterns show up in opinion polls both in the United States and in the international World Values Survey. In both settings, aid to the poor and Left political orientation are more strongly supported by those who have lower incomes, are unmarried, live in cities, and believe that luck determines income. Some results that look different in the international and the U.S. surveys still seem consistent with the self-projection idea. Internationally, being white makes one lean more to the Left politically, whereas being black creates more sympathy for welfare in the United States. This fits self-projection, in that whites in the international sample were disproportionately from relatively homogeneous heavily white countries where the Left program offered safety nets mainly to other whites. In the United States, by contrast, blacks are much more frequent recipients of welfare payments. Being female makes one more politically conservative in most countries, other things equal, but not in Sweden – where women are extraordinarily supported by transfers, as Chapter 11 noted – or in the United States, where poverty is heavily feminized. This is not to say that all patterns reveal self-projection. Higher education makes one more sympathetic to welfare transfers in the United States, even though higher education does not lean one more to the political Left in the international pattern. And having more children makes one more conservative in the international spectrum, but more pro-welfare in the United States. Overall, however, the tendency is clearly toward wanting to help groups for which one feels "that could be me."[12]

The preference for those like oneself leaves its imprint on policy, too. The imprint shows up mainly through the ethnic-racial mix and the income gaps. Social transfers, along with public schools and infrastructure, are resisted more strongly where there is a high degree of ethnic fractionalization. On this issue, some earlier studies matched the findings reported in Chapters 7, 15, and 17 of this book.[13] Ethnic fractionalization pulls down all these kinds of public spending. In the United States the most conspicuous symptom is that welfare spending is more opposed by those states where there are more blacks, other things equal.

Self-projection is also suggested by the fact that social transfers seem to depend on the relative income level and income mobility of middle-income voters. One study found that Americans were more sympathetic to egalitarian redistributions of income if they were closer to the next lower occupational group and also more sympathetic if they were further from the next higher occupational group, as would be predicted by the that-could-be-me theory. In addition, international evidence suggests that social transfers were significantly lower where the prefisc income distribution had a peculiarly wide gap between middle and low incomes, so that relatively few middle-income people would identify with those at the bottom.[14] That wide gap between middle and bottom is a conspicuous feature of the United States and to a lesser extent of a few other countries.[15] It, too, fits the self-projection theory, as Chapter 7 argued.

THE TREATMENT OF OUTSIDERS

Most models of pressure group competition talk as though everybody had the chance to participate in the political fights over redistribution. In most models those who are inactive chose to be inactive, presumably because they had no stake in the political outcome. That is, they were in Table 13.1's inactive I group because the redistributive proposal put them in the unaffected U group.

What about all the outsiders who are denied the option of having any political choice, even though the redistributive fights would affect them? Bringing outsiders into the model is no mere footnote. Every country fights all the time over how to treat disenfranchised foreigners, through its policies about trade, international earnings, and the international flow of humans and capital. Over most of history, most domestic citizens have also been denied the right to vote. The predictive power of any pressure-group model depends on how easily it can incorporate the treatment of the unvoiced outsiders.

Fortunately, it is not hard to incorporate the treatment of outsiders. Let us first note where they fit into the simple basic model above and then discuss some testable predictions about how they will be treated, drawing on some familiar economics.

The first simple link between the basic pressure-group model and voiceless outsiders is through the caring coefficients, the bs and cs. The groups active in the fight might care about one or the other affected group even if it has no political voice. The more likely cases relate to voiceless potential beneficiaries. Nothing in the model said that the S group had to participate in politics. The groups SF and SA could easily be empty, with all Ss being SIs. Children are an obvious example, heavily subsidized and protected without political voice. Another example is the range of animals defended by the power of the animal rights lobby in highly educated high-income countries like Britain.

More at risk in a nation's policy fights are those the politically active groups do not care about, but are quite willing to tax. Let us start with the example of foreigners, whose trade interests can be damaged if this country erects a new trade barrier. The vulnerable foreigners can be represented in either of two ways. Some of the marginal deadweight costs could be lifted from the domestic S and T groups and imposed on foreigners, or we could view the foreigners as part of the potentially taxed T group, a part having zero effectiveness in lobbying (part of $G_A = 0$). Let us take the first approach, since it allows us to plug familiar economic formulae into the basic model. The model remains as before, except that the total deadweight costs equal $D_S + D_T + D_Z$, where D_Z is the net cost borne by the foreigners.

To the extent that the competing political factions are free to ignore the cost D_Z borne by outsiders, the political process should be globally ineffi- cient. The import barriers criticized by economists since Adam Smith offer a venerable case in point. The typical trade barrier lowers world output and welfare. By how much? A useful principle here comes from the literature on the nationally optimal tariff, even though the principle transcends the confines of nationally optimal tariffs or even of tariffs. The principle is that the nation imposing the tariff, a tax on foreign suppliers, gains more the less elastic is the foreigners' supply to us. If they continue to sell us nearly the same quantity of goods despite the tariff, the price we pay them will plummet. We will have successfully exploited their inelasticity. The estimated elasticity of foreign supply is a roughly quantifiable variable that can be used to test the model and to estimate the inefficiency of our policies from a global standpoint.

Of course, different outsiders have different elasticities in dealing with us, since some of them have good alternatives and some don't. We cannot exploit those with high elasticities as much as we can exploit those with low elasticities. One should expect a tendency of national policy debates to put higher taxes on the inelastic outsiders than on the elastic outsiders. Such discriminatory taxation maximizes national gain, which approaches the ex- treme of maximizing the collection of revenue from trade with outsiders. This incentive to levy discriminatory taxes resembles another venerable tra- dition in economics: Ramsey taxation, whereby a government goes to the extreme of taxing each group according to the reciprocal of the elasticity with which it conducts business in the face of the tax. Those who go on buying and selling despite a tax end up paying higher tax rates than those who quit dealing when faced with the same percentage tax.[16]

While the political process is too complex to yield exact Ramsey taxation, one can see hints of it in tax policy and sometimes with international trade bearing part of the burden. Countries gravitate further toward taxing inelas- tic addiction goods, such as tobacco, alcohol, or petroleum, more heavily than elastic demands and more heavily if much of the supply is imported. Again, this would be inefficient from a world point of view, if no redeeming external benefit were captured with the use of the revenues.

So far we have encountered two overlapping principles that we should expect the political process to follow:

The political process (competitive or not) will tend to tax the unvoiced outsiders more heavily, and it will tax inelastic activities more heavily than elastic ones.

Both apply again when the unvoiced outsiders are not true foreigners, but those within our country who have no political voice. Intuitively, one might expect the politics of self-interest to tax the disenfranchised compatriots more heavily, especially when they have no choice but to go on doing nearly the same amount of the taxed activity. Disenfranchised classes within the country are likely to be treated like foreigners by a political process that can ignore, with impunity and inefficiency, the deadweight cost they bear (D_Z). Incorporating their burden into the pressure group model again involves no change other than adding D_Z as a consequence that affects no behavior within the pressure groups, except to the extent that one side or the other directly cares about the well-being of the disenfranchised.

Several historical examples from this book seem to illustrate the Ramsey-like exploitation of disenfranchised compatriots. Chapter 4 implicitly used this framework to explain the oddity of relatively generous poor relief in England before the 1830s. Why would a political process confined to propertied elites pay taxes to give more aid to the poor than earlier or later in history? Why did they give more in the rural Southeast than in other parts of the country, and more than in other countries? There are several ways in which the whole pattern fits the present model. Only two parts of Chapter 4's longer story need emphasis here. One is that the outcome did emerge from pressure-group competition between two groups within local government and again in Parliament. Of the two groups, labor-hiring landlords and farmers tended toward the F group (for taxes and relief) and even toward the S (subsidized) group, despite paying part of the taxes, because relief kept a cheaper labor force at hand throughout the year. The other part of Chapter 4's argument stressed here is that England's policy mix tended to be elasticity-sensitive in that era of the Old Poor Law. Relief policy took care to aid peasants who were at risk of being below subsistence or of emigrating to the cities and therefore elastic in their labor supply (no labor if they die or move away). Yet the combination of strict means testing, strict residence requirements for relief, and the Corn Laws severely taxed the laborers above subsistence, whose exit was less likely.

Another example of the treatment of unvoiced citizens was the generally greater reluctance of elite democracies to pay taxes for mass schooling, noted in Chapters 5 and 15. In this case the model's transfer was actually a payment for educational services that raised national product. On the average, if not at the margin, the deadweight costs ($D's$) were negative. A smoothly efficient process of political competition should have devoted more and more tax revenue to this productive cause, up to the point where diminishing returns made ($D'_S + D'_T$) turn positive. When political voice was restricted to elites, pressure group competition inefficiently ignored a *negative* D_Z of benefits to poorer children and their families.

A case in which the disenfranchised are richer than the rest of society is the case of future generations in the political fight over pay-as-you-go public pensions. Given the persistence of economic growth, our descendents will be different from us because they will have more money. What they lack is direct voice in the current debate over the generosity of public pensions. Granted, participants express great caring for future generations (implying high c_is for unborn taxpayers). Yet as the share of elderly in the population rises, few political processes in prospering countries can resist switching from funded to PAYGO pensions, giving a generation or two a windfall again. As Chapter 8 stressed, it is less likely that countries will switch back to full funding, because this switch would put most of the living into the T group. It remains to be seen whether the switch to PAYGO has a negative or positive effect on overall growth of living standards. It could be positive to the extent that it solves a capital-market problem, the inability of present generations to borrow from their rich unborn relatives. Yet it can also be costly. The main prediction of the minimal theory of transfers is not that switching to PAYGO was good or bad for the present value of all future consumption, but merely that the lack of direct political voice for future generations tipped the scales in favor of more generous pensions for today's elderly.

CHANGING VOICE

Extending Suffrage

How would giving political voice to more and more of the population change fiscal behavior? To answer this requires going beyond the simple optimization calculus of the basic model, since we are changing the population in large discrete steps. Table 13.2 sketches two examples visited at greater length in Chapter 5. The first example imagines that voice is initially restricted to part of the population, called the South. Within the South, the political struggle initially finds only a minority in favor of taxes for public schools (or transfers), so that the South rejects this discrete choice and has neither the taxes nor the schools.

As the economy develops, the share of voters wanting the tax-based schools would rise. This could be because the economic benefits of schooling rise for parents and employers, because the perception grows that schools buy social peace, or because greater and greater shares of people get the vote. As these forces drive up the share of voters favoring public schools, the South would eventually have a majority in favor of the taxes and school and would finally switch in what is called the *advanced era* here.

Extending the franchise to cover the part of the population called the North would tip the political scales. The North, just like the lower- and middle-income groups historically, has a greater taste for taxes and schools. If the franchise is extended from the South alone to both regions centralized together, the pressure-group equilibrium shifts. Taxes and school would arrive sooner, in the *middle era*.

TABLE 13.2. *Changing Voice and Public Choice: Two Simplified Median-Voter Examples*

Suppose that there are two adjacent local governments with equal numbers of voters, who face an all-or-nothing choice of having or not having a public good. Let it be a choice between setting up uniform tax-based public schooling for all children or having no public schools. Let's imagine a more pro-school North and a less enthused South. Decisions are made by majority rule.

| | Share of Voters in Favor of Taxes & Public Schools | | | Whose Children Get Public Schools? | | |
| | | | | If only the South has Voice | If Both Have Voice, | |
Era	South	North	Both		With Centralization	With Decentralization
(1) Backward era	10%	30%	20%	none	none	none
(2) Early rise	25	55	40	none	none	North only
(3) Middle era	40	70	55	none	all	North only
(4) Advanced era	55	85	70	all	all	all

Example 1, extending the franchise: Giving the vote to the North would hasten the day the taxes and schools arrive. If only the South had voice, they would not arrive until the end of the middle era. But if both have equal voice in a centralized government, the taxes and schools would be chosen for the whole nation back at the start of that middle era.

Example 2, decentralization (as in Chapter 5): In a majority-rule nation consisting of both regions, the effect of decentralization on schooling depends on the phase of development. In the most backward and most advanced extremes, it makes no difference whether school decision making is local or centralized. In the intermediate eras, it does matter. Decentralization promotes the taxes and schools in the early rise era, but retards them in the middle era.

Does extending the franchise hinder economic growth or promote it? The traditional presumption fits the interests of the privileged: Extending the franchise hurts growth because it allows the masses to soak the rich and stifle incentives to produce. The basic model certainly allows for this outcome, yet it permits the opposite conjecture as well. Bringing new groups into the political arena means that they are no longer outsiders whose interests can be ignored. They are empowered to fight against D_Z, tipping the political scales against such waste. The rise of democracy could make government efficient as well as more redistributive.[17]

Institutional evidence about the pro-growth side of giving the masses more political voice was sketched in Chapters 10 and 12. As Chapter 12 conjectured, the spread of voting rights and prosperity together may have nudged the tax system toward more efficient ways of raising revenue. As "freedom broadens slowly down," in Tennyson's phrase, the tax system evolves from arbitrary and unpredictable confiscations to more predictable excise and customs taxes, then to direct taxes, and then to uniform universal consumption taxes. The trajectory is toward more and more efficient taxes, partly because it is a drift toward taxes on less and less elastic activities. On the transfer recipients' side, the political decline of means testing and micro-management of individual lives brought down the bureaucratic costs of transfers. The fact that extending the franchise extended mass schooling (Chapters 5 and 15) also promoted economic growth. Overall tests of the link between voice and growth give mildly pro-democracy results: Any democracy grows better than the average autocracy, other things equal, but there is little basis for choosing between the growth records of elite versus full democracies.[18]

Decentralization versus Centralization

The same comparison of sets of active pressure groups serves to map out the possible outcomes of switching from decentralized to centralized governments. As Chapter 5 stressed at greater length, the result is that there is no simple theorem about whether centralization raises or lowers taxes and spending.

The second example in Table 13.2 illustrates the impossibility of a simple unidirectional link between centralization and the size of government taxes and transfers. Given the same plausible pattern in which two parts of the population consistently differ in their taste for taxes and public spending, and given the rise of tastes for public goods over time, decentralization can raise or lower the budget or leave it alone. In the first era, centralized and decentralized pressure-group competition would give the same result: no taxes or schools, because they are not wanted by the balance of power (here, a simple majority) in either half of the population. In the final advanced era, decentralization again makes no difference. Yet decentralization promotes taxes and spending in one of the two intermediate eras and holds it back in the other. The main fruit of the minimal model regarding centralization versus decentralization is this impossibility result: It could go either way, and the effect of decentralization cannot be signed.

SUMMARY OF PREDICTIONS

Once one takes the right cues from history, it turns out that several predictions about social spending and economic growth follow from the smallest of models. Table 13.3 illustrates some of the main ones surveyed here, with reminders about where they appeared in the empirical chapters.

The framework that produced these predictions has cost us very little. Granted, it had to set aside the complexity of the political process. Yet the model required very little in the way of assumptions. All we needed was policy competition among groups of self-interested individuals, who had a fairly correct view of the costs and benefits that a redistributive proposal would impose on them.

TABLE 13.3. *Predicted Influences on Redistribution through Government,
According to the Simple Pressure-Group Model.*

Parameter	The Effect of Raising This Parameter on the Amount Redistributed	Observable Measures of This Parameter
Marginal deadweight loss from extra redistribution, borne by		Administrative costs, elasticities-based
The subsidized group (D'_S)	negative	deadweight cost
The taxed group (D'_T)	negative	formulae
Individuals' caring about		
Own consumption (as)	negative	"Distances"
Subsidized group (bs)	positive	from the affected
Taxed group (cs)	negative	group, in ethnicity or income or other attributes
Size of subsidized group (N_S)	negative per recipient	The group size itself
Size of group to be taxed (N_T)	negative per taxpayer	The group size itself

Some applications:

(1) *Deadweight effects*: The rise of government is limited by the exhaustion of positive-sum programs and the nonlinear rise of deadweight losses (via D'_S, D'_T). The wider is each tax wedge, the greater the perceived and actual waste from further widening it without an offsetting redesign of other incentives. This predicts the budget stakes principle of Chapter 12.

(2) *Affinities*: Affinity for similar groups makes redistribution sensitive to ethnic and economic divisions, as shown by a growing literature (Chapters 7 and 17).

(3) *Poverty effect*: Poverty (high as) makes the poor drop out of political fights, so that redistributions are less progressive and/or more regressive in poorer countries or countries with greater income inequality.

(4) *Group size effects*: For given sympathies, a proposal aimed at larger affected groups evokes less intense political support (via G/N_S and G/N_T), beyond some effectiveness-maximizing group size. An example for a group of rising size: The elderly eventually lose out from further growth in their numbers (Chapters 7, 8, 16, and 17).

(5) *Treatment of outsiders*: When political voice is concentrated in a small minority, that minority behaves like a price-discriminating monopolist toward the relatively voiceless masses. Groups more likely to exit when taxed (by not participating in exchange, rebelling, emigrating, evading taxes, or dying) are taxed less. An example is England-Wales in the era of Corn Laws and the Old Poor Law, as interpreted in Chapter 4.

14

A Guide to the Tests

To test the many plausible theories about social spending and economic growth requires both good historical data and careful test design to make real-world judgments about the different historical forces that theory says could have played key roles. This chapter takes the first step, by introducing the whole empirical framework to be used in this volume.

WHAT KIND OF LABORATORY?

International historical samples should consist of countries and eras for which any differences in the definition of social transfer spending have been ironed out. Such samples are available, but only for several countries and only for three eras. The only available sample period before World War II consists of twenty-one countries' experiences in the six decadal benchmark dates 1880, 1890, 1900, 1910, 1920, and 1930. This sample of 126 observations becomes:

(1) The 1880–1930 sample. The twenty-one countries of the 1880–1930 sample are Argentina, Australia, Austria, Belgium, Brazil, Canada, Denmark, Finland, France, Germany, Greece, Italy, Japan, Mexico, Netherlands, Norway, Portugal, Spain, Sweden, the United Kingdom, and the United States.

All these countries are viewed as sovereign nations, despite limitations on the sovereignty of Australia, Finland, and New Zealand before the turn of the century. World War I brought some territorial changes in our countries. Our "Austria" switched from the Austrian half of the Austro-Hungarian Empire to today's Austria. Germany lost some eastern territories and lost Alsace-Lorraine to France. Italy gained territory from Austria. The United Kingdom lost most of Ireland. The territories and population covered by our nations changed accordingly. For the most part, these changes do not appear to have had any major effects on the variables used here, though I did perform side-tests that included shift terms for Austria and for Finnish independence.

The other two historical samples refer to experience after 1960.[1] The two postwar time periods are the ones for which the OECD developed measures of social transfers that are consistent across countries: their 1960–1981 and 1980–1996 samples of annual data. In both projects the OECD went to considerable trouble to produce standardized estimates across member countries. Unfortunately, the standard definitions are not the same in the two sets, as a detailed study of the overlapping data for 1980–1981 confirms. Therefore two international data sets have to be analyzed separately:

(2) The 1962–1981 OECD data set of ninety-five cases, using five four-year time periods (1962/65 through 1978/81) for nineteen countries: Australia, Austria, Belgium, Canada, Denmark, Finland, France, Germany, Greece, Ireland, Italy, Japan, Netherlands, New Zealand, Norway, Sweden, the United Kingdom, and the United States. This set of OECD estimates had the virtue of including educational spending.

(3) The 1978–1995 data set of 126 cases, using six three-year time periods (1978/80 through 1993/95) for twenty-one countries, consisting of the same nineteen plus Portugal and Spain.[2] The German data series switched from Western Germany to unified Germany in 1991. These OECD estimates allow us to exclude pensions and other payments to government and military employees, payments that are part of the public sector's labor contracts rather than redistributive transfers. The more recent data set also allows a direct view of the tax side, which we examine in the next chapter.

Though both postwar data sets provide annual numbers, there is an econometric reason to prefer data taken only at longer intervals, in the same spirit with which we welcome decadal data for 1880–1930. Social and budgetary policies typically show a great deal of momentum from year to year. This momentum can give misleadingly strong results because of serial correlation from past to current prediction errors. The traditional ways of trying to eliminate serial correlation probably would not work in such an intercountry pooled regression on the history of social spending. Even after introducing lagged values of social spending or of the errors in predicting it, one would get overconfident results from annual data because each observation probably still depends on the errors made regarding the immediately preceding years in the same country. To minimize this problem we have combined the annual observations, first for 1962–1981 and then for 1980–1995, into multiyear averages. Making each observation a four- or three-year period brings the test closer to the true cycle of political climate. With each four-year period closer to statistical independence than each year, it is plausible (and confirmed by the tests that follow) that conventional time-series adjustments can handle the remaining serial correlation.

THE SIMULTANEOUS SYSTEM LINKING SOCIAL SPENDING AND GROWTH

Deciding what could have caused the rise of social transfers, and what could have made it so much greater in some countries than in others, calls for an examination of many forces at once. We need to give as many leading suspects as possible their day in court. Since that compels us to dwell on systematic variables that can be measured for all countries, the task breaks down into two parts. First, we explain as much as possible with these available systematic variables. Then we note which countries seemed to have distinct departures from the overall pattern, departures suggesting unique elements of their national histories.

A freehand sketch and a roadmap of the chapters ahead are offered by Figure 14.1 and Table 14.1. Figure 14.1 sketches the featured influences, and Table 14.1 maps out the sets of equations and variables.

At the center of Figure 14.1 appear the behaviors to be explained in this book: social spending and the growth or level of gross domestic product (GDP) per capita. Let us cast social expenditures as shares of GDP to imitate tax rates or tax effort. In doing so, we follow a rich literature on postwar experience, in which economists, political scientists, and sociologists have all participated, even though almost none of their efforts combined the determinants of both growth and social spending.[3]

The systematic forces that directly shape social spending are shown on the left-hand side of Figure 14.1 and near the top of Table 14.1. The list includes three forces that are measured only in the postwar samples. These could have played roles before 1930 had the data permitted us to explore them systematically. The first of the three forces is the degree of social affinity versus divisiveness. As argued in Chapter 13 and later in this volume, social affinity – the bond with beneficiaries of public programs – can raise social transfers. Conversely, taxes and public spending may be reduced by ethnic or class divisions. A second force is the role of openness to foreign trade. Dani Rodrik has argued that, under certain conditions, being more exposed to international trade can raise a nation's public demand for social spending, especially for safety nets to catch those hurt by trade competition. This can be tested on the postwar data.[4] The third postwar-only variable is military spending as a share of GDP, here interpreted as a claim on government budgets that is causally, and politically, prior to the claims of social programs. A greater pressure to spend on military defense or aggression might lower social spending as a share of GDP.

Some familiar determinants of the level or growth of GDP per capita appear on the right-hand side of Figure 14.1, and toward the bottom of Table 14.1. Product per person can grow better, relative to its past levels, the greater the endowment of prior capital, both nonhuman and human.[5] Growth is also improved by recent technological backwardness if the country in question

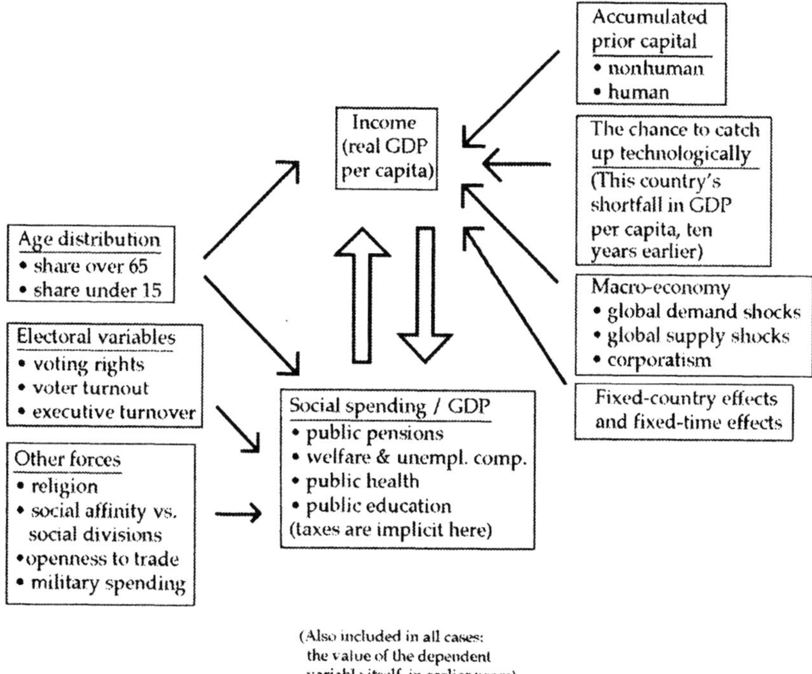

FIGURE 14.1. The simultaneous system linking GDP and social-spending shares.

has institutions as suitable for new growth as those in most OECD countries today. Therefore within the "convergence club" of today's OECD countries, we should expect the extent of a country's lag behind the United States to be a positive influence on its current growth. A country's growth is also influenced by current shocks to aggregate demand and aggregate supply at the level of the world economy. A global aggregate demand shock will be proxied crudely here by the difference between all-country inflation and all-country unemployment. An aggregate supply shock, such as an oil shock, will be proxied by the sum of the all-country rates of inflation and unemployment. The third macro-economy influence is corporatist bargaining among government, organized labor, and organized business to restrain wages in exchange for fuller employment and other policy concessions. Finally, there can be unknown *fixed effects*, fixed attributes of individual countries or time periods. We will explore these growth determinants in detail in Chapter 18, when confronting the free-lunch puzzle about the growth effects of social spending.

Each growth or transfer equation previewed in Table 14.1 must have these attributes stressed in Chapter 10 of Volume 1:

TABLE 14.1. *Forces That Determined Growth, Social Transfers, and Education Since 1880*

| | Equations and Historical Samples | | | | | | Students, Teachers per Child | Public Education Exp./GDP |
| | Growth of GDP/Capita | | | Social Transfers, Taxes as % of GDP | | | | |
	1880–1930	1962–1981	1978–1995	1880–1930	1962–1981	1978–1995	1880–1930	1962–1981
Income								
Real GDP per capita				endog	endog	endog	endog	endog
Its growth rate	Dep	Dep	Dep	endog	endog	endog		endog
Backwardness, lagged	X	X	X					
Social spending/GDP								
Transfers	endog	endog	endog	Dep	Dep	Dep		
Tax rates			endog	Dep		Dep		
Public educ. spending								Dep
School enrollments							Dep	
School, lagged	X	X						
Teachers/1,000 children							Dep	
Age distribution								
0–15s or school-age		X					X	
Young adult share								
Elderly share	X	X		X	X	X		X
Elections and democracy								
Voting rights				X	X		X	X
Voter turnout				X	X	X	X	X
Executive turnover				X	X	X	X	X

24

Social forces

Religions				X	X	X	X	X
Ethnic divisions					X	X		X
Income-group affinity					s	s		
Openness to trade					X	X		X
Military spending					X	X		X
Agriculture, lagged	X							
Capital inputs								
Nonhuman K (or past Is)		s	s					
Educ. attainments of adults		X	X					
Global macro-economy								
Demand shocks (infl. − U)		X	X					
Supply shocks (infl. + U)		X	X					
Corporatist wage-setting		s	s					
Fixed-country effects	s	s	s	s	s	s	X	s
Fixed-time effects	s	s	s	s	s	s	X	s
Lagged dependent variable	s	s	s	s	s	s	X	s

Notes to Table 14.1:

Dep = Dependent variable, to be explained.

endog = Endogenous variable, whose predicted value from another equation is used here.

X = An independent variable used in all variations of this equation (or set of equations).

s = An independent variable used in some variations of this equation (or set of equations).

(a) *Social transfers are big.* Social transfers must take a large share of national product on the average – large enough to show their damage to GDP per capita.

(b) *They vary a lot.* Their share of GDP varies greatly over the sample.

(c) *Polities define the sample.* The units of observation are the polities that set policy toward taxes and social transfers.

(d) *Conventional sources of growth are covered.* We have credible data on most of the usual leading sources of growth, not just the budgetary policies being judged.

(e) *The experience covers both time and place.* The sample is a pooled time-series and cross-sectional analysis, in order to walk the least dangerous line between the perils of time-series analysis and the perils of cross-sectional analysis.

(f) *We take account of simultaneity.* We have enough separate insights on the sources of both social transfer behavior and economic growth to identify both sides of the simultaneous system explaining both social spending and growth.

(g) *The GDP costs can be nonlinear.* We allow the GDP effects of social transfers to be nonlinear, to allow for the likelihood, explained in Chapter 13, that the ratio of deadweight and GDP costs to the amounts transferred would rise quadratically.

It is not only the GDP cost of transfers that we should allow to be nonlinear. Chapter 13 also predicted that the power of different age groups in lobbying for social spending could be nonlinear. An age group's power could rise as it first gains sufficient size to be heard in the political process. It could then decline as further expansion adds too many claimants on the transfers it is lobbying for. This possibility must be tested by using a nonlinear function of the age group's share of the population. In addition, the effect of extra voting rights on transfers and public education may well be nonlinear, as previewed in Chapter 4 of Volume 1 and as confirmed in the next two chapters of this volume.

To this list we should now add two technical econometric requirements:

(h) We allow for the likelihood that the error terms are heteroskedastic across countries and autoregressive over time.

(i) Where the dependent variable is censored to exclude negative values, and often assumes a value of zero, we need to use tobit regressions to estimate both the determinants of positive values and the likelihood of attaining a positive value.

SOME ALTERNATIVE VIEWS

While this sketch and road map capture all the forces to be featured as influences on social spending and economic growth, it is right to ask "Is that all? What about alternative explanations?" Some leading alternative candidates omitted from Figure 14.1 and Table 14.1 deserve a chance to prove themselves in tests.

The first worthy alternative is the role of labor unions and Left or Right political parties. As already admitted in earlier chapters, my approach has been to fold them out of sight in the middle of longer causal chains, the ones now represented as arrows in Figure 14.1. That is, they are viewed as intermediate endogenous variables in any of this book's main displays of empirical results, as if both union power and political parties were the results of such forces as democratic institutions, the age distribution, ethnic fragmentation, and so on. The power of unions and of Social Democrats, in particular, seems to be largely a result of the prior spread of voting and representation rights down the economic ranks of society. Once the causally prior forces are controlled for, Alexander Hicks found in a similar study, Left governments and union-dominated governments have no positive further influence on social spending.[6]

Another view is that the spread of social transfers and public education resulted from a diffusion of knowledge or of tastes from country to country. Perhaps one of the main determinants of how much one country spent on social programs was the tendency of other countries to do the same. The statistical tests of this volume will find little value in the diffusion idea. One version of it has been tested in all the equations having fixed time-period effects, and these turned out not to matter to the effects of the featured forces. A simpler and more direct look at the historical experiences suggests the same. When one country had innovated, why did some fail to follow suit for decades while still other countries seemed to follow the innovator's lead? The forces featured in Figure 14.1 can explain such differences better than any simple historical geography of diffusion.

A particularly serious alternative is historical inertia or momentum. Perhaps the rise of a social program creates a vested interest that fights to have the taxpayers pay more and more to expand that program. Past authors have presented this view in different ways. For critics of bureaucracy in the tradition of Parkinson, once a new program gets started, its bureaucrats succeed in getting it expanded regardless of the social costs or benefits. For social scientists running regressions to explain the rise of social spending, one useful variable has been simply the number of years the social programs were already in place. Whatever the mechanism, there is at least some inertia, some momentum, in social spending as a share of GDP. In the chapters that follow, I represent this momentum by the lagged dependent variable and by adjustments for serial correlation in the error terms. Even with such dependence of one period's social spending on earlier periods' social spending, the other forces featured in Figure 14.1 and Table 14.1 still prove significant.

Finally, some political institutions, such as Parliamentary versus non-Parliamentary government or the degree of federalism, had to be left out because they did not vary enough within the samples or were hard to measure.[7]

HOW COULD ONE COUNTRY BECOME ANOTHER COUNTRY?
THE STAY-IN-SAMPLE RULE

The eventual goal of measuring the effects of social spending on economic growth and vice versa is to give educated answers to some what-if questions. What if U.S. society became more like Swedish society or Sweden became more like Japan? How would social programs change, and what effect would that have on their economic growth? Such quantitative estimates of a what-if world are not idle conjectures. They are basic to any causal inference. No amount of pretending not to need such counterfactuals can ever be persuasive. As Robert Fogel and others rightly insisted, we do need to make, and to empirically defend, counterfactual conjectures in order to have anything to say about how the world works.[8]

Any attempt to interpret patterns over time and space has to have a clear view of what kinds of counterfactual histories it dares to propose. Are we really willing to say that if the United States had had Sweden's values of the independent variables, it would have behaved like Sweden? Would Sweden have behaved like Japan with Japan's independent variable values? Comparisons over time pose the same issue of interpreting counterfactuals. If full democracy had come to all OECD nations by 1880 instead of by 1980, would higher education and welfare states really have bloomed earlier?

How *do* we interpret patterns that emerge from comparing nations and decades? The question is similar to the question of how to interpret cross-sectional differences among individuals. Individuals, like whole nations, are not repeated draws of colored balls from the same statistical urn. Like nations, they have their own personal histories. To deal with these differences among individuals, the micro-economic literature has developed good policy-experiment contrasts between randomly selected treated versus nontreated groups who are similar in the aggregate. That option is not available here, because different national conditions cannot be drawn at random. For example, we can't get dozens of countries to sign up for a major social experiment and only later tell them which ones will be in the experimental welfare-state group and which will remain in the free-market control group, based on random draws. They had their own complex historical reasons for being on different paths already.

Such concerns give either an econometrician or a professor of history serious reservations about believing in just any counterfactual, any what-if history that didn't happen. For the econometrician, the main problem is omitted variables. In a pooled sample of nations and time periods, we know that the observations were not just repeated draws from the same underlying distribution. They differ according to omitted variables, which threatens to bias any causal estimates. The professor of history would voice the same omitted-variable concern differently. Histories evolve differently, in response to more forces than an equation can be assumed to capture. In the most nihilistic variant, every case is hopelessly unique. Certainly, the undeniable role of long history constrains the usefulness of imagining that countries might suddenly shift their independent-variable attributes.

There is a simple rule to follow in deciding what counterfactual changes of historical path are plausibly predicted by the regression data: *Stay within the sample range.* This guideline imposes two kinds of constraints on the counterfactual histories we dare to imagine – a sample-border constraint and a speed-limit constraint.

First, for any set of independent variables, one should not put much stock in any extrapolation that goes beyond the range of values those variables took on in the sampled countries and years. One warning against such extrapolation is sounded whenever we discover nonlinearities within the sample. Once we see that the underlying relationships look nonlinear, we know that any slight misspecification of a nonlinear relationship within the sample can extrapolate into a huge error out of sample. And this book does indeed find those nonlinearities – in the effects of more voting rights, in the effects of population aging, and in the effects of expanding social transfers.

Thus, for example, Chapter 8 in Volume 1 already posted a warning sign at the sample border in projecting the consequences of population aging in the twenty-first century. For each country, it extrapolated the elderly share only up to 20 percent at most, since the oldest country experience in the 1978–1995 sample – Sweden in 1984–1989 – had only 17.8 percent of its population over sixty-five. Predictions within this range were given more emphasis than those beyond it. Another example is the set of welfare state experiments imagined in Chapter 18 below. No OECD country has spent more than 33 percent of GDP on social transfers. We should not extrapolate the effects of transfers on GDP growth beyond that 33-percent welfare state standard without posting a warning sign: Counterfactuals about larger welfare states are especially hazardous beyond this point.

The second constraint to observe is that speed limit: Don't imagine a faster shift than actually occurred in the sample. We know that countries' paths are strongly conditioned by their recent history. Many of the regression variants previewed in Table 14.1 will embody such historical inertia in their use of lagged dependent variables, which stretch the effects of any shock out over many years. In practical terms, following the stay-in-sample rule means imagining that democracy, aging, or the popularity of social programs can advance only as fast as it advanced in the national experiences covered by the sample. We can use our estimates to imagine some shifts toward fuller democracy, as long as some countries democratized that fast within the sample. One of the strengths of our 1880–1930 sample is that it included some abrupt shifts toward democracy – for example, Austria and Weimar Germany after World War I. In the first postwar sample, Portugal, Spain, and Greece all democratized fairly quickly in the 1970s, after the Greek coup had suddenly removed democracy in 1967. Such cases should support, and constrain, conjectures about the effects of quick political change.

The speed limit also applies to our imagining the rise or fall of the welfare state. The fastest five-year jump in the social transfer share of GDP was 10.5 percent in Finland 1988–1993. The fastest five-year drop in the same share was 8.4 percent in Portugal 1979–1984. When it comes to imagining the growth effects of creating or dismantling a welfare state, it would be best to stay within these speed limits. Even the case of Finland 1988–1993 is not to be viewed as an exogenous rise in the welfare state, suitable for imagined counterfactuals. In fact, that jump in the social transfer share was due to Finland's exceptionally severe slump of the early 1990s, resulting from the combination of a world recession and Finland's mistake of tying its currency to the rising German mark. For a more exogenous policy shift toward the welfare state, one should try Germany's social-transfer jump of 5 percent of GDP in the five years (1990–1995) after reunification with East Germany. Chapter 18 will stress how crucial are the sample border and the speed limit in predicting how changes in the welfare state could affect economic growth.

Following the stay-in-sample rule, respecting both the sample borders and the speed limits, cannot do away with all the econometricians' concerns about omitted variables or with all the historians' concerns about missing context. Yet it can assure both parties that the counterfactuals being imagined resemble changes that actually occurred, so that the observed relationships stand a better chance of being well correlated with, and capturing the roles of, hidden variables or events.

PART SIX

ACCOUNTING FOR SOCIAL SPENDING, JOBS, AND GROWTH

Explaining the Rise of Mass Public Schooling

Why did some countries lag so far behind others in finally delivering public subsidies that provided schooling for the entire population? Why did some succumb to the argument that primary and secondary education had to wait for decades and centuries until parents finally had the means and the motive to pay for private education?

A striking early example of this lag was spotlighted in Chapter 5. Victorian Britain lagged behind other leading countries in primary and secondary education before closing the gaps after 1891. Yet Britain's lag was brief relative to the lag of a century or more in Third World schooling. Universal schooling is so important to economic growth that the question "Why isn't the whole world developed?" has rightly been tied to the question "Why don't all children complete their primary education?"[1]

Chapter 5 placed much of the blame for delaying mass education on powerful elites opposed to schooling the masses at taxpayer expense. Where political voice was restricted to those holding substantial property, poor children got little help from the taxpayers. This chapter tells more of that global story about elites, voice, and schooling. We begin with statistical evidence about the determinants of public primary and secondary schooling. While several forces play roles, the results confirm the central role of democratic voting rights. A second section then adds statistical evidence to support the assumption that democracy causes schooling more than schooling causes democracy. Finally, the global role of elitism in delaying development is underlined by some strong circumstantial evidence from Asia in the 1980s. Three elitist fingerprints are displayed, fingerprints that can be used in many national histories without the need for any large statistical sample.

QUANTIFYING THE DETERMINANTS OF MASS SCHOOLING

Enrollments and Teachers in 1880–1937

Fortunately, history has given us panels of international experience that allow tests conforming to the standards stipulated by Chapter 14. The first sample spans from the late nineteenth century through the interwar period. This experience has been sliced into two different samples. The first slicing, already introduced in the last chapter, takes cross-sections for twenty-one countries at each of six benchmark dates from 1880 thorough 1930. It has the advantage of using the dates for which I have estimated social transfer spending, a feature that will be crucial in Chapter 16. This slice is used here as well, partly to explore the numbers of teachers per hundred children of school age. The other slicing yields statistical cross-sections for twenty-four countries every eight years (1881, 1889, 1897, . . . , 1937).[2] The larger 1881–1937 experience, with 192 cases instead of just 126, is possible because the school enrollment series are available annually, unlike the social transfers to be studied in Chapter 16. The two kinds of samples give much the same insights when it comes to understanding mass public schooling.

The level of educational commitment determined by voting and other forces should be measured in terms of public inputs per child. Ideally those inputs would be resource measures, valuing teacher time and other things that go from taxpayers' pockets into each child's learning. For the most part, we must take a less direct approach to judging public inputs per child before World War II. Public inputs will be represented in the statistical analysis by public school enrollments, for want of sufficient data on private enrollments or on educational expenditures back to 1880.

The distinction between public and private enrollments has its own difficulties. In defining the share of children whose schooling is public, the guiding principle should be to imitate the unavailable public share of total expenditures as closely as possible. If public money exactly paid for all public-school enrollments and for none of the private-school enrollments, and if per-student expenditures were the same in both kinds of schools, the public enrollment data would suffice. Yet countries mixed their public and private systems. In some cases, public (government) schools charged tuition and even taught religion. In some cases – including Belgium, France, the Netherlands, and Denmark after World War I – taxpayers paid for part or all of the budgetary costs of private religious schools. What enrollments figure should be used to imitate the public expenditure share? In most cases, we have no choice but to use the public-school enrollments as a guide to the use of taxes. For Belgium, France, and the Netherlands, however, the enrollment figures are adjusted to reflect the fact that public funds dominated many private-school budgets.

To keep differences in definitions of primary enrollments across countries from having much effect on the results, it was necessary to use two different enrollment ratios. The simple ratio of primary-school enrollments to the population ages five to fourteen should be supplemented by a ratio using the combined enrollments of all primary, middle, and secondary schools. Both ratios are explored here. For eleven of these countries, it is also possible to explore the determinants of the number of primary school teachers per 1,000 children in the same five to fourteen age range. The number of teachers gets even closer to the missing expenditure variables, since most of those expenditures went to pay teachers' salaries.

What light does enrollment behavior shed on the political, economic, demographic, and social forces that shaped the commitment to public mass schooling before World War II? The answers come both in Appendix D's coverage of the 1880–1930 experience and in Table 15.1's summary of the 1881–1937 experience from two dozen countries.[3]

Incomes and the numbers of children of school age affect schooling in ways that one would expect. Higher incomes unquestionably raise the share of children who are in school. A crowded birth cohort, represented by a higher share of the five to fourteen age group in the total population, drags down the enrollment rate at all levels of education. The loss of schooling might be due to crowding in the home or to crowding in the schools, both of which happened in the U.S. postwar baby boom generation.[4]

Dominance by the Roman Catholic Church had two opposing effects on the amount of primary schooling. On the one hand, enrollments were significantly lower in heavily Roman Catholic countries, as Table 15.1 makes clear. On the other hand, Catholic dominance also brought more teachers, not only per pupil but also per child of school age.[5] This striking pair of tendencies might be due to Catholic countries' engaging priest and nuns as low-paid extra teachers. Some caution is in order, however, in interpreting both the negative enrollment effect and the positive teacher effect of Catholic dominance. The data count some, but not all, of the students and teachers in church-related schools in the public school data, so that the estimates may be biased. Still, our few indirect hints about overall enrollments suggest that Table 15.1 is correct in announcing that Catholic dominance lowered enrollments at least to some degree.

The most important insight from the enrollment patterns from before World War II comes from the influence of political regimes and political voice. Thanks to recent advances in databases for political history, we can contrast the educational implications of regimes that differ by degree of autocracy and by the share of adults who can vote. The Polity index of autocracy rates each national regime, for each year since 1815, from complete dictatorship (10) down to the most benign or nonexistent autocracy (0).

Among autocracies, where votes are either banned or of little importance, the more dictatorial end of the spectrum tends to provide more schooling, other things equal. This seems to accord with the raw data, which show us that schooling was high, relative to what other forces would predict, in Thailand, Portugal after 1929, pre-Revolutionary Mexico, Hitler's Germany,

TABLE 15.1. *Regression Equations for School Enrollment Rates per 1,000 Children Aged Five to Fourteen in Twenty-Four Countries in 1881–1937*

| | Public-School Enrollments per 1,000 Children 5–14 | | | |
| | (1) Primary Only | | (2) Primary Only | |
Dependent variables	coeff.	|t|	coeff.	|t|
In (GDP/capita), 8 years earlier	167.6	(8.71)**	117.3	(7.42)**
School-age (5–14) share of total population	–7.80	(2.94)**	–4.59	(1.98)[a]
Religion				
Catholic dominance	–418.7	(6.46)**		
Protestant dominance	–154.9	(1.55)		
Political regime variables (see also "Effects" below)				
Autocracy index (0–10)	2.57	(1.11)	4.42	(2.48)*
Did women vote 8 years earlier?	–1.61	(0.10)	–3.36	(0.27)
Franchised as a % of population over 20	–0.80	(0.34)	–0.61	(0.36)
Franchised share, squared	0.060	(1.15)	0.057	(1.47)
Franchised share, cubed	–0.00050	(1.68)[a]	–.00048	(2.10)*
Constant term	–506.6	(2.87)	–149.6	(1.00)
Allowing for 23 fixed country effects?	No		Yes	
"R sq.," equation F-statistic	.574	28.7	.879	46.6
Mean of the dep. var.	550.42		550.42	
Effects of selected shifts toward more electoral democracy				
(a) from benign nondemocracy to 30% franchise	16.6	(0.51)	20.08	(0.85)
(b) from 30% franchise to 80% franchise	48.2	(1.49)	51.26	(2.11)*
(c) from benign nondemocracy to 80% franchise	64.8	(3.21)**	71.35	(4.06)**
(d) from benign nondemocracy to 100% franchise	21.3	(1.21)	31.15	(1.92)[a]
Type of equation	pooled GLS		pooled GLS	

Enrollments per 1,000 Children 5–14

Dependent variables	(3) Primary Plus Secondary (Public)		(4) University (Public + Private)	
	coeff.	|t|	coeff.	|t|
ln (GDP/capita), 8 years earlier	79.3	(6.78)**	6.61	(5.63)**
School-age (5–14) share of total pop.	−2.80	(1.48)	−0.71	(4.21)**
Primary enrollment rate, 8 years earlier	0.82	(17.68)**	−0.0018	(0.52)
Political regime variables (see also "Effects" below)				
Autocracy index (0–10)	1.24	(0.80)	−0.17	(1.16)
Did women vote 8 years earlier?	−3.76	(0.31)	5.02	(5.14)**
Franchised as a % of population over 20	−0.78	(0.39)	0.43	(3.01)**
Franchised share, squared	0.030	(0.63)	−0.011	(3.32)**
Franchised share, cubed	−0.00022	(0.77)	0.000070	(3.40)**
Greece in the 1920s (secondary overcounted)	101.1	(2.83)**	−5.59	(2.16)*
Constant term	−421.3	(4.34)	−31.2	(31.20)
Allowing for 23 fixed country effects?	Yes		Yes	
"R sq.," equation F-statistic	.983	338.0	.793	
Mean of the dep. var.	581.8		5.6	
Number of nonzero observations, out of 192			185	
Effects of selected shifts toward more electoral democracy				
(a) from benign nondemocracy to 30% franchise	−2.6	(0.10)	1.5	(2.46)*
(b) from 30% franchise to 80% franchise	18.8	(0.65)	−2.3	(3.44)**
(c) from benign nondemocracy to 80% franchise	16.2	(0.99)	−0.8	(2.21)*
(d) from benign nondemocracy to 100% franchise	1.3	(0.11)	−0.2	(0.56)
Type of equation	pooled GLS		tobit	

(** = significant at the 1% level, two-tail; * = significant at the 5% level; [a]significant at the 7% level; [b]significant at the 10% level.)

Notes and sources to Table 15.1:

The sample consists of 24 countries over eight benchmark years. The 24 countries are Argentina, Australia, Austria, Belgium, Brazil, Canada, Denmark, Finland, France, Germany, Greece, Italy, Japan, Mexico, Netherlands, New Zealand, Norway, Portugal, Spain, Sweden, Switzerland, Siam/Thailand, the United Kingdom, and the United States. The eight benchmark years are spaced eight years apart: 1881, 1889, 1897, 1905, 1913, 1921, 1929, and 1937. The fact that territorial boundaries changed across World War I (e.g., from the Austrian half of the Austro-Hungarian Empire to Austria alone) should pose no problem here, given that the sample is intended to capture political changes.

(*continued*)

TABLE 15.1. (*continued*)

The only likely violation of the usual statistical assumptions comes from the fact that serial correlation behavior might not be consistent if the geography of the country changed.

The enrollment rates are based initially on the decadal benchmarks in Appendix A. To interpolate between my decadal benchmark estimates, I used some of the enrollment figures from the Arthur S. Banks CD-ROM for 1815–1999. But in some cases, especially the United Kingdom, I prefer my own estimates over those that Banks presents without citing his sources.

The franchised are the shares of the over-20 population legally entitled to vote, in settings where I judged the voting power to be real (see below). For years when women were not yet entitled to vote, the over-20 population refers to men only. Alternative regressions used the actual voter turnout instead of the franchise share used here. The results were qualitatively the same, both in the regressions using voter turnout and in similar regressions on the 1880–1930 decadal benchmark sample results. The franchise and voting shares are from the Arthur S. Banks cross-polity CD-ROM for 1815–1999, which draws them mainly from Mackie and Rose (1991). The autocracy index is from the Polity 98 version of the Gurr–Jaggers Polity data set.

The franchised voting power was judged to be illusory and not real in cases where the Banks indexes and the Mackie description of franchise institutions suggested that voters had little power over the legislature and the chief executive, despite their actually voting in legislative elections. Thus I entered zeroes for the franchise in these cases where elections were actually held: Belgium, Germany, and Italy up to World War I; Norway to 1882; and Sweden to 1907.

Both the autocracy index and the franchised shares are predicted values, rather than actual observed values. The instrumental-variable equations generating these predictions are the political-regime equations in Appendix Table C of the working-paper version of Lindert (2003).

Catholic dominance = the amount of the Catholic majority among religious declarants. It equals the maximum of either 0 or the Catholic share minus .50. It takes on positive values for nine countries.

Protestant dominance = the corresponding majority margin for Protestant countries, with some cases judged to involve no dominance despite a Protestant majority. It equals nearly 0.50 for Denmark, Finland, Norway, and Sweden. It equals 0.16 for the United Kingdom before the separation of Ireland, and 0.10 for 1921–1937.

The religion data are mostly from *Annuaire Statistique de la France* for the 1930s. Those from France, the United Kingdom, and a few other countries are from encyclopedias, in some cases for postwar years.

"Benign" nondemocracy here refers to a polity with an autocracy rating of zero, but with enough impediments to legislative effectiveness and enough power of the monarch for me to disregard any suffrage rates, setting them at zero despite the occurrence of elections. The only pure example in the sample is Norway 1898–1913, though prewar Belgium came close, with autocracy = 1.

For Greece in the 1920s, I used the Banks data series on secondary and higher education rather than the less complete Mitchell series. However, the Banks series seems to overcount secondary enrollments, partly at the expense of tertiary enrollments. This necessitated adding the "Greece in the 1920s" variable to capture the temporary miscount.

The test statistics listed under "effects" at the bottom of the table start from the most limited autocracies, those with a Polity AUTOC index of 0, combined with my judgment that they were nonetheless not democracies. For stricter autocracies, note the autocracy index coefficient.

Regressions were run using the POOL command in SHAZAM 8.0, using the option that sets the same first-order rho coefficient for all countries in making the Cochrane–Orcutt transformation.

and Mussolini's Italy. The opposing examples of benign autocracies, such as Norway 1898–1913 and Belgium up to World War I, indeed had schooling that was not impressive.

To compare democracies with each other or with autocracies, we can use either the share of the adult population entitled to vote or the share that actually votes. Table 15.1 uses the share enfranchised, though using the actual voting share would give similar results. The table presents the voting share effects in two forms. The first, in mid-table, gives the form actually fitted, for those few readers who want to see how the equation was fitted. Of greater interest for most readers is the "effects" presentation of test statistics showing the effects of different political regime shifts on educational enrollments. The first effect, (a), shows little difference between the schooling of benign autocracies, like Norway or Belgium at the start of the twentieth century, and elite democracies with only 40 percent allowed to vote. Examples of this elite democracy group would be the United Kingdom, the Netherlands, and Sweden at the start of the 1880s. Neither group stood out as a high-education context, and the only significant difference between them was at the university level.[6]

As the right to vote was broadened down to lower and lower economic classes, the enrollment patterns shifted in an egalitarian direction. Extending the franchise to 70–85 percent of adults raised primary enrollments and cut university enrollments, other things equal. What mechanism brought this about? Presumably, the egalitarian shift in political power tipped educational finance toward primary public schools and against universities. The universities did not suffer public budget cutbacks, but their budgets failed to grow nearly so much as the rise in incomes would have implied.

Expenditures in 1962–1981

The same issues can be explored further in the postwar era. Of the two OECD samples introduced in the last chapter, the earlier one, for nineteen countries in 1962–1981, conveniently included measures of public education expenditure as a share of GDP. As it turns out, many of the same tendencies reappear in the 1962–1981 results of Table 15.2, even though we have jumped a few decades and have shifted the focus from enrollments to public expenditures. A higher GDP per capita again means higher enrollments, at least when fixed country effects are omitted. A more crowded school-age population cohort receives less support per child. The share of people voting is once again a positive influence, this time on total public education expenditures.

Two new factors enter in the postwar results. Countries that are more open to trade have decided to spend more on children's education, other things equal, probably to help them adjust to changing trade winds during their careers. In addition, military spending tends to crowd out education spending to some extent.

TABLE 15.2. *How Various Forces Affected Public Education Spending as a Percentages of GDP, 1962/65–1978/81*

	Public Education Expenditures as a Share of GDP Over a 4-Year Period: (Standard Errors in Parentheses)			
	Without Fixed Effects		With Fixed Effects	
The effects of unit changes in				
Total social transfers 4 year earlier	0.0053	(0.02)	0.01	(0.55)
Growth in GDP/capita, last 10 years	32.30	(7.18)**	10.41	(1.38)
GDP/capita, 10 years earlier	2.56	(0.35)**	0.18	(0.44)
School-age population, starting				
at sample mean	−13.89	(1.82)[b]	4.56	(0.95)
The effects of selected shifts in electoral politics				
From 40% voting to 70% voting	−0.33	(1.02)	−0.529	(1.18)
From 70% voting to 85% voting	0.54	(0.22)*	0.703	(4.13)**
Faster turnover of chief executive	0.020	(0.03)	0.031	(1.68)[b]
The effects of changes in these other forces				
Catholic majority	0.64	(0.69)		
Ethnic fractionalization	0.21	(0.94)		
Openness to foreign trade/1,000	17.66	(4.97)**	0.0036	(0.51)
Military spending/GDP	−0.15	(0.07)*	−0.242	(4.04)**

Sources and notes to Table 15.2:
  (** = significant at the 1% level, two-tail; * = significant at the 5% level; [a]significant at the 7% level; [b]significant at the 10% level.)
For the fuller regression equations, see Appendix Table E1.

Democracy and active voter participation, then, seem to have left a deep footprint. This result confirms the link between unequal political power and underdeveloped human capital recently suggested by Engerman, Mariscal, and Sokoloff.[7] It adds a twist relating the concentration of power to the distribution of public funding (enrollments) across levels of education. What fuller democracies delivered, relative to nondemocracies or elite democracies, was *primary* education, the kind of tax-based education that redistributed the most from rich to poor.[8]

While the results in Tables 15.1 and 15.2 confirm a tendency of elite democracies to block public education, they do not support one particular elite theory, namely the optimal-exploitation model of Martin McGuire and Mancur Olson.[9] As mentioned in Chapter 5, McGuire and Olson predicted that a democracy with more widespread voice brings either no change or a decline in public educational spending and enrollments. Yet the regression results clearly show a significant rise in schooling as democracy spreads, even when income is held constant.

The distribution of voting power thus played a systematic role in explaining why countries differed in their schooling in the late nineteenth century. Still, the equality of political voice does not explain all of the observed differences between countries. The uniqueness of each nation's history still has a role to play.

THE EXOGENEITY OF DEMOCRACY

To emphasize the role of democracy is to invite suspicions about reverse causation. Scholars already familiar with the chicken-and-egg puzzle involving whether income causes education or vice versa will have little trouble remembering to ask "Ah, but what if it's the education that is causing the democracy? Doesn't that raise doubt about whether democracy is causing the extra public schooling?"

Suspicions about reverse causation can be dealt with by looking more closely at either the historical sequences of events or the simultaneous-equation statistical nexus linking democracy and schooling. This book takes both of those closer looks. Chapter 5 in Volume 1 argued that the historical sequences showed jumps in voting rights that were not preceded by any great change in, or level of, educational attainment among adults. Democracy looked exogenous and not heavily dependent on the schooling that it is promoting.

A closer look at the simultaneous-equation system involving political regimes, education, and growth reinforces the conclusion that the advance of democracy promoted schooling, much more than schooling promoted democracy. The closer look takes the form of Table 15.3's regressions predicting the index of autocracy and the share of adults allowed to vote in terms of regime history, national income, global growth, war losses, urbanization, and schooling. Since the dependent variable equals zero in about half the cases (there was either no autocracy or nobody allowed to vote), the regression type is tobit, rather than conventional least-squares.

The political regime depends on its own past history. Autocracies are hardened (up to an index of 10) by a more autocratic history. They are softened (down to 0) by a democratic experience in the more distant past, here represented by the extent of voting twenty-four years earlier. The franchised share, in turn, tends to follow its own recent past. If political regimes were a random walk, equaling the latest value plus a zero-mean random error, then all the coefficients in the equation would be zero. The equations in Table 15.3 do not quite conform to the random walk, despite the prominent role of first-order (eight-year) lagged terms.

The political regime also depends on some other national attributes – but not very much on the level of schooling, the issue of most immediate concern. Autocracy seems quite independent of any systematic influence, coming closer to being a random walk. The franchised share, by contrast,

TABLE 15.3. *Regression Equations for Political Regimes: The Autocracy Index and the Franchise Share, Twenty-Four Countries in 1881–1937*

Dependent variable	The Autocracy Index (Polity)		The Franchised Share of Adults	
	coeff.	|t|	coeff.	|t|
The regime depends on its own history				
The autocracy index, lagged 8 years	0.976	(6.25)**	1.10	(0.53)
The autocracy index, lagged 16 years	−0.278	(1.36)	0.38	(0.14)
The autocracy index, lagged 24 years	0.254	(1.56)	−1.48	(0.71)
Franchised as a % of adult population, lagged 8 years	0.011	(0.90)	0.96	(6.54)**
Franchised as a % of adult population, lagged 16 years	0.003	(0.22)	−0.13	(0.74)
Franchised as a % of adult population, lagged 24 years	−0.069	(4.25)**	0.12	(0.78)
The regime also depends on other forces				
In (GDP/capita), 8 years earlier	0.132	(0.16)	31.58	(2.89)**
Growth of the global economy	3.654	(1.42)	−26.17	(0.94)
Lost a war in the last 8 years	−17.154	(0.01)	82.78	(3.44)**
Lost a war 9–16 years ago	−14.825	(0.01)	51.20	(2.40)*
Share of population in cities > 50,000, 8 years earlier	1.139	(0.25)	−67.59	(1.78)[b]
Primary + secondary enrollment rate, 8 years earlier	−0.0011	(0.82)	0.029	(1.61)
Constant term	−1.466	(0.25)	−259.83	(3.25)
Allowing for 23 fixed country effects?	No		No	
"R-squared"	.693		.763	
Mean of the dep. variable, std. error of estimate	1.302	2.521	26.86	30.779
Number of nonzero observations, out of 192	104		98	
Type of equation	tobit		tobit	

Notes and sources to Table 15.3:

The autocracy index is from the Gurr–Jaggers Polity 98 data set.

The variable "lost a war in the last 8 years" = 1 for France 1881, and for Germany and Austria in 1921 and 1929, otherwise = 0.

The share of the population living in cities greater than 50,000 in population is from the CD-Rom of the Arthur S. Banks (1971) data set for 1815–1999.

In the case of tobit regressions the "R-squared" parameter is the squared correlation between observed and expected values, and the mean of the dependent variable is the expected value at the mean values of all independent variables.

Regressions were run using the TOBIT command in SHAZAM 8.0.

has behavioral links to GDP per capita, military defeat, and urbanization. Still, the key parameter is virtually zero: Recent school enrollments hardly affect the political regime. There is good reason to talk as though democracy's independent effect on schooling has been captured fairly enough by Tables 15.1 and 15.2.

Combining the political effects of Table 15.3 with the effect of democracy on schooling suggests a corollary about war, democracy, and schools. Within this 1881–1937 sample, losing a war to a foreign power was good for democracy and schooling. So hinted the in-sample cases of France after 1871 and Germany and Austria after World War I, Hitler's later rise notwithstanding. Outside of the sample, the same constructive effect of military defeat advanced German schooling after the defeat at Jena in 1806, as Chapter 5 noted. Both democracy and schooling were similarly advanced in Germany, Italy, and Japan after World War II. No sweeping general law has been discovered here, since history contains many more defeated nations than postwar births of democracies or of mass education. Yet it is possible that the probability of a link between defeat and democracy might be on the rise. Perhaps the strong demand for postwar government legitimacy is increasingly fixing on democracy as a mandate.

ELITIST FINGERPRINTS IN THIRD WORLD EDUCATION POLICY

A main purpose of exploring the determinants of education before World War II is to search for patterns that tell us something about Third World countries today, where incomes and other measures of development are often similar to those of the OECD countries before 1939. To search for instructive parallels and patterns, one logical next step is to turn to statistical samples that are global, to see if the same patterns hold there. That line of research has already begun, and indeed there are similarities to the historical patterns noted here.

Let us pick up a simpler tool, however, one that works in more settings. The comparative history of education policy in fact reveals a simpler test for elite bias, a test that does not require a data panel of many years, many countries, and many variables. The test therefore applies to less data-rich settings in the deeper past and in today's Third World, where something is more likely to be amiss with the financing and allocation of public education.

Three Fingerprints

Past writings on education in developing countries offer strong incomplete evidence that poor societies systematically underfinance primary education. The evidence is incomplete because it is confined to so-called social rates of return on the attainment of a higher level of schooling. These rates of return are as encompassing as they can be, but they still omit some kinds of human investments. For one thing, such rates of return can only capture the returns and costs of extra school years, not the returns and costs of raising the quality of schooling at each level. That is, they can show only the damage done by rationing schooling, not the damage from poor schooling. For another, they cannot measure the net external or intergenerational benefits of education and are social only in that they include the public-budget effects of public financing and later tax collection from more educated adults. They miss primary education's external benefits related to making everybody a fuller citizen, one less likely to put claims on later transfer budgets. For what they are worth, however, those studies consistently show that the social rate of return on the extra (unattained) primary schooling is much higher in today's Third World than either the marginal returns on higher education in the same countries or the rates of return measured for any level of schooling in high-income countries.[10]

Underinvestment in primary schooling reflects two defects at once. First, it reflects the usual imperfections of capital markets, which block low-income families from borrowing to educate their children, whose high later incomes could have repaid a loan at low prime interest rates. Second, it also reflects insufficient use of taxpayer funds to conquer this capital market imperfection. Given the pervasiveness of capital market imperfections and of external benefits from education, taxpayer effort on behalf of public education has been key to raising educational performance. For two centuries now, the global leaders in educational attainment, test scores, and human earning power have been countries that have relied on public funding at the primary and secondary levels. Tax money does not simply displace private or philanthropic funding.[11]

The failure to equilibrate social rates of return suggests an elitist policy bias, one that sacrifices GDP growth and discriminates against those who would benefit from extra primary education – particularly the poor, the rural, and females.

Some simple indicators can reveal such an elitist bias in a country's educational policy, even without sufficient data to estimate rates of return. Compare that country's public-education expenditure and admissions patterns with those of high-income high-technology countries in the same era. The *first fingerprint* that an elitist bias would leave relates to the primary-school *support ratio*

> Primary-school support ratio =
> (public funding for primary school per child of primary-school age) divided by (GDP per capita).

Note that the school-age population here is an entire age group, not just pupils, in order to combine both support per pupil and the attendance or enrollment rate.[12] Such a support ratio will typically rise with GDP per capita. A country's educational policy leaves such an elitist fingerprint, *Fingerprint 1*, if it has a lower support ratio for primary education than a typical country of the same income level, or of poorer countries, in the same historical time-period. In such a case, this Fingerprint 1 means that the country is passing up some economic growth, either to keep powerful groups from paying taxes or to keep the masses unschooled as an object in itself. We will illustrate the use of this clue in the next section. For the eighteenth and nineteenth centuries, this support ratio test is our best prima facie clue to an elitist bias in educational policy, one that sacrifices some economic growth. Chapter 5 found such fingerprints in Victorian Britain.

Other clues can support this one. For the twentieth century, elite bias can also show up as relatively generous public funding for higher education, given that higher-income and politically privileged families typically have better access to that higher education. With taxpayers now subsidizing all levels of education and with greater data availability, we can use two other clues that suggest elite bias at the expense of overall GDP growth:

> Relative support ratio for higher education =
> (public support for tertiary education per pupil) divided by
> (public support for primary education per child of primary-school
>   age),

and

> Inequality of support favoring the best-off =
> A direct measure of the concentration of public support into educating
>   those with the highest levels of educational attainment, such as a gini
>   coefficient or a share of education subsidies received by the
>   best-educated 10 percent.

Fingerprint 2 is left when policy gives a higher relative support ratio for higher education than other countries with the same or higher average incomes.[13] Granted, it is conceivable that a poorer country might need to concentrate its education budget on training at the top, so that national leaders and teachers are trained first, before advances in schooling can trickle down to the masses. But the rate-of-return evidence, plus smoking-gun historical narratives of elite antipathy to mass schooling for its own sake, suggests a growth-sacrificing elite bias if Fingerprint 2 is found.

Similarly, *Fingerprint 3* show up whenever a direct measure of inequality of public funding favors the best educated groups, relative to typical practice in high-income countries. The calculated social rates of return are lower for tertiary education than for primary, and there is no clear externality argument in favor of subsidizing higher education more than primary education in a lower-income setting.

TABLE 15.4. *Two Fingerprints of Elite Bias in Asian Education Policy in the Mid-1980s*

	Fingerprint 1 (Below-Average Values Suggest Elitist Bias) Public Primary Expenditures per Child of Primary-School Age as a % of GDP/Capita Mid-1980s	Fingerprint 2 (Above-Average Values Suggest Elite Bias) Public Tertiary-Education Expenditures per Pupil/Public Pre-Prim. + Primary Expend. per Child of Primary-School Age
Bangladesh	3.4	83.3
China	7.9	25.2
India	5.4	36.8
Indonesia	13.7	6.7
Korea, Repub. of	12.7	5.6
Malaysia	14.0	13.6
Nepal	7.0	35.5
Pakistan	4.0	31.8
Philippines	5.8	8.7
Singapore	8.4	7.7
Sri Lanka	6.2	13.4
Thailand	13.7	2.9
Papua New Guinea	19.8	53.0
Ten Asian nations	8.5	17.5
Japan, 1995	17.3	0.9
United States	15.7	1.4
OECD average, 1988	17.3	2.0

Sources and notes to Table 15.4:
See sources and notes under Table 15.5.

Finding the Fingerprints in Asia for the 1980s

Tables 15.4 and 15.5 expose all three of those elitist fingerprints in educational policy using estimates for Asia in the 1980s. First, the support ratio for public primary education, the same measure used in Chapter 5, gives prima facie evidence against India and Pakistan. Either country's primary-school support ratio is below that of poorer Nepal. Bangladesh's support ratio is even worse, but we have no poorer country with which we can compare Bangladesh.

The next two fingerprints, the ones showing the relative generosity of taxpayer support for higher education, confirm that the problem is not just meagerness of public funds. For any given budget, it should not be the case that a poorer country spends more of a given budget on the tertiary education of top students, given the rate of return evidence and the stronger external benefits of primary education. On the second fingerprint in Table 15.4, most

TABLE 15.5. *A Third Fingerprint of Elite Bias in Asian Education Policy in the Mid-1980s*

	Fingerprint 3 (Above-Average Values Suggest Elitist Bias)		
	Mid-1980s Inequality of Public Funds Among Students Ranked by Educational Attainment		Memorandum: GDP/Capita for 1985, in 1990 $, per Maddison
	Gini	For 10% Best-Educated	
Bangladesh	.82	72.0	577
China	.44	31.0	1522
India	.66	61.0	1079
Indonesia	.27	21.0	1972
Korea, Repub. of	.16	13.0	5670
Malaysia	.38	32.0	4157
Nepal	.57	54.0	713
Philippines	.19	14.0	1964
Sri Lanka	.33	28.0	2234
Thailand	.33	23.0	3054
Papua New Guinea	.62	54.0	3497[a]
Ten Asian nations	.43	36.3	

Sources and notes to Tables 15.4 and 15.5:
[a] From Penn World Tables 6.0. Other GDP/capita figures are from Maddison (2001).
  The sources are UNESCO (1998) and Tan and Mingat (1992).
  The ten Asian nations averaged together are Bangladesh, China, India, Indonesia, Korea, Malaysia, Nepal, Philippines, Sri Lanka, and Thailand.
  For Fingerprint 3, a one-year profile is used to synthesize the whole educational cycle.
  The UNESCO source, used here for Pakistan, Singapore, and Japan, allows the calculation of the support ratio through two different methods. They do not give the same answers, however. One possible source of discrepancy is the inclusion of pre-primary expenditures with the primary school estimates.

Asian nations seem to have overspent in favor of higher education. The worst offenders are Bangladesh, Papua New Guinea, India, Nepal, and Pakistan. A similar bias is evident for these same countries in Table 15.5 (except that detailed data are lacking on the distribution of subsidies in Pakistan). To these three fingerprints, one could add that the Indian subcontinent's teaching profession at all levels has been dominated by males, more so than in any other Asian nation except Cambodia.

South Asia's elitist distortion has not gone unnoticed. India has drawn repeated criticism in this respect. At the start of the 1990s, as India was beginning to emerge as an exporter of software and other highly skilled services, almost half of Indian adults – 36 percent of men and 61 percent of women – were illiterate. A consensus of in-depth studies has found a serious distortion of Indian public funds in favor of higher education at the expense of mass primary education.[14] For example, the World Bank in 1992 was clear in its recommendations for Indian educational policy:

> The aggregate level of public spending on education is probably adequate. . . . But some changes are called for in the allocation of those resources. In particular, more spending should be allocated to primary education, mainly to improve its ability to retain students. . . . The shift in funding in favor of primary education can be achieved by increasing the contribution of private financing in higher education. . . . The structure of enrollments and financing arrangements result[s] in a distribution of public spending that is skewed toward the privileged.[15]

While the performances of Bangladesh and Pakistan look just as bad, let us dwell on the Indian case a bit. Why is India, "the world's greatest democracy," the locus of much of the world's illiteracy? Doesn't this one case do great damage to the notion that democracy and widespread political voice are key to mass education?

There is at least a prima facie case that political voice in India has been highly restricted and disproportional, despite the holding of full-suffrage elections. India, in other words, is not the democracy it seems, especially in the distribution of control over public education.

India's history has featured an educational system designed for the elite, at least back to the infamous and influential "Minute on Indian Education" that Thomas Babbington Macauley penned for Parliament in 1835.[16] Granted, every generation of British and Indian leaders in the twentieth century gave lip service to free public education for all. In the transition to Indian provincial autonomy the 1930s and 1940s, most provinces passed compulsory education laws. But in the absence of funding and enforcement, these were no more effective in India than in any other polity where unfunded compulsion tried to precede the private demand for mass schooling. The gap between grants per university student and subsidies per primary student widened further under provincial autonomy in the 1930s and 1940s. Gandhi and the Congress Party leadership continued the rhetoric, but declined to provide the funds needed for the daunting task of conquering illiteracy. Gandhi himself added to the problem by demanding that alcohol could not be legal, and therefore not taxed for schools and other programs, and by refusing to abandon his scheme for "self-supporting" education in which illiterate children would learn all they needed to know by working at menial jobs.[17]

Both in the transition to independence and since 1947, political voice in India was limited, first in law and then in practice. The differences in democracy among Sri Lanka, India, and Pakistan were already evident in the 1930s. Britain gave Ceylon (Sri Lanka) universal adult suffrage in 1931, only a few years after the last restrictions on women's suffrage were removed in Britain itself. Provincial elections were held under this new franchise in

1931 and 1936.[18] In India, by contrast, the Montague–Chelmsford reforms approved by Parliament in 1919 extended suffrage only to include more property taxpayers, persons with educational qualifications, and landholders. The landless and urban workers were still not included; in most municipal areas the electorate was about 14 percent, and in rural areas it remained a tiny 3.6 percent.[19] For its part, the Muslim League wanted little to do with democracy.

The differences in franchise and voting persisted into the Independence era. Voter turnout in Sri Lanka rose from 55.8 percent of the electorate in 1947 to 76–78 percent in two elections of 1960, to 86.7 percent in 1977. By contrast, in India it rose only from 46.6 percent in 1952 to 60.5 percent in 1977, and dropped back to 57 percent in 1980, even though the legal franchise share had risen from 55 percent to 99 percent across the 1960s and 1970s, and Pakistan has remained autocratic.[20] These differences correlate with Sri Lanka's much better performance in primary education, though not in higher education, than either India or Pakistan. And within India, the voter turnout rate again correlates with the relative development of primary education and average incomes. Voting, primary schooling, literacy, and income all continue to be higher around the rim in the South, Punjab and Haryana, and lower in the heartland states of Bihar, Madhya Pradesh, Rajasthan, and Orissa.

What mechanism might have linked limited political voice with the discouragement of primary education? We know that single-member pluralities, like the electoral institutions of India and the United States, create a bias in favor of the largest and longest-organized political parties. The Congress Party was given decades of clear primacy among political parties during its leadership of the Independence movement. In the first thirty years of Independence its leadership was hard to dislodge, and it won a majority of seats despite never capturing a majority of votes.[21] Once Congress's educational policy had set the favoritism for higher educational into the five-year plans, no lower-class or lower-caste opposition could easily overturn that policy. Voice was effectively restricted by history and by political institutions. One could view India under the "Congress Raj" as a case of Mancur Olson's institutional arteriosclerosis. Political elites became increasingly entrenched, and institutions were frozen in practice. In India's case, that transition may have secured the power not only of the well-off in the heartland states, but also of teachers as a tenured lobby against parental voice, competition, and reform.

Surely a bedrock of political exclusion in India has been its tradition of caste, tribe, class, and ethnicity. No matter how full the franchise or how much power has devolved to provinces and to village *panchayats*, even the most local rule seems to remain concentrated into long-organized groups. For its part, the central government had tried to equalize power with affirmative actions giving the "backward classes," "scheduled castes," and tribes not only job quotas, but even reserved legislative constituencies. Yet control over taxes and especially education remains largely provincial, an arrangement that appears to have perpetuated the handicap of primary schooling for the disadvantaged groups and the heartland states.[22]

Tentatively, the answer might be that the world's greatest democracy fell behind because it was not much of a democracy in ways that were crucial for education policy. In this respect, twentieth-century India may have been the mirror image of nineteenth-century Germany: an ostensible democracy that failed to be democratic on the education front, as opposed to an ostensible autocracy that led the world in locally initiated education. Sometimes the truth "on the ground" differs from the stories written in statutes and decrees.

SUMMARY

Multinational statistical tests and simpler fingerprint clues on individual countries repeatedly underline the same point: There is a strong link from the spread of political voice to the rise of tax-based primary education and from primary education to economic growth. When it comes to judging types of political regimes by their contribution to education, the ranking favors fuller political rights, but not linearly so. The average dictatorship in the 1880–1937 era, like the communist dictatorships thereafter, did more to promote education than less oppressive autocracies or elitist democracies where fewer than half of adults were allowed to vote. Yet the greatest aid to mass education was delivered in the fullest democracies, those where the universal right to vote was both granted and enforced in practice.

16

Explaining the Rise of Social Transfers, 1880–1930

With social transfers as with public schooling, the half century from 1880 to 1930 provides the earliest consistent numbers for over twenty countries and our first chance to quantify the main influences on those transfers to the poor, the unemployed, the sick, and the elderly. This chapter conducts tests that are as close as possible to the tests that Chapter 17 will perform on post-1960 data, so that the two chapters together can illuminate how the larger patterns of policy behavior have evolved over more than a century.

SOME FORCES THAT LED THE WAY

Several forces determine a country's commitment to tax-based social transfers. Some of these forces are unique to their historical settings. Others are more systematic, and we pursue both here.

Some things *not* pursued here should be noted at the outset. The reasons vary. For simplification, this chapter pays no attention to such political mechanisms as the conflicts and bargaining among political parties, and the specifics of legislative caucuses, budgetary appropriations rules, and legal precedents. That is, as warned in Chapter 13, I do not open the black box of political machinery, but take a reduced-form approach featuring prior forces that are inputs into that black box and the economic outcomes it produces. Some other forces are set aside here because I lacked the data series to chart them. So it is with income distribution, unionization, and military spending.[1] One idea omitted here because it has already proven unhelpful as an explanation of social transfers is Mancur Olson's hypothesis that long-peaceful countries develop an institutional arteriosclerosis.[2]

One idea that serves well in this era will be passed over because it is tested elsewhere. The national economy's openness to international trade has been featured in Dani Rodrik's (1997a, 1998) work as a facilitator, or necessitator, of the development of social spending. For the period 1880–1930 Rodrik's openness hypothesis has already been tested by Michael Huberman

51

and Wayne Lewchuk.[3] They find the same tendency before World War I that Rodrik finds for the late twentieth century: Smaller and more open economies tended to develop stronger social safety nets. We shall test this theme at greater length in Chapter 17, using postwar data.

The historical laboratory for estimating the key influences on social transfers is one already introduced in Chapters 5, 7, and 14. We are able to use systematic data for the six years 1880, 1890, 1900, 1910, 1920, and 1930 from twenty-one countries.[4] The resulting statistical estimates, summarized in Table 16.1 and detailed in Appendix D, offer some insights into the rise of social spending and direct taxes. The strategy followed here is to survey and interpret the systematic influences on social spending and then to see which of them contributed most to an explanation of the rise of tax-based social transfers. It will turn out, of course, that the systematic forces do not explain all of the movements in social transfers during that half-century. The remaining prediction errors, combined with fixed country and fixed-time effects, reveal the roles of unique historical elements.

The role of momentum, featured in the first row of Table 16.1, shows smallish results. The coefficient on total transfers ten years earlier is sometimes positive and sometimes negative. Its small positive coefficient for social transfers can be viewed in different ways. Some would emphasize that it shows how programs gather momentum by building up a vested set of interests that continues to push for more of the same. Others would emphasize that it shows the difficulty of changing anything immediately, suggesting that the history of social programs reveals a slow protracted response to earlier changes in the political and economic climate. Either way, the share of transfers in gross national product (GNP) ten years earlier was itself just a reflection of earlier movements in more fundamental forces, such as income growth, population aging, democracy, or religion.

Higher incomes raise the share of government in GNP, here as in studies of the later twentieth century. Table 16.1 divides the role of income into two parts, the ten-year growth rate predicted by other factors and the log-level of GNP per capita ten years earlier. The combination of the two income terms has a clearly positive effect of income on total social transfers, as well as on the introduction of income taxes. The results thus offer slight support for the Wagner's Law belief that higher incomes mean a greater share of government spending in national product. On the other hand, higher incomes meant a lower likelihood of having introduced public pensions. This odd result is not sustained in the next chapter and may reflect a pre-1930 tendency of the richest countries to keep supporting their elderly through classic poor relief rather than through new separate pension programs for the elderly.

An older population devoted a significantly greater share of national product to all kinds of social transfers and to inheritance taxes. Some of this was probably an automatic population-base effect. For any given set of rules about age-specific benefits and inheritance taxes, a bigger elderly population

TABLE 16.1. *Unit Impacts of Various Forces on Social Transfers and Direct Taxation, 1880–1930*

	Impacts on These Kinds of Government Behavior in the Same Decade (Standard Errors in Parentheses)					
	(1) Total Social Transfers as % of GNP		(2) Poor Relief and Unempl. Compens. as % of GNP		(3) Public Pensions as % of GNP	
The effects of unit changes in						
Total social transfers 10 year earlier	0.151	(0.13)	−0.021	(0.08)	0.062	(0.07)
Growth in GNP/capita, last 10 years	5.590	(2.50)*	0.329	(1.33)	−6.740	(2.91)*
GNP/capita, 10 years earlier	0.105	(0.49)	0.081	(0.26)	−0.514	(0.30)[b]
Elderly share	0.111	(0.04)*	0.056	(0.03)[a]	0.032	(0.03)
Effects of selected shifts toward more electoral democracy						
(a) from nondemocracy to 40% voting	−1.805	(0.77)*	0.348	(0.89)	−5.487	(1.54)**
(b) from nondemocracy to 55% voting	−0.750	(0.80)	0.296	(0.92)	−2.656	(1.33)[a]
(c) from nondemocracy to 70% voting	0.254	(0.84)	0.755	(0.89)	−0.288	(1.21)
(d) from 40% voting to 70% voting	2.059	(0.57)**	0.407	(0.58)	5.199	(1.12)**
(e) from 70% voting to 85% voting	0.313	(0.56)	1.220	(0.68)[b]	−0.446	(0.75)
Do women vote?	0.342	(0.12)**	0.134	(0.07)*	0.003	(0.07)
Turnover of chief executive	0.077	(0.02)**	0.054	(0.01)**	0.017	(0.01)
Religion						
Catholic majority	−208.8	(219,857)	131.4	(169,068)	71.8	(81,280)
Protestant dominance	0.009	(3.77)	−1.997	(2.15)	8.545	(2.45)**
Average value of dependent variable	0.553		0.253		0.122	

(*continued*)

TABLE 16.1. (*continued*)

| | Impacts on These Tax Shares in the Same Decade (Standard Errors in Parentheses) | | | |
	(4) Income Tax as % of GNP		(5) Inheritance Tax as % of GNP	
The effects of unit changes in				
Same behavior 10 year earlier	−0.10	(0.09)	−0.30	(0.09)**
Growth in GNP/capita, last 10 years	2.89	(8.12)	−0.38	(1.60)
GNP/capita, 10 years earlier	4.09	(0.93)**	−0.05	(0.13)
Elderly share	−0.04	(0.16)	0.07	(0.03)*
Effects of selected shifts toward more electoral democracy				
(a) from nondemocracy to 40% voting	−0.57	(0.67)	−2.06	(1.03)a
(b) from nondemocracy to 55% voting	−0.03	(0.72)	−1.59	(1.16)
(c) from nondemocracy to 70% voting	0.58	(0.76)	−1.39	(1.06)
(d) from 40% voting to 70% voting	1.15	(0.55)*	0.67	(0.62)
(e) from 70% voting to 85% voting	0.82	(0.56)	−1.04	(1.03)
Do women vote?	2.01	(0.57)**	0.35	(0.09)
Turnover of chief executive	−3.42	(1.40)*	2.72	(15,107)
Religion				
Catholic majority	5.04	(5.99)	−6.04	(7.01)
Protestant dominance	16.63	(17.22)	1.78	(2.32)
Average value of dependent variable	1.11		0.13	

Notes to Table 16.1 :

The figures in parentheses are the standard errors of the coefficients.

Growth in GDP/capita, last 10 years is measured as the natural-log differential.

GDP/capita, 10 years earlier is a natural log of the Maddison figure in 1980 international dollars.

The elderly share is total persons over 65 as a percentage of persons over 20.

The turnover of the chief executive is the number of times the chief executive (monarch, president, prime minister) was replaced by a nonally in the previous ten years.

The Catholic majority is either zero or [the share (not percentage) of religious declarants declaring they are Roman Catholic minus .50], whichever is greater.

Protestant dominance is either zero or [the share (not percentage) of religious declarants declaring they are of a particular Protestant church minus .50], whichever is greater.

The cases of Protestant dominance in this sample are Denmark, Norway, Sweden (each .50), and the United Kingdom (.16 prewar, then .10).

The results for teachers per 1,000 children in (4) are based on an 11-country subsample, not the full 21-country sample. Those for the income- and inheritance-tax shares are from a 19-country sample.

The standard errors reaching into the thousands are the result of tobit regressions' inability to set confidence limits on coefficients that apply mainly to the cases where the dependent variable is zero. The large standard errors for Catholicism in the social spending equation would translate into much smaller standard errors if the regression had combined Catholocism with the fixed-country effects for the Catholic countries.

For fuller reporting of the regressions, see Appendix D.

share would have meant greater benefit payments and inheritance tax receipts as a share of national product. Yet the effect of pre-1930 population aging on total social transfers was probably greater than that. In fact, raising the elderly share of the adult population raised total social transfers *per elderly person* in those days. To see this corollary of the coefficients in Table 16.1, consider the partial response of the support ratio per elderly person to the elderly share of the population. The relevant support ratio here is defined as

$$\text{Support rate } S = (B/Y)/(N_{\text{old}}/N),$$

where B = transfer benefits, Y = national product, and (N_{old}/N) is the share of the adult population (N) that is over the age of sixty-five. When a population gets older, the response of the support ratio is not the same thing as the coefficient on B/Y shown in Table 16.1. To focus on the response of the support ratio, let us examine the slope of the support ratio with respect to the elderly share, or

$$\text{Slope } s = \partial[(B/Y)/(N_{\text{old}}/N)]/\partial(N_{\text{old}}/N).$$

By the quotient rule,

$$\text{Slope } s = [(N_{\text{old}}/N)b - (B/Y)]/(N_{\text{old}}/N)^2$$
$$= (b - S)/(N_{\text{old}}/N),$$

where b = Table 16.1's regression coefficient of (B/Y) with respect to (N_{old}/N). Note that the sign of the effect (slope) on the support ratio depends not just on the sign of the coefficient b, but on the difference between it and the prevailing support ratio S. As it happens, the coefficient (b) of total social transfers' share of GNP with respect to the elderly share is 0.111, which exceeds the sample-average support ratio 0.054. The effect of an older population on the support ratio for all social transfers per elderly person is therefore positive.[5]

One may fairly ask at this point why I have just explored the effect of the elderly population share *on total social transfers*. Why not just the effect on pensions? Why include transfers that did not go to the elderly? The answer lies in Table 16.1's results and in pre-1930 social institutions. Note again, in Table 16.1, that raising the elderly share of the population raises social transfers other than pensions. It is as if the policy impact of having a more elderly population spilled over to include benefits to the younger poor and disabled. It did, and for good institutional reasons. In most countries the elderly still did not have separate noncontributory pension systems that gave them benefits from the younger taxpayers. Rather, their public benefits were still mainly means-tested benefits as part of the larger lingering system of poor relief. Thus if they wanted to lobby for greater benefits for themselves, they needed to lobby for poor relief in general. The political package was bundled together in a way that allied the elderly with other beneficiaries of taxpayers' money.

Given the nonlinearities in the effect of lobbying group size on its redistributive success, predicted back in Chapter 13, one might go beyond the linear age-share effect in Table 16.1 and test for a polynomial curvature of this effect. In extra tests not reported here or in Appendix D, there are indeed hints of nonlinearities, ones congenial to Chapter 13's theoretical predictions about group size effects. Having more elderly raises social transfers strongly as the elderly (over-sixty-five) share of the population rises up to 11 percent of the over-twenty adult population. That range takes us most of the way through the sample. Only as one approaches the sample's maximum elderly share of 14.4 percent does the effect of aging on social transfers as a share of GDP start to decline. There is little harm in using a linear positive effect of aging on social transfers before 1930, when populations were still relatively young.

Several effects of shifts toward more electoral democracy also emerge from Table 16.1. The effects labeled (a) through (e) capture the contrasts between autocracies and democracies and also between elite narrow-suffrage democracies and fuller ones. The striking pattern here is that elite democracies tended to supply the least in overall social transfers and in public pensions, a result already sketched in Figure 4.2 in Volume 1. So say the coefficients contrasting those elite democracies with the average nondemocracy (the row labeled (a)) and with democracies where 70 percent or more of men could vote (row (d), or (d) plus (e)). What about societies in which women were granted their right to vote, as many were before 1930? These devoted significantly more taxpayer money to all kinds of social transfers, mainly to nonpension transfers. Here as in Chapter 7, I interpret this result as reflecting on the kind of society in which women's right to vote was finally granted and not as reflecting a wide gap in women's and men's voting preferences on redistributive issues.

The rate of turnover of the chief executive also mattered. Perhaps less secure regimes tried to offer more redistribution from rich to poor, and more social spending, in an attempt to hang onto power. This is a possibility, as Chapter 7 noted, even though there is no clear theoretical reason why insecurity should make incumbents pander more to those in favor of taxes and spending than to those opposed.[6] The results in Table 16.1 suggest that there may indeed be such an effect. Regime insecurity here is represented by the turnover-of-chief-executive variable, the number of times, over the previous ten years, that a president, prime minister, or monarch was replaced by someone who was not that chief executive's political ally. As Table 16.1 shows, such turnover, presumably representing the expectation of still more turnover to come, has raised poor relief and other social transfers. Perhaps a compilation of detailed political histories from several of these countries might confirm that endangered political incumbents did use social-transfer increases to pander to marginal voters in this era, just as they have done more recently.

Religion also mattered, apparently. Before 1930 Scandinavia and Britain, the nations dominated by a single Protestant sect, were more supportive of social spending and taxes than Roman Catholic countries. Of course, one might imagine that Catholic nations preferred church aid rather than government aid. It seems implausible, however, that the church made up the amounts withheld by governments in Catholic countries.[7]

The more negative influence of Roman Catholicism contrasts sharply with the role of Catholic political parties in Northern Europe after World War II. In 1880–1930 Catholic countries seem to have been against every kind of social spending, yet the Catholic countries of Western Europe have been in the forefront of social spending since World War II. Harold Wilensky found that in 1946–1976 Catholic political-party power appeared to raise social spending in Italy, Austria, Germany, Belgium, and the Netherlands.[8] Possibly, as he suggests, the later setting found them in direct political competition with socialist parties.[9] Papal social policy itself was probably endogenous, driven by competition from socialism and economic development.

ADDING UP THE EXPLANATIONS

Of the influences that significantly shaped the rise of social transfers, which ones shaped it the most? As Dierdre McCloskey has repeatedly warned, we must go beyond asking about statistical significance and ask what influences are truly large according to our best unbiased estimates.[10]

To weigh how much each influence contributed to an overall explanation of what happened to social transfers before 1930, one can multiply the coefficients from Table 16.1 and Appendix D by the actual historical changes in each influencing variable. Table 16.2 does this for a sample of countries, contrasting the shares of national product that countries spent on all social transfers. Reading down the rows of Table 16.2 tells stories about both the international differences and the changes in each country over time.

To clarify why countries differed in their early commitments to social transfer programs, Table 16.2 starts by comparing seven other countries to France for the year 1930.[11] France makes a useful comparison base for at least two reasons. First, it is a large country, with low social spending before World War II, so that most departures from France appear as positive numbers in the table. Second, France was not an outlier in social spending given its values of the independent variables, so that the elements of historical uniqueness can be attributed to the other countries in each comparison.

A small part of each international contrast for 1930 was due to sheer historical momentum: Countries behaved differently in 1930, for example, because they behaved differently in 1920. The first row of Table 16.2 says so by displaying estimates of the small contribution of the effect of earlier

TABLE 16.2. *Explaining Some Differences in Total Social Transfers as a Share of GNP, 1880–1930*

(A) Explaining the Deviations of Other Countries from France's Behavior in 1930

Sources of the Deviations	Australia 1930	Denmark 1930	Italy 1930	Japan 1930	N.Z. 1930	U.S. 1930	U.K. 1930	Simple Average
Total social transfers, 10 years earlier	0.13	0.24	−0.03	−0.03	0.15	0.05	0.12	0.09
Income per capita, present and past	−0.06	0.04	−0.09	−0.13	0.02	0.06	0.01	−0.02
Elderly share (over 65s as % of pop.)	−0.36	−0.22	−0.16	−0.50	−0.47	−0.51	−0.27	−0.36
Democracy and electoral variables	−0.16	−0.21	−0.46	−0.15	−0.12	−0.49	−0.18	−0.25
Religion and fixed-country effect	1.00	1.83	−0.61	0.33	1.37	0.70	1.52	0.88
Sum of these predicted differences	0.56	1.67	−1.34	−0.48	0.95	−0.19	1.20	0.34
Actual differences	1.03	2.32	−0.98	−0.86	1.35	−0.52	1.61	0.56

(B) Explaining the Growth from 1880 to 1930 (in Social Transfers/GNP)

Sources of the Growth	Australia	Denmark	France	Japan	N.Z.	U.S.	U.K.	Simple Average
Total social transfers, 10 years earlier	0.17	0.17	0.03	0.01	0.19	0.06	0.12	0.10
Income per capita, present and past	−0.04	0.13	0.10	0.05	0.06	0.10	0.08	0.07
Elderly share (over 65s as % of pop.)	0.79	0.09	0.10	−0.07	0.74	0.25	0.27	0.32
Democracy and electoral variables	0.92	1.07	0.43	0.61	1.02	0.15	0.96	0.70
Fixed time effect	0.19	0.19	0.19	0.19	0.19	0.19	0.19	0.19
Predicted growth	2.03	1.64	0.85	0.80	2.19	0.75	1.62	1.38
Actual growth	2.11	2.44	0.62	0.17	2.26	0.27	1.83	1.31

Sources and notes to Table 16.2:

The contributions are based on the equation for total social transfers as a percentage of GNP given in Appendix Table D3. For comparable results using a slightly different equation, and for an explanation of how tobit is adapted to this accounting purpose, see Lindert (1994).

Each cell is a contribution to the overall percentage change. For example, the third entry in the first columns says that Australia's being a much younger population than France would have made Australia spend 0.36 percent of GNP less on social transfers than France did (other things equal).

The "democracy and electoral" entry for Japan in the lower panel reflects a rise in executive turnover, not a switch to democracy.

social transfers on current social transfers. As already noted in connection with Table 16.1 above, momentum is probably not a separate force but rather a channel for transmitting the effects of earlier movements in the behavioral forces featured here.

International differences in income per capita played only a modest role in most of the contrasts shown in the upper half of Table 16.2. That is partly because most of the countries chosen here had income levels not too different from that of France. Only Japan and Italy were enough poorer than France in 1930 to show much effect of income differences on social transfers. Income effects would have been more visible had the table included additional poor countries from the sample, such as the Latin American countries, Portugal, Spain, and Greece. Incomes also played a secondary role in explaining why social transfers grew between 1880 and 1930, as shown in the lower half of the table.

Population aging played a noticeable and understandable role in both the international differences and the growth of social transfers. One of the main differences between France and other countries was that the French were older than the populations of other countries. Since an older population tends to have more political demand for such programs as poor relief, public pensions, and public health subsidies, we would expect France to have higher transfers (other things equal). This is why the entries in the "elderly share" row of the international contrasts for 1930 are all negative. Younger national populations, especially those outside of Europe, saw less need to pay taxes for social programs. To this extent, what some might view as international cultural or ideological differences could have been driven by demography. Population aging also left its fingerprints on the growth of social transfers between 1880 and 1930. As the lower half of Table 16.2 shows, the especially rapid aging of the populations of Australia and New Zealand seems to have accelerated their development of new social programs by about half a percent of GNP.

Some of the strongest effects on social transfers came from democracy and electoral forces. In the international contrasts for 1930, these political variables played a particularly large role in explaining the departures of Italian and American behavior from that of France. One political source of the Franco-Italian and Franco-American contrasts was peculiar to the era around 1930. At that juncture France had come through a series of rapid turnover in governments, which in general is a force raising social transfers. By contrast, in 1930 Mussolini's Italy and Herbert Hoover's America were historical settings in which the incumbent administration was already of long standing, which tends to act against social transfer programs. Aside from their differences in political turnover, the same countries differed in their voter turnout. Relative to France, the United States had become a nation of low voter turnout after the 1910s, as noted earlier. Lower voter turnout meant less national commitment to social programs. Italy too had lower effective turnout in that Mussolini's Italy was not an electoral democracy at all. Again, the general international pattern translates that lack of democratic voice into lower social transfers. Turning to the changes in social transfers between 1880 and 1930 in the lower half of the table, the whole set of democracy and electoral variables again played a leading role. As this book notes repeatedly, extending political voice to the full adult population is perhaps the greatest single source of the rise of social spending.

The link between dominant Protestant religions and taxed-based social transfers also separated Australia, Denmark, New Zealand, and the United Kingdom from Catholic France, as shown in the lower panel of Table 16.2.

Once all these forces have been given their due, some international differences and some growth of social spending still remain unexplained. This was expected, since countries and time periods do have unique elements that are not captured by systematic variables. Of the seven countries contrasted to France in the upper half of Table 16.2, the only one where the chosen systematic forces should have caused a higher relative commitment to social transfers than we actually observe for 1930 is the United States. The Americans spent fully half a percent of GNP less on social transfers than France, whereas the systematic variables would have predicted that the Americans should have been spending only a fifth of a percent less (−0.19 percent). The growth accounting in the lower half of Table 16.2 also points to the American case as one for which social transfers as a share of GNP should have grown more by 1930 than predicted. Between 1880 and 1930, that share should have grown by 0.75 percent, yet it grew by only 0.27 percent. By the low-spending standards of 1930, these are wide gaps. Aside from these error terms, fixed country effects in the underlying regression also bespeak historical and cultural influences not captured in Table 16.2. In particular, Canada, Greece, and the Netherlands gave much less in social transfers than the systematic forces would have predicted. The explanation for these national peculiarities awaits further study.

There are many possible, and popular, explanations for the extra anti-social-transfer bias of the Americans, and any of these is consistent with the results shown here. One strong likelihood is that the greater ethnic fractionalization of the United States makes voters extra reluctant to pay taxes for collective social programs, since there is less feeling in an ethnically fragmented society that "our" tax money gets returned to "us" in government programs. Chapter 17 will confirm that ethnic divisions have fostered resistance to taxing and spending in the postwar era.

SUMMARY

As of 1930, three main forces, some lesser systematic forces, and some unique historical elements combined to explain most of the differences in social transfers across countries and over the half century between 1880 and 1930.

The three are income, demography, and democracy. That raising income per capita raises the share of income given to taxes and social transfers, an idea known as Wagner's Law, received modest but noticeable support here. On the negative side, low income helped to explain the lack of social programs in the vast impoverished majority of the world's countries, represented in the sample by four Latin American countries, Japan, and Mediterranean Europe. On the positive side, income growth helped to account for the claim of social transfers on a greater and greater share of national product.

The drift toward a noticeable share of over-sixty-fives in the population also contributed to the historical emergence of social transfers. An older adult population leaned toward more social transfers, mainly transfers other than pensions. The likely reason for this look of altruism toward the young is that the elderly before 1930 still got their safety net support from general poor relief systems, not yet from a separate public pension system. And before 1930 the rise in the share of over-sixty-fives in the population seemed to evoke not only a greater share of transfers in national product, but also a slightly higher level of social transfers per old person, relative to the level of GNP per adult. There were hints of an emergence of "gray power" even before 1930.

Democracy also affected social transfers. The real contrast was not between all democracies and autocracies, however. Rather, the type of regime that stood out for its low social transfers was the same type that most staunchly resisted taxes for public schools: elite democracies, where only 40 percent or less of men were franchised to vote. Elite democracies, such as Great Britain before 1900, transferred less than either the average autocracy or a typical heavily voting populace.

Beyond these three leading forces, religion also played a role in international differences, though not in the rise of transfers over time. The greater propensity of dominant Protestant churches to back government transfers helps to explain how they transferred a greater share of GNP than France, even though elderly France might have had greater transfers than other countries on demographic grounds.

What Drove Postwar Social Spending?

The postwar growth of welfare-state social transfer programs has dwarfed the earlier pioneering attempts to build comprehensive insurance programs. Social transfers have risen even faster than public education. How did that happen? A lesser part of the answer is a story of the generations that lived through the Great Depression and the Second World War. The greater part of the answer rests on the same broad social forces that were already acting in the half-century after 1880. This chapter reintroduces the three main forces of democracy, demography, and income, and adds other social differences to give a fuller explanation of both the growth and the diversity of the movement toward welfare states.

To highlight how policy behavior has and has not changed since 1880, this chapter follows the same historical forces and same format we just followed in Chapter 16. The fuller postwar data coverage allows us to expand the inquiry, however. We can compare time periods of only three or four years, yielding more dynamic information from a thirty-five-year span than the ten-year stretches could give for the fifty years between 1880 and 1930. Public education expenditures are also conveniently available for the 1962–1981 period, allowing more direct comparison of social budget priorities than for the pre-1930 era, for which we had to be content with counting enrolled students and teachers.

It will turn out that the same three leading actors are at center stage for the postwar era, but with altered behavior and with two others now sharing the stage. Electoral politics continued to play a key role in international differences in social transfers, but with voter turnout performing more visibly than voter rights. The effects of population aging became more problematic, in ways that have shaped this book's exploration of how the aging crisis will change social policy in the twenty-first century. Income growth still plays a strong role but is now joined by openness to international trade and social divisions as key determinants of international differences in social policy.

Deciding what could have caused the postwar rise of social transfers, and what could have made it so much greater in some countries than in others, again calls for an examination of many forces at once. Here again, as in our look at the forces that set the pioneers apart in the 1880–1930 period, we need to give as many leading suspects as possible their day in court. Since that compels us to dwell on systematic variables that can be measured for all countries, the task breaks down into the same two parts noted in Chapter 16. First, we explain as much as possible with the available systematic variables. Then we note which countries seemed to have distinct departures from the overall pattern, departures suggesting unique elements of their national histories.

To explore the possible causal forces in the experience since World War II requires choosing a sample of countries with high quality data. As noted in Chapter 14, the two time periods visited here are the ones for which the OECD developed measures of social transfers that are consistent across countries: their 1960–1981 sample and their 1980–1996 sample. The samples are, again,

The 1962–1981 OECD data set of ninety-five cases, using five four-year time periods (1962/65 through 1978/81) for nineteen countries: Australia, Austria, Belgium, Canada, Denmark, Finland, France, Germany, Greece, Ireland, Italy, Japan, Netherlands, New Zealand, Norway, Sweden, the United Kingdom, and the United States; and

The 1978–1995 data set of 126 cases, using six three-year time periods (1978/80 through 1993/95) for twenty-one countries, consisting of the same nineteen plus Portugal and Spain.

The OECD data offer insights on the sources of postwar social spending that can be compared with the prewar patterns of Chapters 15 and 16. The results are summarized in Table 17.1 and detailed in Appendix Tables E1 and E3.[1]

THREE MAIN FORCES

Elections

The uneven rise of democracy before 1930 offered a clear view of the social-policy impact of giving new voting rights to workers and to women. After World War II, the same central role for the spread of democracy would show up in global samples that have varying degrees of democracy. The OECD countries studied here, however, offered little variation in voting rights. All were electoral democracies in our sample periods, except for Greece 1967–1973. All OECD democracies recognized women's right to vote, except for pre-1972 Switzerland. Given this historical setting, one should not expect differences between autocracy and democracy, or differences in female suffrage, to play the major role it played on the pre-1930 period.

Yet two electoral influences – the rate of voter turnout for elections and the rate of turnover of top government leaders – continue to affect governments' social spending and taxes, just as they did a hundred years ago. The voting share of adults again raises social transfers. Specifically, raising the voting share from 70 to 85 percent of eligible voters significantly raises pensions and educational spending. This impact resembles the impact of extra voters back in 1880–1930. Yet the postwar differences in countries' voting shares reflect differences in people's willingness to use the votes they are allowed and not differences in the right to vote. It is striking that in Switzerland and the United States fewer than half of eligible voters actually vote and that this has apparently weakened the political will of both countries to raise public pensions, relative to countries in which 85 percent of eligible voters show up at the polls.

Who are the nonvoters in Switzerland and the United States and other countries? U.S. information suggests that the nonvoters are not elderly on the average, since the elderly vote at least as faithfully than younger adults. Thus the bias against pensions cannot be due to any relative absence of pro-transfer elderly from the polls. Rather the nonvoting pattern that lowers social transfers is probably the heavier nonvoting by low-income and low-education voters.[2] Their unwillingness to vote probably serves to lower transfers they would benefit from.

The other electoral influence with almost a century of impact on social transfers is the rate of turnover of the top executive – the president or prime minister – in most postwar democracies up to 1981. As Table 17.1 shows, a greater number of changes at the top over a ten-year span raises the share of GDP spent on welfare, on public health, and on total social transfers in the 1962–1981 era, just as it did between 1880 and 1930.

Population Aging Again

Most national populations aged across the twentieth century, and Europe continued to be the continent with the greatest share of persons over sixty-five. Several outside clues predict that this should have raised total social spending, and pension spending, as a share of GDP. In fact, it could even have raised the relative generosity of pensions per elderly person, if an older population gave the elderly more political clout, more gray power. So said the historical experiences of twenty-one countries in 1880–1930, as discussed in Chapter 16. A recent literature on postwar social spending agrees with at least the premise that an older population means a greater share of public pension budgets in GDP.[3]

Yet gray has shifted its focus away from supporting transfers in general to lobbying more narrowly for pay-as-you-go public pensions. Comparing the coefficients in the first two columns of Table 17.1 with their counterparts in Chapter 16 suggests such a historical reversal. Instead of raising the social

TABLE 17.1. *How Various Forces Affected Social Spending as Percentages of GDP, 1962–1995*

Panel A. In the 1962–1981 Sample of 19 Countries

Effects on These Public Expenditure Shares Over a 4-Year Period
(Standard Errors in Parentheses)

	Total Social Transfers as % of GDP		Old-Age Pensions as % of GDP		Old-Age Pensions Support Ratio		Welfare and Unempl. Comp. as % of GDP		Public Health Expenditures as % of GDP		Public Education Expenditures as % of GDP	
The effects of unit changes in												
Total social transfers 4 years earlier	0.90	(0.05)**	0.20	(0.13)**	0.02	(0.004)**	0.20	(0.05)**	0.08	(0.03)**	0.01	(0.02)
Growth in GDP/capita, last 10 years	59.17	(12.99)**	4.38	(11.36)	0.71	(1.03)	19.51	(10.52)[a]	22.21	(7.41)**	32.30	(7.18)**
GDP/capita, 10 years earlier	3.53	(0.56)**	1.92	(0.68)**	0.18	(0.06)**	1.02	(0.55)[a]	2.26	(0.42)**	2.56	(0.35)**
The effects of a 1% rise in the elderly share of adults												
For a young adult population	0.01	(0.23)	0.09	(0.24)	−0.01	(0.02)	−0.18	(0.19)	0.03	(0.16)		
For a medium adult population	−0.08	(0.10)	0.33	(0.12)**	−0.02	(0.01)*	−0.07	(0.11)	0.05	(0.08)		
For an old adult population	0.15	(0.27)	0.29	(0.30)	−0.03	(0.02)	−0.04	(0.24)	0.25	(0.21)		
The effects of selected shifts in electoral politics												
From 40% voting to 70% voting	−0.74	(1.09)	−1.67	(1.38)	−0.20	(0.11)[b]	3.47	(0.86)**	−1.07	(0.89)	−0.33	(1.02)
From 70% voting to 85% voting	0.45	(0.30)	0.72	(0.35)*	0.08	(0.03)**	0.17	(0.34)	0.35	(0.25)	0.54	(0.22)*
Faster turnover of chief executive	0.14	(0.07)*	0.02	(0.06)	0.003	(0.01)	0.13	(0.05)*	0.06	(0.03)[b]	0.02	(0.03)
The effects of changes in these other forces												
Catholic majority	1.57	(0.80)[a]	2.00	(1.25)	0.18	(0.10)[b]	0.77	(1.29)	−0.05	(0.87)	0.64	(0.69)
Ethnic fractionalization	−2.19	(0.82)**	−2.78	(1.12)*	−0.22	(0.10)*	0.65	(1.35)	−2.38	(0.95)*	0.21	(0.94)
Openness to foreign trade/1,000	32.98	(6.67)**	−12.5	(8.65)	−1.29	−(0.71)[b]	30.26	(9.76)**	5.80	(6.35)	17.66	(4.97)**
Military spending/GDP	0.16	(0.09)[b]	−0.00	−(0.10)	0.003	(0.01)	0.06	(0.09)	−0.16	(0.07)*	−0.15	(0.07)*

Panel B. In the 1978–1995 Sample of 21 Countries

Effects on These Public Expenditure Shares Over 3-Year Period
(Standard Errors in Parentheses)

	Total Social Transfers as % of GDP		Old-Age Pensions as % of GDP		Old-Age Pensions Support Ratio		Welfare (Basic Assistance) as % of GDP		Unemployment Compensation as % of GDP		Public Health Expenditures as % of GDP	
The effects of unit changes in												
Total social transfers 3 years earlier	0.93	(26.01)**	0.29	(8.68)**	0.02	(9.09)**	0.14	(7.67)**	0.11	(5.83)**	0.08	(3.67)**
Growth in GDP/capita, last 3 years	−4.51	(1.85)ᵃ	−1.84	(1.39)	−0.17	(1.73)ᵇ	0.47	(0.71)	−1.65	(2.86)**	−0.30	(0.28)
GDP/capita, 3 years earlier	0.58	(0.98)	1.13	(1.97)*	0.07	(1.61)	0.90	(2.53)*	0.48	(1.31)	2.71	(5.73)**
The effects of a 1% rise in the elderly share of adults												
For a young adult population	0.02	(0.05)	0.01	(0.02)	.0001	(0.00)	−0.18	(0.93)	−0.11	(0.63)	0.15	(0.51)
For a medium adult population	0.13	(1.15)	0.46	(4.22)**	−0.01	(0.84)	−0.01	(0.01)	−0.11	(1.88)ᵃ	−0.04	(0.44)
For an old adult population	0.05	(0.07)	−0.32	(0.63)	−0.08	(2.84)**	0.57	(1.34)	−0.47	(1.48)	0.41	(0.67)
The effects of selected shifts in electoral politics												
From 40% voting to 70% voting	−0.64	(0.54)	−0.84	(0.91)	−0.08	(1.20)	0.70	(1.40)	0.87	(1.15)	−0.84	(1.02)
From 70% voting to 85% voting	0.24	(1.07)	0.58	(2.77)**	0.05	(3.13)**	−0.09	(0.84)	−0.22	(1.89)ᵃ	0.15	(0.89)
Faster turnover of chief executive	−0.01	(0.21)	0.04	(0.72)	0.002	(0.47)	−0.04	(1.36)	−0.03	(0.91)	0.07	(1.47)
The effects of changes in these other forces												
Catholic majority	1.05	(1.50)	3.22	(4.34)**	0.22	(4.18)**	0.44	(1.02)	0.37	(0.92)	1.12	(2.05)*
Ethnic fractionalization	0.02	(0.30)	−1.41	(2.18)*	−0.10	(1.94)ᵃ	−1.34	(3.23)**	0.71	(1.24)	−0.64	(1.12)
Openness to foreign trade/1,000	−0.004	(0.93)	−0.01	(2.45)*	−.001	(2.55)*	0.01	(3.055)**	0.01	(2.311)*	0.01	(2.091)*
Military spending	−0.03	(0.32)	0.16	(1.93)ᵃ	0.01	(1.56)	0.06	(1.03)	0.04	(0.78)	−0.10	(1.27)

Sources and notes to Table 17.1:

(** = significant at the 1% level, two-tail; * = significant at the 5% level; ᵃsignificant at the 7% level; ᵇsignificant at the 10% level.)

The source for all social spending was OECD (1985) for the 1962–1981 sample, and the OECD's CD-ROM for social expenditures 1980–1996 for the 1978–1995 sample, with splicing of 1978–1980 averages using both sources.

The pension support ratio = (public pension spending/person over 65) / (GDP/total population). Its sample mean = 0.558 for the 1962–1981 sample, and 0.598 for the 1978–1995 sample.

Growth in GDP/capita is measured as the natural-log differential predicted in a first-stage regression. Its mean = 0.0354 per annum in the 1961–1981 sample, and 0.0665 for a 3-year growth span (0.0222 per annum) in the 1978–1995 sample.

GDP/capita, 10 years earlier (in the 1962–1981 sample) is a natural log of the Summers–Heston (1988) figure in thousands of 1980 international dollars. Its mean = 1.536. For the 1978–1995 sample, GDP/capita 3 years earlier is the log of the Penn World Tables 5.6 figure in 1985 international dollars. Its mean = 9.302.

(continued) Sources and notes to Table 17.1:

The elderly share of adults is the percentage of the over-65 population in the total population. For the 1962–1981 sample its mean = 11.5%. Its values used here are 8% for the young population (e.g., Japan 1974–1977), 11.5% for the medium-age population, and 15% for the old population. This last is close to the sample maximum, 16.2% for Sweden 1978/1981. For the 1978–1995 sample, its mean is 13.3%. Its value for the young population here is 9% (e.g., Japan 1980), 13% for a medium-age population, and 18% for an old population (near the sample maximum of 18.72% for Sweden in 1985–1987). The main data source is United Nations (1998).

The voting share is the share (not percentage) of adults of voting age who actually voted in the most recent full (or presidential) election, including an election held in the same year. For Switzerland 1962–1971, that meant males only. Its mean is .790 for the 1962–1981 sample. For the 1978–1995 sample it refers to a share of those eligible to vote, rather than a separately calculated "voting-age" group, and its mean is .768. The source is Mackie and Rose (1991, 1997).

The turnover of the chief executive is the number of times the chief executive (monarch, president, prime minister) was replaced in the previous ten years.

The Catholic majority is either zero or [the share (not percentage) of religious declarants declaring they are Roman Catholic minus .50], whichever is greater. Its mean = .121 in the 1962–1981 sample, and .157 in the 1978–1995 sample (which includes Portugal and Spain). It is positive only for Austria, Belgium, France, Ireland, Italy, Portugal, and Spain. See Taylor and Hudson (1972).

Ethnic fractionalization is the index of ethnic and linguistic divisions, circa 1960.

Openness is exports plus imports as a share of GDP at current prices, from Penn World Tables 5.6. Its mean is 53.15% for the 1962–1981 sample, and 62.49% for the 1978–1995 sample. The table above reports the coefficients on 1/1,000 of this to allow a display of significant digits.

Military spending as a percentage of GDP is from Stockholm International Peace Research Institute. The source warns that the basis of measurement changes often. The mean = 3.13% for the 1962–1981 sample, and 2.66% for the 1978–1995 sample.

For fuller reporting of these variables and regressions, see Appendix E.

transfer budgets significantly and having a considerably smaller effect on separate programs, as in 1880–1930, postwar aging tends to raise pensions more clearly than it raises total social spending. The reversal makes political sense. Before 1930, an older population tended to favor more social transfers of all kinds, including more welfare and unemployment compensation, as we saw in Chapter 16. That was apparently because an older population supported poor relief in general, given that much of the government support for the elderly was administered by the same institutions. A society wanting more pensions for an aging population would, in those days, have given more support to the whole set of poor-relief institutions. Yet in the postwar period, public pensions had become a separate program of their own, and the larger population could decide to expand them without expanding welfare or the dole.

In the postwar era population aging did not raise the combination of welfare assistance and unemployment compensation. The impact of population aging on welfare and unemployment might even have become negative since 1962. The overall effect is insignificantly negative in the 1962–1981 sample, as shown in Panel A of Table 17.1. In 1978–1995, the negative effect of aging seems to have been felt more on unemployment compensation than on welfare payments. In the equations that include fixed country effects (Appendix Table E3), the effects look even more negative. The negative effect on the dole is not yet statistically robust, however, and a related study actually finds a positive effect of aging on the dole.[4] The overall effect thus wavers around zero. Subject to further tests, the tentative conclusion is that having the population become older no longer raises welfare and unemployment compensation the way it did before 1930.

The consensus that older populations want bigger public pensions needs to confront an obvious limit to this political force. Sooner or later, something has to give, as we have been warned repeatedly since the 1980s. If the elderly became, say, half the adult population someday, how much generosity of pension support could they extract from younger adults in a pay-as-you-go system of the sort that still generally prevails? If half of all adults were retired, they could receive 100 percent of a typical young adult's after-tax income only if the young were willing to work and pay a 50 percent tax rate to get no more than retirees get. At some point on the way to such an extreme, protests by the young would check the rise in pension benefits. As theorized in Chapter 13, there should be an eventual downslope in the relationship between a lobby's share of the population and the rate at which it gains net transfers per member from the rest of the polity. In other words, gray power should eventually fall as the elderly share of the population rises. The empirical literature on the aging effect needs to allow for such a downturn, especially as aging continues in the early twenty-first century.

The regression results reinforce this fear about the implications of aging for the generosity of public pensions per elderly person. The estimates do not yet allow us to reach a firm answer on who pays for the rise in the elderly share of the population: perhaps taxpayers, perhaps recipients of welfare and unemployment compensation, perhaps the elderly themselves. The estimates do offer some strong hints, however. The hints are consistent with part of Chapter 13's predictions, and they have shaped the forecasts of Chapter 8 in Volume 1.

The generosity of the taxpayers toward each individual oldster can decline even though the pension share of GDP may rise with the elderly share of the population. The link between these two shares should be evident from the definitional link between the budget share and the support ratio:

Pension support ratio

= pension budget share of GDP

divided by the share of oldsters in the population.

The slope of the pension budget share with respect to the elderly population share probably declined a bit across the twentieth century. Even if it had remained constant, however, the mere fact that the elderly share rose must have pulled down the pension support ratio, other things equal. Indeed, both in 1962–1981 and in 1978–1995, this negative effect stands out in Table 17.1, just as it did in Chapter 16's equation for the support-ratio slope with respect to aging. Thus, over the whole century, as well as in the separate nonlinear regressions for each historical sample, the implications of aging for the relative support of each elderly person must eventually turn negative.

Income Growth

As in the pre-1930 history, and as in most research on the postwar era, Panel A of Table 17.1 reports strong income effects in 1962–1981, on the share of social in GDP. Wagner's Law is again confirmed for social spending, though its underlying mechanism remains open to interpretation. There are a couple of twists, however, for the 1978–1995 period. Without fixed effects, the income effects evaporate. Yet with conventional effects added to the equation, the positive income effects re-appear for 1978–1995. While one could choose to remain agnostic about Wagner's Law, on the grounds that the fixed effects may reflect unmeasured forces, I tend to view Wagner's Law as receiving support once again. Within the positive overall effects on social spending, increasing income tends to raise spending in all categories, including public education.

OTHER VERDICTS

Momentum from Past Transfers

A strong influence on the current rate of social transfers is the recent history of that rate itself. Such momentum is revealed here by the role of the share of total social transfers in GDP.[5] There is indeed a large carry-over from one period to the next, when the periods are three- and four-year averages. This momentum fits various theories. One is that the self-interested government group paid by the programs effectively lobbies for their continued expansion. Alternatively, and more likely, the carry-over reflects the slowness with which the political process adjusts only incrementally to a longer-standing rise in the demand for social programs. In effect, each period's behavior is a weighted average of the level of social transfers it would prefer if transition were costless and the level inherited from the previous time period.

Religion and Ethnic Fractionalization

After World War II, Catholic-majority countries no longer lagged behind in their support for public pensions and social transfers. Table 17.1 confirms this historic shift, previously described in Chapters 7 and 16.

The social divisions highlighted in Chapter 7's section on social affinity also should be tested statistically. The postwar setting provides historial data, which allow two tests that were not possible in Chapter 16 for lack of pre-war information. The first test, also employed in earlier publications, uses the income gaps described in Chapter 7 to represent the pre-fiscal income gaps among the rich, middle-class, and poor. That test found some support for the view that wider gaps between the middle-class and poor indicated society's reluctance to spend on social transfers, but the results were fragile. The second, more robust test of social divisiveness takes advantage of a set of ethnographers' indexes of ethnic fractionalization for most of the world's nations in the 1960s. Using indices from the Soviet *Atlas Narodov Mira* reveals the predicted negative effects on some, though not all, kinds of social spending. Ethnic divisions reduce public funds for pensions and public health, though not for unemployment or public schooling, as Table 17.1 shows. The overall effect on total social spending is clearly negative, as expected. This accords with other studies' findings that ethnic divisions reduce all sorts of public spending.[6]

Openness

A nation's being open to foreign trade, and vulnerable to foreign-trade shocks, could make its politicians more sensitive to the need for safety nets, as Dani Rodrik has argued. In Rodrik's own version of the story, openness has two opposing tendencies.[7] On the one hand, he grants, others may be right that being open to foreign trade and to foreign investment could cause a race to the bottom, in which countries cut their social programs to remain competitive internationally. On the other hand, he predicted that vulnerability to terms-of-trade shocks would cause the safety net demand already mentioned. Rodrik's own tests supported both predictions. Openness by itself had a negative effect on social spending, à la "race to the bottom," but it had a strongly positive effect when interacted with terms-of-trade movements.

The tests conducted here are simpler than Rodrik's own bifurcated hypothesis, and some of the effects are strikingly more straightforward than in his tests. Openness is represented simply by the share of exports plus imports in GDP at current prices, notwithstanding the literature's fears about such a simple measure.[8] Table 17.1 reports that openness is indeed a significantly positive influence on social spending. The kinds of spending it raises are the nonpension varieties: welfare unemployment and education. That it raises these seems consistent with Rodrik's emphasis on supplying support for those of working age in the face of trade competition. Yet Appendix Table E.3 shows no positive effects of openness once fixed country effects are included.

Military Spending

It seems inevitable that a political mandate to raise military spending as a share of GDP would cut into social programs, in the traditional ugly trade-off between guns and butter. What kinds of social spending do a military commitment displace? The results in Table 17.1 say that the main victims are public health and public education. The military expenditures did not move drastically in these postwar samples, however, and all-out wars might have had different effects.

Fixed Country Effects

Thus far we have ignored the econometric bogeyman of fixed effects, which threaten to cast a cloud over any pooled or cross-sectional regression analysis. Perhaps, the traditional fear goes, what look like clear behavioral influences are just the result of unseen and unmeasured fixed attributes of places and times. What attributes? Scholars are free to fear them without being able to name them.

The distinct possibility of fixed effects calls for three kinds of response here. The first two are interpretive, and the third is directly empirical.

One interpretive response is to repeat others' concern that conventional time and fixed effects are often used in a way that throws away information on the behavioral structure we seek to explore. Adding $n-1$ fixed country dummies and $t-1$ fixed time dummies, in a pool of n countries and t time periods, threatens to give interpretive credit to these mystery variables when some or all of that credit is due to the behavioral variables already under study. In history's laboratory, part of the effect of income, age, or voting takes a form that is fixed for a country or for a time period. The influence of income, age, or voting is often embodied in, not competitive against, fixed attributes of country and time. There is the danger of underrating these behavioral forces by crediting them only with the part not fixed by country or time in the historical laboratory we are given.

The second interpretive concern is that some of the behavioral forces we wish to study consist entirely of linear combination of fixed country or time effects. In this chapter, religion, ethnic fractionalization, and the circa-1970 upper and lower incomes gaps are all combinations of fixed-country effects. To test for their influences, one must omit the fixed country effects. Similarly, Chapter 18's exploration of the sources of growth must omit the full battery of fixed-time effects in order to discuss global demand shocks and global supply shocks effectively.

The third, directly empirical, response is that the conventional battery of fixed effects has been tried here. In regressions relegated to Appendix E, the conventional fixed effects had only two impacts on the qualitative roles of the behavioral variables. The more important impact, already noted, is that fixed effects reduce the income and openness effects for 1978–1995. Aside from this impact, fixed effects left little mark on the other behavioral influences and serve mainly as a clue for investigating which unique historical elements need to be added to achieve a fuller explanation.

ACCOUNTING FOR DIFFERENCES IN SOCIAL SPENDING

Which of the driving forces played the biggest role in making some countries into welfare states and committing other countries to a more free-market system? To determine which of the factors loomed largest in the overall explanation requires a more elaborate algebra than was needed in Chapter 16. The postwar history is characterized by a stronger momentum effect than the 1880–1930 experience. The reason may simply be that the postwar sample uses three- and four-year averages rather than benchmark years spread ten years apart. The lagged dependent variable therefore has more power in the equation for total social transfers, as testified by the 0.90 and 0.94 terms in Table 17.1. To replace this less informative momentum effect with the earlier systematic behavior that created it requires a sequential decomposition back to the earliest data. Appendix G derives the accounting algebra we need to break down our best predictions of social spending into meaningful systematic forces plus an error term. This algebra succeeds in shrinking the role of the lagged transfer variable, which has been pushed five or six periods earlier.[9]

For the easiest interpretation of the international differences in social spending, Tables 17.2 through 17.6 compare all other countries to the United States, a large and low-spending country. The historical contrasts will be for the four-year period 1978–1981, to make use of the fact that the 1962–1981 sample allows some story telling about public education as well as about social transfers. Let us begin reading the historical interpretations with Table 17.2's contrast in overall social transfers and with the eighteen-country average in the top row.

TABLE 17.2. *Accounting for International Differences in Total Social Transfers as a Percentage of GDP, in 1978/81*

Relative to the United States in 1978/81

	Total Observed Diff.	Total Predicted Diff.	Error	Diff. Due to to Diff's in Transfers c. 1960	The Part of Total Transfers Explained by Behavior Since 1962						
					All	Income Effects	Age Effect	Electoral Effects	Religion & Ethnic Divisions	Trade Openness	Milit. Exp./ GDP
18 nations[*]	5.6	6.4	−0.8	1.7	4.6	−4.5	−0.2	2.8	3.4	5.7	−2.5
Australia	−1.5	2.3	−3.7	0.1	2.2	−3.2	0.4	3.5	1.6	2.2	−2.4
Austria	9.1	10.9	−1.9	4.6	6.4	−4.5	−0.3	2.5	5.9	6.3	−3.6
Belgium	16.0	15.1	0.9	3.1	12.0	−3.3	−0.6	3.4	2.6	12.2	−2.4
Canada	0.4	−0.1	0.6	1.0	−1.1	−1.5	0.4	0.8	−2.2	4.2	−2.9
Denmark	12.4	11.6	0.8	2.6	8.9	−2.0	−0.5	4.0	4.0	6.3	−2.8
Finland	5.2	3.1	2.1	0.8	2.3	−4.5	0.0	2.0	3.0	5.1	−3.4
France	8.0	8.0	0.0	3.3	4.8	−2.2	−0.6	1.2	5.2	2.7	−1.6
Germany	11.4	11.9	−0.4	5.7	6.1	−2.7	−0.3	3.0	4.2	3.9	−2.0
Greece	−3.4	−1.8	−1.6	1.7	−3.5	−13.2	−0.2	4.4	3.6	3.0	−1.0
Ireland	3.9	4.2	−0.3	0.8	3.5	−12.6	−0.2	2.3	6.9	10.4	−3.4
Italy	7.3	7.6	−0.3	3.1	4.6	−7.5	−0.3	4.5	7.3	3.1	−2.6
Japan	−2.7	−1.6	−1.1	−1.7	0.1	−4.0	0.3	2.1	4.4	1.1	−3.8
Neth.	13.4	14.2	−0.8	2.3	11.9	−4.1	0.0	4.4	3.6	10.2	−2.1
N.Z.	0.6	2.8	−2.2	1.6	1.2	−5.7	0.4	3.4	1.2	5.1	−3.2
Norway	7.0	13.5	−6.5	0.3	13.2	−1.5	−0.6	3.7	4.1	9.7	−2.3
Sweden	11.3	8.8	2.5	1.9	6.9	−2.2	0.0	2.4	3.8	5.0	−2.1
Switz.	−0.1	1.1	−1.2	−1.2	2.3	−1.3	−0.4	0.1	0.0	6.9	−2.9
U.K.	2.3	3.1	−0.8	1.6	1.6	−5.7	−0.5	2.6	1.6	4.7	−1.1
U.S.	0.0	0.0	0.0	0.0	0.0	0.0	0.0	0.0	0.0	0.0	0.0
Correlation with observed change	.94	.31	.69		.86	.24	−.53	.35	.41	.58	−.06

TABLE 17.3. *Accounting for International Differences in Public Pensions as a Percentage of GDP, in 1978/81*

Relative to the United States in 1978/81

	Total Observed Diff.	Total Predicted Diff.	Error	Diff. Due to to Diff's in Transfers c. 1960	The Part of Public Pensions Explained by Behavior Since 1962						
					All	Income Effects	Age Effect	Electoral Effects	Religion & Ethnic Divisions	Trade Openness	Milit. Exp./ GDP
18 nations*	1.5	0.8	−0.7	0.0	0.8	−1.0	−0.7	0.5	1.3	0.7	0.0
Australia	−1.5	0.1	−1.6	0.0000	0.1	−0.7	−0.6	1.0	0.6	−0.2	0.0
Austria	6.5	3.2	3.3	0.0005	3.2	−1.2	1.7	1.2	2.3	−0.8	0.0
Belgium	1.9	0.5	1.4	0.0004	0.5	−0.9	1.3	0.6	1.0	−1.5	0.0
Canada	−2.7	−2.6	−0.1	0.0001	−2.6	−0.3	−0.3	−0.6	−0.9	−0.5	0.0
Denmark	0.9	2.2	−1.3	0.0003	2.2	−0.5	1.3	0.6	1.6	−0.7	0.0
Finland	1.8	0.0	1.7	0.0001	0.0	−1.2	0.4	0.2	1.2	−0.6	0.0
France	4.4	1.6	2.9	0.0004	1.6	−0.8	1.2	−0.6	2.0	−0.3	0.0
Germany	5.6	2.5	3.0	0.0007	2.5	−0.7	1.7	0.4	1.6	−0.5	0.0
Greece	−1.3	−1.2	−0.1	0.0002	−1.2	−2.9	0.8	−0.1	1.4	−0.4	0.0
Ireland	−2.5	−1.1	−1.4	0.0001	−1.1	−2.3	−0.1	0.1	2.7	−1.3	0.0
Italy	5.2	4.6	0.5	0.0004	4.6	−1.6	0.8	3.0	2.8	−0.4	0.0
Japan	−2.8	−1.1	−1.6	−0.0002	−1.1	−1.4	−0.7	−0.6	1.7	−0.1	0.0
Neth.	5.7	0.4	5.3	0.0003	0.4	−0.9	0.1	1.0	1.4	−1.2	0.0
N.Z.	0.3	−1.0	1.3	0.0002	−1.0	−0.9	−0.5	0.6	0.5	−0.6	0.0
Norway	1.2	1.4	−0.2	0.0000	1.4	−0.6	1.4	0.0	1.6	−1.0	0.0
Sweden	3.9	3.3	0.6	0.0002	3.3	−0.7	1.9	1.2	1.5	−0.6	0.0
Switz.	0.9	1.3	−0.4	−0.0001	1.3	−0.2	1.0	1.3	0.0	−0.8	0.0
U.K.	−0.2	0.1	−0.3	0.0002	0.1	−1.0	1.4	−0.4	0.6	−0.5	0.0
U.S.	0.0	0.0	0.0	0.0	0.0	0.0	0.0	0.0	0.0	0.0	0.0
Correlation with observed difference		.80	.81	.74	.80	.17	.62	.54	.45	−.17	.01

TABLE 17.4. *Accounting for International Differences in Welfare and Unemployment Compensation as a Percentage of GDP, in 1978/81*

Relative to the United States in 1978/81

	Total Observed Diff.	Total Predicted Diff.	Error	Diff. Due to to Diff's in Transfers c. 1960	The Part of Welfare and Unemp. Comp. Explained by Behavior Since 1962						
					All	Income Effects	Age Effect	Electoral Effects	Religion & Ethnic Divisions	Trade Open-ness	Milit. Exp./ GDP
18 nations[*]	2.4	1.9	0.5	0.0	1.9	−0.4	−0.1	1.0	−0.1	1.7	−0.2
Australia	−0.8	1.4	−2.1	0.0000	1.4	−0.3	0.2	1.3	−0.1	0.5	−0.2
Austria	1.9	2.1	−0.2	0.0005	2.1	−0.3	−0.2	0.8	0.1	2.0	−0.3
Belgium	12.9	4.9	8.0	0.0003	4.9	−0.2	−0.2	1.1	0.5	3.8	−0.2
Canada	1.7	2.0	−0.3	0.0001	2.0	−0.1	0.1	0.8	0.2	1.2	−0.3
Denmark	9.8	2.2	7.6	0.0003	2.2	−0.2	−0.2	1.5	−0.4	1.7	−0.2
Finland	2.3	1.5	0.8	0.0001	1.5	−0.4	−0.1	0.9	−0.3	1.6	−0.3
France	1.4	1.5	0.0	0.0003	1.5	−0.1	−0.2	0.7	0.3	0.9	−0.1
Germany	3.3	1.4	2.0	0.0006	1.4	−0.2	−0.2	1.1	−0.4	1.2	−0.2
Greece	−1.6	0.9	−2.5	0.0002	0.9	−0.9	−0.1	1.2	−0.3	0.9	0.1
Ireland	2.7	3.4	−0.7	0.0001	3.4	−1.0	0.0	1.3	0.0	3.4	−0.3
Italy	0.1	1.5	−1.4	0.0003	1.5	−0.6	−0.1	1.3	0.1	1.0	−0.2
Japan	−0.6	1.1	−1.7	−0.0002	1.1	−0.2	0.3	1.4	−0.4	0.2	−0.3
Neth.	5.3	3.3	2.0	0.0003	3.3	−0.4	0.0	1.3	−0.3	2.9	−0.2
N.Z.	−0.6	2.1	−2.7	0.0002	2.1	−0.6	0.2	1.4	−0.1	1.5	−0.3
Norway	3.0	3.4	−0.3	0.0000	3.4	0.0	−0.2	1.6	−0.4	2.5	−0.2
Sweden	2.8	1.5	1.3	0.0002	1.5	−0.3	−0.2	1.1	−0.3	1.5	−0.2
Switz.	−2.4	−1.9	−0.6	−0.0001	−1.9	−0.3	−0.1	−3.1	0.0	2.0	−0.3
U.K.	1.5	1.8	−0.3	0.0002	1.8	−0.6	−0.2	1.4	−0.1	1.3	−0.1
U.S.	0.0	0.0	0.0	0.0	0.0	0.0	0.0	0.0	0.0	0.0	0.0
Correlation with observed difference		.73	.94	.44	.73	.22	−.37	.33	.19	.63	−.06

TABLE 17.5. *Accounting for International Differences in Public Health Spending as a Percentage of GDP, in 1978/81*

Relative to the United States in 1978/81

	Total Observed Diff.	Total Predicted Diff.	Error	Diff. Due to to Diff's in Transfers c. 1960	The Part of Public Health Spending Explained by Behavior Since 1962						
					All	Income Effects	Age Effect	Electoral Effects	Religion & Ethnic Divisions	Trade Open-ness	Milit. Exp./ GDP
18 nations*	1.7	1.2	0.6	0.0	1.2	−0.9	0.2	0.4	0.7	0.3	0.4
Australia	0.8	0.8	0.0	0.000000	0.8	−0.7	−0.1	0.5	0.5	0.1	0.5
Austria	0.6	2.1	−1.5	0.000002	2.1	−0.9	0.6	0.4	0.9	0.3	0.7
Belgium	1.2	0.9	0.3	0.000001	0.9	−0.7	0.4	0.4	−0.2	0.7	0.4
Canada	1.5	−0.2	1.7	0.000000	−0.2	−0.2	0.0	−0.1	−0.6	0.2	0.6
Denmark	1.8	2.3	−0.6	0.000001	2.3	−0.5	0.3	0.5	1.2	0.3	0.5
Finland	1.2	1.1	0.0	0.000000	1.1	−1.0	0.1	0.2	0.9	0.3	0.7
France	2.2	0.6	1.5	0.000001	0.6	−0.5	0.3	−0.1	0.6	0.2	0.2
Germany	2.5	2.1	0.3	0.000002	2.1	−0.5	0.6	0.3	1.2	0.2	0.4
Greece	−0.5	−1.0	0.5	0.000001	−1.0	−2.4	0.2	0.2	1.0	0.2	−0.2
Ireland	3.7	0.5	3.2	0.000000	0.5	−2.2	0.0	0.4	1.2	0.6	0.6
Italy	2.0	1.5	0.6	0.000001	1.5	−1.4	0.2	0.8	1.2	0.2	0.5
Japan	0.7	1.3	−0.6	−0.000001	1.3	−0.9	−0.1	0.2	1.3	0.0	0.8
Neth.	2.5	1.6	0.8	0.000001	1.6	−0.8	0.0	0.5	1.0	0.5	0.4
N.Z.	0.9	0.6	0.3	0.000001	0.6	−1.1	−0.1	0.5	0.3	0.3	0.6
Norway	2.8	2.5	0.4	0.000000	2.5	−0.4	0.4	0.4	1.2	0.4	0.4
Sweden	4.7	2.3	2.4	0.000001	2.3	−0.7	0.8	0.5	1.1	0.3	0.4
Switz.	1.5	1.5	0.0	0.000000	1.5	−0.4	0.2	0.8	0.0	0.3	0.6
U.K.	1.1	0.4	0.7	0.000001	0.4	−1.1	0.4	0.3	0.5	0.2	0.1
U.S.	0.0	0.0	0.0	0.0	0.0	0.0	0.0	0.0	0.0	0.0	0.0
Correlation with observed difference		.55	.67	.18	.55	.04	.42	.25	.35	.43	.23

TABLE 17.6. *Accounting for International Differences in Public Education Spending as a Percentage of GDP, in 1978/81*

Relative to the United States in 1978/81

	Total Observed Diff.	Total Predicted Diff.	Error	Diff. Due to to Diff's in Transfers c. 1960	The Part of Public Education Spending Explained by Behavior Since 1962						
					All	Income Effects	Age Effect	Electoral Effects	Religion & Ethnic Divisions	Trade Openness	Milit. Exp./ GDP
18 nations[*]	0.2	1.0	−0.8	0.0	1.0	−0.9	0.0	0.7	0.0	0.8	0.4
Australia	0.3	1.2	−0.9	0.000	1.2	−0.8	0.4	0.9	0.0	0.3	0.4
Austria	−1.8	1.8	−3.6	0.000	1.8	−0.8	−0.1	0.9	0.2	1.0	0.6
Belgium	2.4	2.4	0.0	0.000	2.4	−0.6	−0.4	0.9	0.3	1.9	0.3
Canada	0.5	1.2	−0.7	0.000	1.2	−0.3	0.1	0.2	0.1	0.6	0.5
Denmark	2.3	1.3	1.0	0.000	1.3	−0.6	−0.2	0.9	−0.1	0.8	0.5
Finland	0.7	0.6	0.1	0.000	0.6	−1.0	−0.5	0.8	−0.1	0.8	0.6
France	0.1	0.6	−0.5	0.000	0.6	−0.5	0.0	0.2	0.3	0.4	0.2
Germany	−0.6	0.6	−1.2	0.000	0.6	−0.5	−0.5	0.8	−0.1	0.6	0.3
Greece	−3.2	−1.4	−1.7	0.000	−1.4	−2.3	0.0	0.7	−0.1	0.5	−0.2
Ireland	0.8	1.5	−0.7	0.000	1.5	−2.2	0.5	0.8	0.2	1.7	0.5
Italy	0.0	1.0	−1.0	0.000	1.0	−1.3	0.0	1.1	0.2	0.5	0.4
Japan	−0.6	0.5	−1.1	0.000	0.5	−0.8	0.1	0.4	−0.1	0.1	0.7
Neth.	1.7	1.9	−0.3	0.000	1.9	−0.9	0.2	0.9	−0.1	1.4	0.3
N.Z.	−1.2	1.4	−2.6	0.000	1.4	−1.3	0.5	0.9	0.0	0.7	0.5
Norway	0.9	2.0	−1.1	0.000	2.0	−0.3	0.1	0.8	−0.1	1.2	0.4
Sweden	0.9	0.6	0.2	0.000	0.6	−0.8	−0.5	1.0	−0.1	0.7	0.3
Switz.	−0.2	1.0	−1.2	0.000	1.0	−0.6	−0.3	0.4	0.0	1.0	0.5
U.K.	−0.1	0.0	−0.1	0.000	0.0	−1.2	0.0	0.6	0.0	0.6	0.1
U.S.	0.0	0.0	0.0	0.0	0.0	0.0	0.0	0.0	0.0	0.0	0.0
Correlation with observed difference	.62	.75	−.02		.62	.41	−.16	.13	.12	.49	.22

Sources and notes to Tables 17.2–17.6:
[*]The "18 nations" figures in the top row refer to a simple average of the 18 country rows other than the United States.
The fuller regressions are given in Appendix Table E1.
The underlying accounting algebra is presented in Appendix G.

What made the eighteen other countries spend 5.6 percent more of GDP on social transfers than the United States? Income effects have a negative explanatory role. That is, since the United States has a higher income than any of the other countries, and given that higher incomes tend to raise social transfers, taking income into account roughly the task of interpretation. Had income been the only difference between the Americans and the others, the United States would have spent 4.5 percent more of GDP on social transfers than the other countries. With the income effect extracted, we now need to explain a bigger 9.1 percent gap (4.6 plus 4.5 percent of GDP). The age effect no longer helps account for the international differences, the way it did in the 1880–1930 period. One of the keys to the gap between the eighteen countries and the United States is provided by electoral democracy, which has become a stalwart explanatory factor throughout this book. The Americans paid less in taxes for social transfers because fewer of them voted. The Democratic Party has long rued the fact that a small share of its registered partisans actually show up at the polls, whereas registered Republicans show up more regularly. As Chapter 7 noted, low voter turnout seems to have played a major role in defeating budget-raising candidates in Switzerland and the United States.

Other countries also differ from the United States in the role of religion and ethnicity. In the postwar setting, as we have seen, religion translates into a positive effect of Catholicism on social transfers, especially pensions. Ethnic fractionalization, a negative influence on most kinds of social spending, is greatest in Canada, followed by Switzerland and the United States. Religion and ethnic divisions together explain a large part of why the average social transfers for the other eighteen countries (still including Canada and Switzerland in the eighteen) are higher than in the United States.

Trade openness is also a large factor in the contrasts shown here, because the United States is the least trade-exposed of the nineteenth countries. Out of the original task of explaining why the eighteen others spent an extra 5.6 percent of GDP on transfers, openness explains a 5.7 percent gap, or more than the whole net difference. The small-country effect is big, even when one has held constant some potentially correlated factors such as ethnic homogeneity. Yet openness may be getting credit from unknown fixed-country effects.

Finally, military spending played a slightly negative role in the total social expenditure difference. The reason is that the United States spent slightly more than the average on military goods and services, which the regression results of Table 17.1 translated into a slight positive influence on social transfers. This is not a robust difference, however.

Three other kinds of contrasts emerge from Tables 17.2 through 17.6. The first contrast is in the relative roles of different factors in different kinds of social spending. For pensions (Table 17.3), the contrasts in income, openness, and voter turnout fade away, leaving relatively greater roles for age differences and for religion and ethnicity. What props up welfare and unemployment compensation outside of the United States is mainly trade openness (Table 17.4). The non-Americans' extra health and education expenditures are raised largely by their lower military expenditures, stronger voter turnout, and ethnic homogeneity.

A second contrast is that between the United States and other low-spending nations. Setting aside low-income Greece, an interesting contrast is between the offsetting influences on Canada, Australasia, Japan, and Switzerland that make these countries end up similar to the United States in their general approach to social spending. Since all of them have lower average incomes than the Americans, what kept their social expenditures from being much lower? In the case of Japan, ethnic homogeneity appears to have propped up public spending on health and pensions. For the others, trade openness played a key role, along with the greater voter turnouts of Australia (where voting is compulsory) and New Zealand.

Finally, which nations' contrasts with the United States are least well explained by the systematic forces featured in the statistical regressions? The most conspicuous error terms differ by type of spending. In overall social transfers, Norway, Australia, and New Zealand spent noticeably less in 1978–1981 than the regressions could explain, while Sweden and Finland spent more than predicted. Public pensions were unexplainably high in the Netherlands, Austria, Germany, and France – and perhaps unjustifiably high, as we have seen in Chapter 8. In welfare and unemployment spending, the outliers were the unexplainably high transfers in Belgium and Denmark. Here again, earlier chapters have identified these as cases in which public debate has strongly questioned the generous unemployment compensation and early retirements. In the case of public schooling, the outliers are on the negative side: Why did Austria and New Zealand spend so little around 1980? Such unexplained contrasts call for deeper histories.

SUMMARY: HOW HAVE THE DETERMINANTS CHANGED SINCE 1880?

What we have learned from countries' experience since 1960 reinforces some insights from the pre-1930 history of social spending and adds other insights that could not be developed on the basis of the more limited pre-1930 information.

That populations continue to get older has pushed a now-evident influence toward its predictable limit. The influence of population aging on social transfers should have been positive as long as the shift toward an older population brought more gray power. That rise in power must erode, however, as the elderly share of the population exceeds some margin. Beyond that point, the balance of power over public transfer programs must shift because transfers sought by the elderly become increasingly expensive to younger adults and must be spread over more and more oldsters. This chapter has illustrated the pressure over this issue on the pension front. It found that the aging of OECD populations can continue to push up pensions as a share of GDP, but with resistance because somebody must be made worse off. Who will pay for the aging of the population is still uncertain. So far, we have found that there is likely to be a sharing of the burden between the elderly themselves, who will probably suffer a decline in relative support *per person* even though pensions take more of GDP, taxpayers, and younger recipients of nonpension transfers.

Income, program momentum, social affinity, and openness to foreign trade were also strong positive influences on social spending. One might have predicted as much by knowing that the welfare-state countries tend to be prosperous, mature in their programs, ethnically homogenous, and exposed to the winds of international trade.

Electoral politics continued to exert a strong force on social spending, but a different type of electoral influence has done most of the storytelling in the OECD countries since World War II. In an OECD world in which virtually all countries are full democracies and women vote, differences in voting rights no longer play the crucial role they played in the same countries before 1930 or in today's Third World. Rather, if it is differences in the willingness to vote, and differences in the belief that one's vote matters, that explain why most countries have more social transfers than Switzerland and the United States, where more than half the voters stay home on election day.

18

Social Transfers Hardly Affected Growth

In his presidential address to the American Economic Association, Nobel Laureate Robert Lucas offered two findings about the huge costs of taxation and, by implication, of the social transfers that are the excuse for most taxes:

"[S]tudies found that reducing capital income taxation from its current U.S. level to zero (using other taxes to [replace it]) would ... imply an increase of consumption along a balanced growth path of 7.5 to 15 percent."

"Edward C. Prescott ... shows that ... [t]he steady-state welfare gain to French households of adopting American tax rates would be the equivalent of a consumption increase of about 20 percent ... with *no* increase in work effort! ... in the neoclassical growth model."[1]

Such findings have two distinctive features. First, they show big numbers. Second they are not really findings. Contrary to the words offered so traditionally and casually by economists, none of these authors actually "found" or "showed" their results. Rather, they *chose to imagine* the results they announced. In every study Lucas cited here the crucial ingredient was a theoretical model laden with assumptions.[2] It is educated, intelligent, plausible fiction – but fiction nonetheless, just like the blackboard diagrams, parables, and simulations we questioned in Chapter 10.

Theory and fiction cannot be dismissed out of hand, of course. Every theoretical model, like every good novel, is inspired by observation of the real world. Yet for every theoretical conclusion worth debating, some scholar will imagine and derive the opposite conclusion, if only because scholarly self-interest generates such a dialectic. We need empirical tests that can choose among competing views on the basis of factual evidence. The empirical tests offered in the past have been incomplete and defective because they fail to satisfy the requirements of a convincing test, requirements laid out in Chapter 14. This chapter elaborates on those requirements, shows how past studies have failed to meet them, and offers better tests. The tests firm up our understanding of Volume 1's free lunch puzzle. They confirm the common

82

intuition about huge costs of the welfare state by predicting such hypothetical costs *out of sample*, that is beyond the range historically experienced. They also confirm that social transfers did not deliver a significant net GDP cost in the real-world welfare states.

BASIC REQUIREMENTS FOR FINDING THE GROWTH EFFECTS OF SOCIAL TRANSFERS

Getting the growth effects right calls for tests meeting some requirements introduced in Chapter 14. The sample and the regressions must span a large number of years and governmental units, over which social transfers are large and variable. The regression must control for conventional sources of growth and nonlinearity in the effects of social transfers. They must allow for simultaneity and for heteroskedasticity and serial correlation in the error terms. Two of these requirements – attention to simultaneity and to nonlinear costs – deserve some emphasis here.

The level of GDP per capita is both a cause and a consequence of social transfers and the taxes usually associated with them. This simultaneity threatens to bias any statistical estimates of the effects of social transfers on growth. One kind of feedback from GDP to social transfers can make the welfare state look deceivingly bad for growth, and two other feedbacks can make it look deceivingly good for growth. A deceivingly negative growth effect results from short-run cyclical feedbacks when social transfers are used as to represent the welfare state. Any outside force that creates a slump in the economy will raise transfer payments to the poor and unemployed. Failure to correct for such feedback will create the impression that the higher transfer payments are causing the slump in GDP per capita. The same bias would falsely attribute a boom to the automatic cut in social transfers that accompanies the boom. To eliminate such bias, one would have to take a two-stage approach in estimating the effects of transfers on growth. First, one would have to use truly exogenous variables to predict social transfers. In the second stage, one should then use the predicted, rather than the observed, values of transfers in sorting out the determinants of the growth of GDP per capita. Yet, as we shall see, past studies have failed to eliminate such cyclical bias.

By contrast, two other feedbacks threaten to make the growth effects of the welfare state look too good. One is a short-run cyclical bias that arises in studies portraying the welfare state by its total tax collections rather than by its social transfers. Whenever an outside force causes a cyclical boom in GDP, tax collections will automatically rise. A naive growth equation would pick up a positive falsely effect of taxes on the growth of GDP. The other kind of false credit for the welfare state arises in studies of the determinants of longer-run growth trends. Here again, there is a positive feedback from increased GDP to taxes and social transfers. The vast literature on growth and the state tends to confirm Wagner's Law, which predicts that long-run growth in average incomes will make governments tax and spend a greater share of those incomes. On this, the present book agrees with most other studies. Such a feedback from income, or GDP per capita, to transfers threatens to give transfers too much credit for the long-run growth in income. This longer-run simultaneity bias, like its cyclical counterparts, must be eliminated statistically.

The other requirement deserving emphasis here stresses the nonlinearity that theory plansibly attributes to the costs of transfers. No theoretical discussion of the marginal costs of taxes and transfers has imagined that the marginal costs are fixed, making total costs rise linearly with total taxes and transfers. Rather we assume that the marginal costs rise as more and more is taxed and transferred. That is, we assume that the cumulative share of GDP or well-being lost because of taxes and transfers has a slope that is both positive *and rising*, not a fixed linear slope. Chapter 13's minimal theory agreed with the past literature on the plausibility of this assumption. If there is so much theoretical agreement that the costs of taxes and transfers can rise nonlinearly, then an empirical test of the growth effects of taxes and transfers must allow for, must test for, this possible nonlinear rise in costs. Yet, as we shall see, the statistical literature on transfers and growth has almost never taken this simple precaution.

WHAT PAST GROWTH TESTS HAVE FOUND

Key public issues deserve a lot of attention, and social scientists have not ignored the possible growth effects of social transfers. Yet, as so often happens in the study of aggregate human behavior, they have reached conflicting conclusions, partly because they have used different kinds of tests. Even the overall summaries of past studies disagree on what the studies add up to. Most summaries report a hung jury, with studies dividing fairly evenly between positive, negative, and agnostic conclusions about the growth effects of transfers and of the taxes that pay for them. Others disagree, however, claiming that the studies finding a negative growth effect are better-based than the rest of the literature.[3]

To capture the varied nature of these past tests, and to show what they have missed, I have selected the past studies arranged chronologically above the line in Table 18.1. Most authors drew on the experience of the main OECD countries since the 1950s, though two of the studies used a larger global database. Most succeeded in testing across different time periods, though a couple were just cross-sections in a single time period. Yet like the larger literature they represent, they did not agree about the effect of social transfers on GDP. Five studies could not find any consistent effect. Five others displayed here found a negative effect of transfers on output, though one of them featured an effect on just private output, ignoring the expansion of public outputs such as public health. Contradicting these findings were two studies finding that transfers significantly increased GDP. The two studies that found a positive effect on GDP were written earlier than the five that found a significantly negative effect, and covered slightly earlier periods.

Every past study failed to meet some of the good test requirements, as suggested by the three columns on the right side of Table 18.1. Only about half of them are truly studies of social transfers. The other half come from the larger literature on total government and economic growth, so that inferences about the effects of transfers have been guessed at by using extra taxes or total government spending or government consumption in GDP to represent extra transfers. Almost none of the studies dealt with the feedback from GDP to transfers by noting and estimating it. Finally, only one study estimated the nonlinear curvature of the cost function.

The studies finding negative growth effects from transfers were not better based than those finding positive effects. On the contrary, the only study to use a theoretically correct quadratic function for GDP costs (the McCallum–Blais study) found that transfers increased GDP growth for a typical OECD country. Each of the five studies finding that transfers significantly cut GDP had a number of other limitations. Three of the five estimated the effects of taxes or government consumption, not transfers. Three of them failed to endogenize the public budget and are thus subject to unknown simultaneity biases. And all five of them failed to test for the theoretical nonlinearity of the GDP costs. This last omission is particularly odd, since the GDP costs should look quadratic whether the underlying supply and demand curves are linear or log-linear.[4] These shortcomings are not necessary, and we turn to new estimates that address all these issues.

BETTER TESTS

The right historical base for getting the growth tests right is still the OECD experience since 1960, as with past studies. To be sure, earlier experience does have something to say on the subject. The 1880–1930 experience actually suggests a significant positive effect of transfers on economic growth.[5] This positive effect might have reflected the positive role of early poor relief in improving workers' health and productivity. Let us set aside this early positive growth effect, however. The real controversy about social transfers centers on their effects when they get to be large shares of GDP, and that did not happen to the OECD countries before World War II. Similarly, for the post-1960 period itself, it is better to focus on the high-spending OECD countries alone, rather than folding them into a global sample that is likely to mix too many different structures – even though an initial foray into such global samples also supports the conclusions advanced here.[6]

TABLE 18.1. *The Growth Effects of Postwar Social Transfers: Summary of Recent Studies*

Authors	Publication Year	Sample Countries	Sample Years	Other Growth Sources (Control Variables) Included	Results: The Effect on Annual GDP Growth From Raising Social Transfers by 5% of GDP	Was the Dependent Variable Really Social Transfers?	Were Public Expenditures Endogenized to Address Simultaneity Bias?	Were the GDP Costs Allowed to be Nonlinear?
Landau	(1985)	16 OECDs	Annual 1952–1976	Yo, educ, I/Y, tot changes, time trend	Not signif.	Yes	No	No
Korpi	(1985)	17 OECDs	4 periods, 1950–1973	Yo, agric	Up by 0.9%	Yes	No	No
McCallum and Blais	(1987)	17 OECDs	4 periods, 1960–1983	Yo, unions, pop. growth, G/Y, Choi	Up by 0.4%	Yes	No	Yes, quadratic
Castle and Dowrick	(1990)	18 OECDs	4 periods, 1960–1985	Yo, pop. growth, Choi	Not signif.	Yes	Yes	No
Weede	(1991)	19 OECDs	4 periods, 1960–1985	age, employ-ment, agric, democracy	Not stable (c)	Yes	No	No[c]
Easterly and Rebelo	(1993)	53 countries 14 OECDs,	1970–1988	Yo, educ, upheavals	Down by 0.3%	No, tax rates	No	No

Hansson and Henrekson	(1994)	14 private sectors	4 periods, 1970–1987	I/Y, pop. growth, other gov't exp, tax mix	Private output Down by 0.7%	Yes	No	No
Persson and Tabellini	(1994)	13 OECDs ($n = 13$!)	1960–1985	Yo, educ, ineq	Down by 0.3%	Yes	No	No
Commander et al.	(1997)	132 countries	3 decades, 1964–1993	Yo, educ, pop growth, I/Y, gov't quality, tot changes, ffx	Down by 0.1%	No, gov't consumpt'n	Yes	No
Mendoza et al.	(1997)	18 OECDs	5 periods, 1966–1990	Yo, I/Y, tot changes	Not signif.	No, tax rates & G/Y	No	No
Fölster and Henrekson	(1998)	23 OECDs	5 periods, 1970–1995	Yo, age	Down by 0.5%	No, taxes	Yes[a]	No
Agell et al.	(1999)	23 OECDs	5 periods, 1970–1995	Yo, age	Not signif.	No, taxes	Yes[a]	No
This chapter	(2004)	19 OECDs	5 periods, 1962–1981	Yo, age, lagged I, educ, OECD macro	Not signif.[b]	Yes	Yes	Yes, cubic or quadratic
This chapter	(2004)	21 OECDs	6 periods, 1978–1995	Yo, age, lagged I, educ, OECD macro	Not signif.[b]	Yes	Yes	Yes, cubic
This chapter	(2004)	21 OECDs	6 periods, 1978–1995	Yo, age, lagged I, educ, OECD macro	Not signif.[b]	Yes	Yes	Yes, quadratic

(continued)

TABLE 18.1. *(continued)*

Notes to Table 18.1:

This table expands on an earlier one by Tony Atkinson (1999, 32–33).

(a) In one variant, Fölster and Henrekson instrumented taxes by their own lagged value, fixed effects, initial GDP, population, and population growth. Agell et al. improved slightly on this.

(b) To estimate the effects of a 5% rise in the transfers' share of GDP, I took the most-populated range from 10% of GDP (U.S. or Japan) to 33% of GDP (Sweden), and multiplied the effect by (5%/23%). The three (insignificant) effects were +0.3%, +0.21%, and −0.32%, respectively.

(c) Weede (1991) found a growth effect that was either significantly positive or significantly negative, depending on whether dummies for Japan and two time periods were included. His regression were OLS, with no allowance for intercountry differences in error variance. As for nonlinearity of the cost effects, some of Weede's results allowed for it, but he dismissed his own quadratic cost curves as unstable (see esp. p. 435).

Control variables: Yo = log of initial or lagged GDP per capita; educ = adult educational attainment or lagged enrollments; pop. growth = rate of population growth; I/Y = private investment/GDP; gov't quality = indices of bureaucracy or policy distortion; ffx = fixed effects; upheavals = assassinations, revolutions, and war casualties per capita; OECD macro = aggregate demand (inflation minus unempl.) and misery index (inflation + unempl.), both at the level of the whole OECD; G/Y = government spending share of GDP; Choi = the Choi index of Mancur Olson's institutional arteriosclerosis; agric = agriculture's share of total employment; ineq = a measure of income inequality.

Log-linear GDP costs are here considered "linear."

For the Castles–Dowrick study, I used their Equations 9a and 9b in Table 5, which did not control for employment. Controlling for employment would yield a significantly positive effect of transfers on growth, but this hides the negative effect of transfers on employment, to which we return in Chapter 19.

For the McCallum–Blais study, I used their preferred quadratic equation, evaluating the effects of raising social security transfers from 10% to 15% of GDP.

The post-1960 OECD experience has to be split into two periods, as mentioned in earlier chapters, because the OECD changed its way of measuring social expenditures. For the period from 1960 through 1981, the OECD statistical team worked up moderately aggregated social expenditure data that were comparable across countries.[7] Later, it offered a more detailed set of estimates for 1980–1996.[8] The two series cannot be spliced together into a unified panel, however, since the figures for the overlapping years 1980–1981 did not mesh. For each of these two periods, it is better to take average behaviors for multiyear periods, because using annual data as observations leads to severe serial correlation that will overstate the precision of the estimates. Accordingly, I have developed those two separate pooled samples already introduced in earlier chapters:

- the 1962–1981 sample, which covers the four-year averages from 1962/1965 through 1978/1981 for nineteen countries, yielding ninety-five observations; and
- the 1978–1995 sample, covering the three-year periods from 1978/1980 through 1993/1995 for twenty-one countries, yielding 126 observations.[9]

The basic growth equation needs to allow for nonlinear costs of transfers, as already noted. Theory most strongly recommends a quadratic functional form relating GDP loss (or net deadweight welfare loss) to the share of transfers in GDP. While theory prefers the quadratic form, let us use a cubic function, which includes the quadratic as a special case:[10]

$$\text{Growth} = a_0 + a_1 \hat{T} + a_2 \hat{T}^2 + a_3 \hat{T}^3 + a_4 X + e_1,$$

where Growth = the growth rate in GDP per capita over three to four years, $\hat{T}$ = the predicted value of the share of social transfers in GDP, and the Xs = exogenous influences on economic growth. This growth equation interacts simultaneously with the equation for social transfers as a share of GDP:

$$T = b_0 + b_1 \hat{\text{Growth}} + b_2 Z + e_2.$$

The predicted value Grôwth is generated by running the first-stage equation

$$\text{Growth} = c_0 + c_1 X + e_3, \text{ and discarding its error term } e_3.$$

The Zs are exogenous influences on the share of social transfers in GDP. Similarly, the predicted value of the transfer share, $\hat{T}$, is the value predicted by fitting the first-stage equation

$$T = d_0 + d_1 Z + e_4, \text{ and discarding its error term } e_4.[11]$$

The exogenous Xs and Zs are those already introduced in Chapter 14.[12]

No growth equation should be presented as the best guess without a supporting expedition to explore other variations that also look plausible at the outset. There are some plausible variations on the theme of the basic Barro-type growth equation that deserve to be explored:

- The dependent variable could be either the level or the growth rate of GDP per capita – or per worker, or per labor hour. This dimension alone suggests six variations.
- Transfers as a share of GDP could enter the equation either in the theoretically preferred quadratic form or in a more generalized cubic form.
- Fixed effects by country and time period could be included or excluded, depending on one's hunches about what such effects capture.
- Capital inputs per worker could be represented by a past history of capital formation, measured directly for a narrower group of countries, or omitted on the grounds that it is endogenous.
- Employment could be either omitted as endogenous or included if one wanted to explore how transfers affect productivity rather than GDP itself.
- The lagged value of the dependent could be either omitted or included, depending on how one wanted to interpret the dynamics of growth.

These dimensions alone imply $6 \times 2 \times 2 \times 3 \times 2 \times 2 = 288$ possible variants of the growth equation in each historical sample, and exploring other choices would entail even more regression runs. Readers will not want to endure a discussion of all these variants. Overloaded with regression results, especially in the empirical growth literature, we long for refreshing summaries with little or no regression display. Xavier Sala-i-Martin recently offered such refreshment when he titled an article "I just ran two million regressions" – and spared his readers by displaying none of them.[13] Indeed, even the cost of running and reading all the 288-plus variants was more than I could bear. Instead, I have taken a neighboring-variants approach. Of the alternatives just listed, I explored those that differed from the preferred variant in only one or two dimensions at a time. These shorter expeditions suggested that none of the 200-plus unexplored compound variations would overturn the conclusions presented here.

Tables 18.2 and 18.3 summarize the determinants of GDP growth in the 1962–1981 sample and the 1978–1995 sample, respectively. Starting from the top of each table, let us look first at the roles of some other forces before turning to the verdict about social transfers and taxes.

As the convergence literature often finds, growth is faster in countries that had a greater shortfall behind the United States ten years earlier, an effect that presumably represents technological catching-up among countries in the OECD "convergence club." Greece's falling 63 percent below the United States in GDP per capita ten years earlier would have raised Greek GDP growth by 3.5 percent a year in the 1962–1981 era, with a similar effect in the 1978–1995 era. A familiar source of growth that showed little effect

TABLE 18.2. *Sources and Nonsources of Growth in GDP per Capita, 1962–1981*

	Dependent Variable = Log-Growth of GDP Per Capita (Here Converted to %/Annum)					
	Equation (1) Quadratic Costs		Equation (2) Quadratic Costs		Equation (3) Cubic Costs	
Independent Variables	Coeff.	|t|	Coeff.	|t|	Coeff.	|t|
Shortfall in GDP/capita, 10 years earlier	3.38	(9.58)**	3.29	(9.08)**	3.31	(9.13)**
Capital formation/capita, one year earlier	1.67	(7.88)**	1.50	(7.14)**	1.51	(7.28)**
Capital formation/cap., 10 years earlier	−1.11	(5.13)**	−1.01	(4.51)**	−1.03	(4.59)**
Prim. + sec. enroll'ts/5–14s, 10 years earlier	3.10	(3.29)**	2.99	(3.16)**	2.84	(2.95)**
University enroll'ts/5–14s, 10 years earlier	2.95	(1.27)	3.97	(1.85)[a]	4.04	(1.87)[a]
Global demand and supply shocks						
Inflation − unemployment, all OECD	0.33	(4.67)**	0.39	(5.39)**	0.39	(5.25)**
Inflation + unemployment, all OECD	−0.21	(5.33)**	−0.24	(5.67)**	−0.23	(5.41)**
Effects of raising social transfers by 1% of GDP, starting from their average shares						
(a) total social transfers			0.043	(2.63)**	0.034	(1.59)
(b) public pensions	0.099	(2.96)**				
(c) welfare and unemployment compens.	0.030	(1.14)				
(d) public health spending	−0.015	(0.25)				

Source and notes to Table 18.2:

(** = significant at the 1% level, two-tail; * = significant at the 5% level;[a] significant at the 7% level;[b] significant at the 10% level.)
For a fuller review of these equations, see Appendix Table E2.
The social spending and tax variables are predicted values based on the first-stage regressions.
The equations presented here are the ones without the full set of fixed effects for time periods and countries. As stated in the text, and as suggested by the total-transfer effects in Equations (2) and (3), including fixed effects (in additional regressions) had no effect on the main conclusions reached here.
The "average" share of total transfers in GDP, used to evaluate the growth effect of 1% more, is actually the average for the 1978–1995 sample (18.72% of GDP), for better comparison with Table 18.3.

TABLE 18.3. *Sources and Nonsources of Growth in GDP per Capita, 1978–1995*

	Dependent Variable = Log-Growth of GDP, Per Capita (Here Converted to %/Annum)							
	Equation (1) Quadratic		Equation (2) Quadratic		Equation (3) Cubic		Equation (4) Cubic	
	Coeff.	|t|	Coeff.	|t|	Coeff.	|t|	Coeff.	|t|
Shortfall in GDP/capita, 10 years earlier	−0.26	(0.10)	4.02	(2.34)*	3.60	(2.08)*	3.22	(1.47)
Capital formation/capita, 1 year earlier	0.88	(1.96)[a]	0.33	(0.66)	0.29	(0.58)	−0.11	(0.23)
Capital formation/cap., 10 years earlier	−0.97	(1.72)[b]	−0.86	(1.41)	−0.86	(1.42)	−0.88	(1.44)
Prim. + sec. enroll'ts/5–14s, 10 years earlier	0.01	(3.17)**	0.004	(1.94)[a]	0.005	(2.10)*	0.009	(3.96)**
University enroll'ts/5–14s, 10 years earlier	−0.01	(1.41)	−0.003	(0.40)	−0.004	(0.52)	−0.012	(1.48)
Global demand and supply shocks								
Inflation − unemployment, all OECD	0.86	(5.87)**	1.07	(7.11)**	1.04	(6.85)**	1.00	(6.81)**
Inflation + unemployment, all OECD	−1.41	(5.96)**	−1.75	(7.94)**	−1.75	(7.91)**	−1.85	(8.42)**
Effects of raising expenditure shares by 1% of GDP, at sample-average social transfer share (18.72%)								
(a) social transfers, with typical tax mix			−0.05	(0.63)	0.003	(0.03)	0.28	(1.96)[a]
(b) social transfers, all financed by personal income tax	−0.24	(1.55)						
(c) social transfers, all financed by corp. income tax	−0.84	(1.15)						

(d) social transfers, all financed by property tax	−0.47	(0.70)		
(e) social transfers, all financed by consumption tax	−0.39	(1.82)[a]		
Effect of a permanent tightening of employee protection laws, by 1 index point			−0.40	(1.18)
Effect of raising the unemployment compensation support ratio by 1% (when it is 20%)			−0.13	(3.30)**

Source and notes to Table 18.3:
(** = significant at the 1% level, two-tail; * = significant at the 5% level; [a]significant at the 7% level; [b]significant at the 10% level.)
For a fuller review of these equations, see Appendix Table E4 , Equations (1)– (3), and (6). The underlying data sources are listed at the start of Appendix E. The social spending and tax variables are predicted values based on the first-stage regressions.

The equations presented here are the ones without the full set of fixed effects for time periods and countries. As stated in the text, including those effects (in additional regressions) had no effect on the main conclusions reached here.

Capital formation per capita is measured in thousands of international dollars of 1985 per person. The capital formation has the stated lag in years, but the denominator is current (not lagged) population.

in either sample is capital per worker, here proxied by earlier net capital formation per worker this year. Growth was strongly raised by extra schooling,
especially extra primary and secondary schooling.

The state of the global macro-economy strongly affected the rate of
growth, as one would expect. To capture global demand and supply shocks,
I have combined the rate of inflation and the unemployment rate at the level
of the whole OECD. Global demand shocks are proxied by the difference
between inflation and unemployment, and global supply shocks are proxied
by the sum of inflation and unemployment, often called the misery index. In
all periods a rise in global demand raises the GDP growth rate, as it did in
the Vietnam War. Conversely, any global slump in aggregate demand cut the
growth rate, as in the early 1990s. The main aggregate supply shocks were,
of course, the two oil crises, which raised both inflation and unemployment
and hurt GDP growth for the OECD as a whole.

Three kinds of government policy that are separate from social transfers
have had their own understandable, though small, effects on growth.[14] A
higher share of government jobs in total employment tends to be associated with slower growth, though one cannot say for certain that the true
association is not zero. The same suspicion arises about employee protection laws. While they have no clear effect when first instituted, their effect
seems slightly negative after three years. Corporatism, or national collective
bargaining over wages and jobs, seems to have a positive effect on growth.
While it lasts, that is: As we saw for Sweden in Chapter 11, corporatism is
likely to break down sooner or later. Each of these three side-policies of a
welfare state – public employment, job protection laws, and corporatism –
affects growth in the same direction as it affects employment in the results
revealed in Chapter 19.

Raising social transfers, the influence featured in this chapter, has no negative effect on GDP in an average OECD country. Tables 18.2 and 18.3
report this confirmation of the free lunch puzzle in the form of the slope
of growth with respect to social transfers. When such transfers are 18.72
percent of GDP, the OECD average for the 1978–1995 period, no equation
shows their effect to be significantly negative. On the contrary, the 1962–
1981 experience shows in Table 18.2 that more social transfers implied better
growth, other things equal. The mechanism linking social transfers with improved growth seems to have been correlated with public pensions, to judge
from the first equation. Only for the later period, 1978–1995, did any slope
reported in Table 18.3 suggest a negative effect of transfers on growth, and
that slope was small and insignificant.

Are there no other ways to reveal that social transfers have damaged
GDP? There are, but they illustrate the importance of the stay-in-sample
rule introduced in Chapter 14. That is, every show of a big GDP cost of
social transfers occurs *out of sample*. Such a display appears first when we
turn to particular kinds of social transfer finance, rather than overall social

transfers, and again when we search for a particular pessimistic twist to the overall cost function.

There are two kinds of taxes that would seem to cut GDP noticeably. Just as in the conjectures by Robert Lucas that opened this chapter, raising social transfers and paying for them entirely with taxes on capital could slash GDP. If any country had financed all of its social transfers, average and marginal, out of taxes on corporate income or personal property, GDP might have dropped noticeably, according to the first equation in Table 18.3. That is a big drop from raising transfers by just another percent. Yet no country ever taxed corporate income or property that much on the average, nor was any 1-percent expansion of an existing welfare state financed that way. The only two significant costs of social transfers and taxes in Table 18.3 were far out of the historical sample range, just like the tax rollbacks that Lucas imagined.

Another possibility is that social transfers might hurt growth more if they were concentrated in that most antiwork of transfer categories, unemployment compensation. Table 18.2 suggests the opposite for 1962–1981. Still, the last equation in Table 18.3 does give a hint for 1978–1995 that supports our usual intuition. If the social transfer budgets did not grow at all but were shifted toward giving the unemployed more support while they stay out of work, then GDP would be lowered by 0.13 percent for each extra 1 percent of support for an unemployed person. Chapter 19 will confirm this suggestion, by showing that a more generous dole cuts work and offsets only part of that work loss with greater productivity by those still at work. In searching for the growth effects of all transfers, however, we should set the costs of the dole aside, both because they failed to show up for 1962–1981 and because their appearance for 1978–1995 required holding the total social budget constant.

Seeking a pessimistic twist to the GDP cost function, one could come up with a particular functional form that somehow manages to make the welfare state look costly. Such a partisan search would be rewarded by the cubic function introduced earlier, the one for which the theoretically preferred quadratic function is a special case. Suppose that we allowed the relationship between social transfers and economic growth to take a couple of twists and turns, as the cubic function allows. Might it show the economic superiority of the small-government approach of the United States, Switzerland, and Japan? Or is there an intermediate peak, in which semi-welfare states achieve better growth than either the small-government states or the welfare-state Leviathans? Or would it allow the relationship between transfers and growth to have peaks at both ends, suggesting what Richard Freeman called "diversified," as opposed to "single-peaked" capitalism?

Variations on the growth curve traced out by changing the share of social transfers in GDP appear in Figure 18.1.[15] The curves follow both the theoretical quadratic shape and the more flexible cubic shape for our two

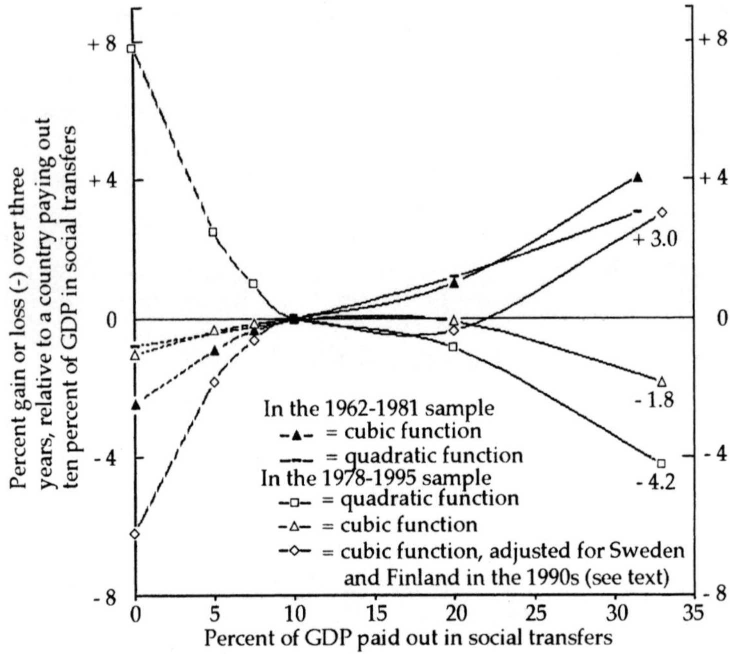

(Dashed lines = extensions out of the sample range.)

FIGURE 18.1. Estimated three-year effects of social transfers on GDP, relative to a country transferring 10 percent of GDP.

historical sample periods. All growth effects are compared to the experience of a country transferring 10 percent of GDP, such as the United States around 1980 or Japan around 1990. The earlier experience, 1962–1981, has good things to say about the welfare state. A greater social transfer share raised GDP in that era, regardless of the functional form. Social transfers look more costly if we follow the twisting cubic curves from the 1978–1995 era, setting aside the quadratic curve that fails to trace significant cost effects. The most intriguing curve is the cubic-function curve traced with triangles. Starting from social transfers around 8 percent of GDP, the lowest experienced since 1978, the curve suggests that there were large and significant costs from the welfare state by the time social transfers passed above 25 percent of GDP and rose toward the Swedish maximum of 33 percent. The triangle curve for 1978–1995 implies that shifting from a Japanese or American 10 percent of GDP to Sweden's 33 percent would cost the nation 3.0 percent of GDP over three years' time. At last, it might seem, we have found the regression that reveals the true (but statistically insignificant) costs of social transfers.

The large cost is not robust, however. It hinges completely on a particular interpretation of what happened to Sweden and Finland between 1990 and 1995. As we saw in Chapter 11, the early 1990s were Sweden's darkest hour of the postwar era. The same period was even worse for Finland, whose unemployment had soared from 3.5 to 18.4 percent of the labor force between 1990 and 1994. Yet the crisis was not due to social transfers and the welfare state. Rather it owed much to the macro-policy mistake of fixing both the krona and the Finnish mark to the German mark in the hopes of joining the European currency union. At that moment in history, the German mark was soaring in value, and the world was entering a U.S.-led recession. Swedish and Finnish goods were priced out of world markets. The growth tests need to separate this macro-policy crisis from the effects of social transfers. An equation adding a special recession effect for Sweden and Finland in the early 1990s gives the much-altered cubic curve shown with diamonds in Figure 18.1.[16] With this adjustment, the contrast between the Japanese–American minima and the Swedish maximum actually favors the welfare state. Here again, what might look at first like the hidden truth about GDP costs of the welfare state turns out to be a mirage.[17]

An econometrician might have waited patiently for this chapter's presentation of fixed country effects, knowing that many effects that other scholars have attributed to behavioral variables have turned out to be just fixed effects. That is, there may be unmeasured special features of each country's economy that deserve credit for growth effects that would be wrongly attributed to other forces if the fixed effects were not introduced into the regression. Would introducing fixed country effects unmask the negative effects of social transfers on economic growth?

It turns out that including fixed country effects in the regressions from 1978–1995 reproduces the virtually-zero net growth effect of transfers but with a bizarre splitting of that zero into two strongly opposing effects. The cubic curve for the effects of social transfers on growth tilts suddenly upward, suggesting that a shift from the Japanese–American minima to the Swedish maximum would raise GDP by 5 percent within three years. Yet the growth impacts implied by the fixed country effects are negatively correlated with the countries' social transfers. Plausibly interpreting the fixed country effects as driven by the countries' average social transfers cancels out but never greatly reverses, that gain in GDP. Tentatively, I conclude that when fixed country effects are included, the net costs are still not negative.

Thus all the seeming paths to showing large growth costs of social transfers turn out to be dead ends. The negative effects were extensions far beyond sample, either into the unexperienced *laissez faire* range below 8 percent of GDP or into burdensome tax packages that were never tried. The negative effects of higher unemployment compensation held total transfers constant and were thus not a test of the effect of greater transfers. The cubic function that seemed to reveal a high cost without fixed effects was driven by the macro-policy crisis of Sweden and Finland in the early 1990s. And adding fixed effects left the growth impact near zero. All in all, the free lunch puzzle is hard to dismiss.

WHAT NET COSTS REMAIN?

The free lunch puzzle continues to pose a challenge for anyone who devoutly believes that the welfare state, like any government intervention, drags down economic performance. Could it be that tax-financed social transfers are costly only in distant hypothetical worlds, and not in the real world, as the estimates seem to imply? Must one accept this book's suggestion that offsetting mechanisms make the net cost effectively zero?

The best hope for devout opponents of the welfare state lies in leaning on selected side-results of this study. One could stress the shift from net benefits to net costs as the historical sample shifted toward the present day. The 1880–1930 experience showed positive GDP-growth effects of much-needed tiny transfers, 1962–1981 showed effects that were generally positive, and only the 1978–1995 experience showed that the welfare state could have become costly. Perhaps that shift from benefits toward costs across the historical samples shows a gradual behavioral rot, in which people develop an addiction to handouts and entitlements. In addition, the recession and unemployment that hit Sweden and Finland in the early 1990s might be the harbinger of soaring costs in the twenty-first century, not just an aberration. Maybe the drift toward negative estimates and the brief crisis in Sweden and Finland are showing us that the worst is yet to come. Perhaps the welfare state will eventually collapse under its own weight, even if that took longer than a conservative expected in the heyday of Reagan and Thatcher. Perhaps.

Yet the evidence still leaves little support for believing that big costs have entered the real world. Take the worst present estimates of the GDP cost shown at the bottom of Table 18.1. At a growth-rate loss of 0.32 percent per annum from a 5-percent rise in the transfer share, like that in Germany from 1990 to 1995, the cost reaches 1 percent of GDP only after three years and 5 percent of GDP only after 15.3 years. Even this cost trajectory comes from the worst-case estimates traveling at the historical sample's speed limit, and other estimates from the same postwar datasets imply no cost at all.

Next, the estimates contain some biases that invite an overstatement of GDP costs. Even the fitted values of transfers contain some cyclical bias, as noted earlier. In addition, the estimates fail to capture any rise in shadow-economy production and consumption caused by the rise of taxes to finance social transfers. Curiously, many writers have cited the higher shadow-economy production as if it were a negative side-effect of the taxes that support transfers. It is referred to as tax avoidance, as if that were something costly. Yet that side-production in the shadow market should be *added to* the visible GDP achieved in the higher-tax countries.

Above all, the effects on GDP per capita are too pessimistic about the effects on well-being. The effects on GDP per capita miss the favorable effects of public health systems on the length of life, as argued in Chapter 10. They also fail to value the extra leisure time of those who respond to the social transfer system by working fewer hours or fewer years. That extra free time is indeed valuable. We should stop assuming that time outside of work is worth zero, as the whole GDP debate implies.

So great is the value of free time that adding it to GDP actually cancels the American lead in well-being. This wake-up call is clear even if we look only at the free time per year of working age, without adding in the longer life expectancy under the more public health systems of Europe, Canada, and Japan. As Nick Crafts has shown, the United States ranked only ninth in GDP per working hour in 1992, behind Belgium, France, Netherlands, West Germany, Norway, Switzerland, Canada, and Austria.[18] If we value each hour of free time at the salary rate people passed up, then these same rankings hold for any measure of well-being per year of working age. Economists have warned, of course, that an hour of free time is not necessarily worth the same as an hour of salary. For some people, it is worth more than that, and they choose not to work at all. For others, it is worth less than the wage, and their not working is partly involuntary.[19] Yet it is surely more accurate to value Europeans' extra vacations – and their longer life expectancy – at the wage rate than at zero, which is what the debate over GDP effects has assumed.

Thus even if social transfers had any slight cost in terms of GDP because they reduced work time, such a cost is even closer to zero in welfare terms than in GDP terms. Almost any positive effect of the social programs on productivity and well-being would be enough to cancel the net cost altogether, and leave a substantial net gain from the overall welfare-state package.

19

Reconciling Unemployment and Growth in the OECD

By Gayle J. Allard and Peter H. Lindert

It is time for a showdown between the findings of two separate strands of empirical literature. On one side, studies of jobs and unemployment find that giving more to the unemployed cuts the number of jobs and raises unemployment. On the other, as we have seen, studies of the effects of total social transfers on the growth or level of GDP find no reliable statistical effect. The conflict stares at us directly in the raw data and is not just a subtlety revealed by the buildup of statistical studies. Just looking at the postwar record, we can see that unemployment rose dramatically in many countries after the 1960s, yet their GDP did not visibly drop relative to countries with less unemployment.

How can these two strands be tied together? How can GDP not be cut if jobs are cut? Is it just that transfers to the unemployed cut jobs and output, while other transfers actually raise output? If the story of no clear GDP cost is correct, did more generous unemployment compensation really not destroy any jobs, contrary to past findings? If subsidizing the unemployed makes fewer people have jobs, is the GDP literature overlooking true costs? The reconciliation cannot simply hinge on differences between the GDP effects of the dole and the GDP effects of total social transfers, since Chapter 18 found that even the dole itself did not have a significant GDP cost. Alternatively, could more unemployment compensation remove only completely unproductive workers, whose marginal product is zero?

We offer a reconciliation using better data and better tests than the past literature on the job effects of unemployment compensation, alias the dole. The first task is to use new measures of different labor-market policies. That affords a clearer view of all the separate determinants of jobs and joblessness. Once the impacts of many forces are determined, we can account for the huge international differences in recent unemployment history. Labor market institutions are an important part of the story of why some countries have suffered high unemployment for the last quarter century, while others managed to return to full employment in the 1990s.

Sorting out the various determinants of jobs and joblessness also allows firm conclusions about the separate effect of giving more social transfers to the unemployed. Yes, giving more to the unemployed costs jobs. So do some other labor market policies, such as employee protection laws, once their impact is measured correctly. At the same time, more generous unemployment compensation seems to raise productivity per person still employed, so that the net effect on GDP is indeed close to zero. In this respect, the dole is very different from employee protection laws.

UNEMPLOYMENT SINCE 1960

The history of employment and unemployment has been eventful in the industrialized market economies since 1960, and there is much to explain. The share of the population that holds jobs has risen slightly, mainly because more and more married women hold jobs. Despite a slight trend toward work, the rate of *un*employment also rose, dramatically and unevenly. Both jobs and joblessness rose together because the share of people seeking work rose even faster than the share actually holding jobs. To sharpen our focus on what needs most to be explained, this section traces the contours of recent unemployment history, first following the average experience for the OECD as a whole and then exploring the enormous differences between countries' rates of unemployment. What happened to the employment ratio, the share of the adult population holding jobs, is a softened mirror image of the contrasts revealed by the history of unemployment.

For most of the 1960s unemployment remained low, and even improved a bit, across the OECD, as shown in the thick curve that plots the OECD average in each of the five panels of Figure 19.1. There was little hint of the problems that were to follow. The quiet discussion of comparative unemployment rates posed a question that soon became obsolete: Why was unemployment persistently higher in the United States and Canada? The general verdict was that the North Americans somehow lacked the right institutions for helping people find new jobs.

A major transformation set in between the late 1960s and the early 1980s. Unemployment rose in virtually every OECD country, partly because of the two oil shocks of 1973–1974 and 1979–1981. However, something else must have been going on in the background. Average unemployment was already on the rise between the 1969 cyclical peak and the 1973 cyclical peak, before the oil shocks took effect. Another background clue is that unemployment remained severe for the OECD as a whole even after its peak in 1983. Granted, the improved growth of 1983–1991 brought down average unemployment, yet these gains had vanished by 1993, and the century closed with the whole OECD having an average unemployment rate of almost 7 percent.

The international contrasts in the rise of unemployment were sharper than the average rise itself between the late 1960s and the early 1980s. In some

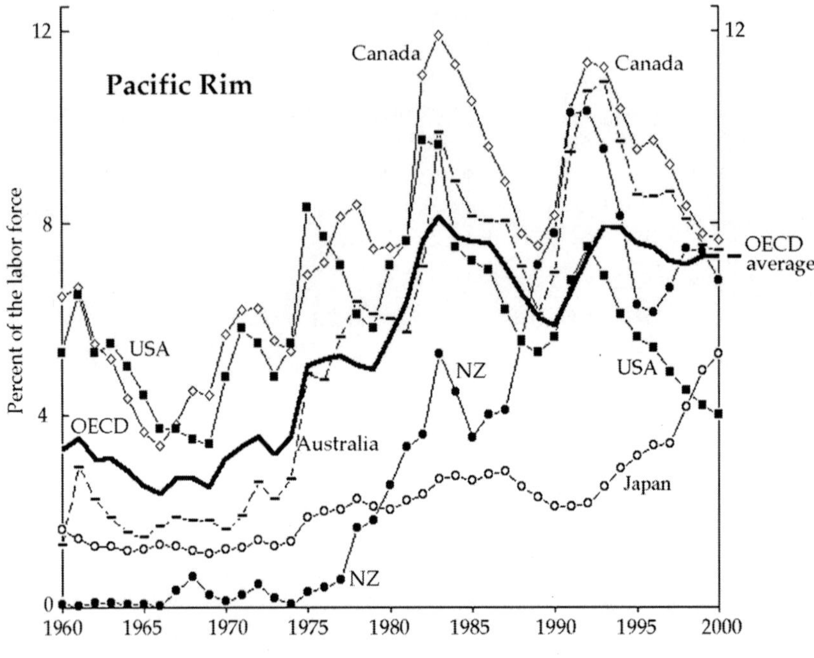

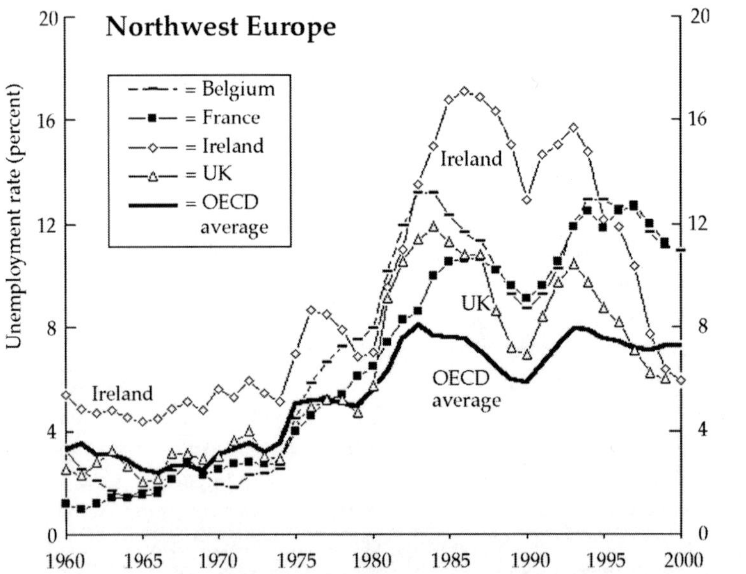

FIGURE 19.1. Standardized unemployment rates, OECD countries 1960–2000.

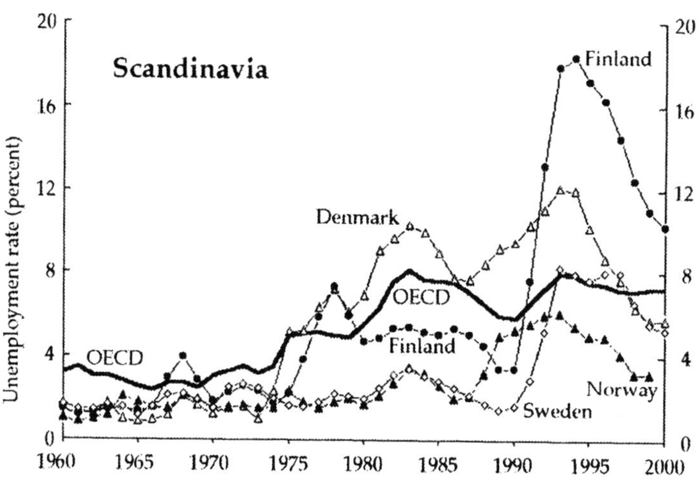

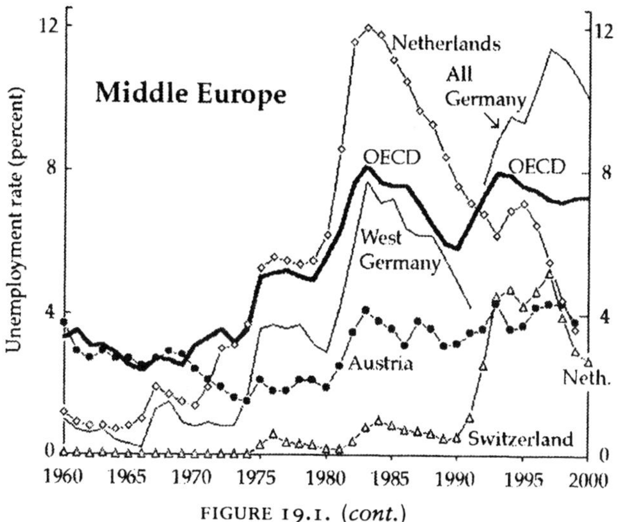

FIGURE 19.1. (*cont.*)

countries the unemployment rate soared into double digits. Spain reported the worst rates, exceeding 20 percent in several years. While these rates were somewhat inflated by Spain's nonreporting of paid work in the unofficial shadow economy, even Spain's true unemployment probably remained in double digits across the 1980s and 1990s. Also hitting unemployment rates of 12 percent or higher in the 1980s were Ireland, the Netherlands, Belgium, the United Kingdom, and Canada. By contrast, no such crisis had visited Japan, Switzerland, Austria, Norway, or Sweden by the early 1980s.

Since the early 1980s, the geography of high unemployment has shifted. By the late 1990s, Ireland, the Netherlands, the United Kingdom, and the

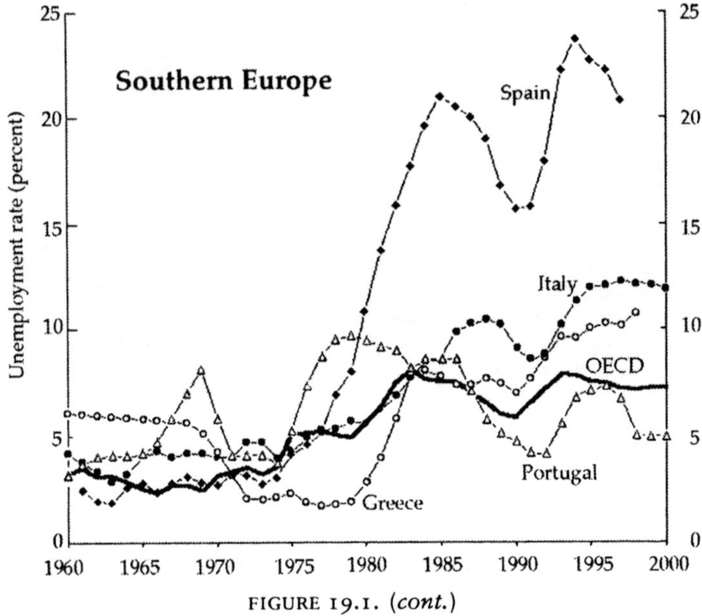

FIGURE 19.1. (*cont.*)

United States had cut their unemployment impressively. News began to spread about the Dutch and Irish miracles and the superiority of Anglo-American labor market institutions. By contrast, unemployment soared as never before in Finland, Germany, France, Italy, and Greece. By the late 1990s the set of OECD countries with high unemployment was clearly European, even though some European countries had escaped to virtually full employment.

Why did joblessness soar between the late 1960s and the early 1980s? What explains the stark international contrasts in that rise? And since 1990, why did some countries seem to work full-employment miracles, while others had higher unemployment than ever before?

EXPLAINING EMPLOYMENT AND UNEMPLOYMENT

Any forces affecting either labor demand or labor supply can affect the rates of employment and unemployment. On the demand side, our training and instincts usually focus first on the determinants of the aggregate demand for a country's national product, such as global booms and slumps, shifts in world demand for the particular country's exports, or national monetary and fiscal policies. These surely matter and must be controlled for. So must aggregate supply shocks, which in the era since 1960 mean those two great oil shocks of 1973–1974 and 1979–1981, plus any measurable shifts in technology that might augment or cut the demand for labor. On the supply side, labor supply can be affected by shifts in demography, in leisure preference, and in policies and institutions.

To trim this long list down to a short list of prime candidates for key roles in explaining jobs and joblessness, let us first drop some natural candidates that do not fit the symptoms, either in raw correlations or in multivariate analysis. That seems to be true of the labor-demand explanations, which cannot explain much by themselves.[1]

The oil shock story cannot do the explaining by itself. Neither the timing nor the international geography of high unemployment rates fits the oil-shock story. The two great oil shocks were replaced by falling real oil prices after 1982, yet unemployment failed to drop much over the next two decades. Nor were the countries hardest hit by the oil shocks the ones that had the greatest jumps in unemployment. Of the three economic superpowers – the United States, Japan, and the European Union – Japan clearly suffered the greatest declines of national purchasing power from the oil crises, because Japan had the greatest oil imports as a share of national product. The Japanese economy should have been the one to nosedive into recession and high unemployment, yet Japan suffered the least recession, and the least unemployment, of the three.

Another labor-demand story that did not explain much of the rise in unemployment is demand-shift or mismatch unemployment. In some cases, unemployment rises and persists because demand suddenly shifts away from certain sectors, leaving workers in those sectors with skills that fail to match the available jobs. That happened to coal, textile, and shipbuilding workers in the North and West of Britain after World War I, and those regions continued to suffer more unemployment than the Southeast over the next eighty years. It also happened to coal miners all over the world. Workers who have lost jobs in an injured sector will remain unemployed if they are older and less trainable. However, the demand shift phenomenon seems to explain very little of the overall rise in OECD unemployment. Even in Britain, multivariate analysis finds that mismatch unemployment explains only a very modest share of the rise in unemployment from the 1950s to the 1980s.[2]

Demography can also be put aside as a source of rising unemployment. There was no compositional shift toward those age groups that have perennially higher unemployment rates. The highly unemployed young adult age groups declined as a share of all adults after 1980, a shift that should have lowered unemployment instead of raising it. The shift toward an increasingly female labor force, while profoundly important in many respects, has not had much effect on unemployment rates. Even though women were a rising share of the workforce and usually have higher unemployment rates, the male–female differences in unemployment rates remained too small to explain much of the aggregate trend, or the international differences, in unemployment.

Union membership, as a clue to labor unions' political power, also fails to take center stage. It is only slightly correlated with unemployment. To be sure, closed union shops and the heavy political hand of national labor organizations did have effects that must have raised unemployment in some countries. Organized labor pressure imposed high minimum wage rates in some core countries of the European Union, particularly France and Italy, and unions were surely behind some of the job-killing employee protection laws that we discuss below. However, the damage done to employment in some of these cases was reversed in some other countries where unions were equally strong. The contrast in unions' impact is between their job-restricting effect in core countries of the old European Community and their full-employment cooperation with business and governments in Scandinavia, the Netherlands, and Austria. Differences in the rate of work stoppages give a useful clue here: Where strong unions still fought with business and government (old European Community), unemployment remained stubbornly high; where they made peace, jobs were created. Yet union membership and union power as such cannot be at the center of any overall explanation of unemployment in the OECD.

If these actors did not deserve leading roles, which ones did? We turn now to those institutional variables that made the short list as leading candidates to explain the stark contrasts in rates of jobholding and joblessness.

The Role of Benefits for the Unemployed

To see the key roles played by institutional forces, let us turn first to a traditional leading actor, one that involves social transfers directly to the unemployed. Unemployment compensation takes a number of forms. Here we confine our view to the classic payment to unemployed workers in the early and middle parts of their careers. Later we shall look at subsidies for early retirement.

Unemployment compensation is unavoidably a tax on work for persons able to work. How much it gives a work disincentive depends on five things:

(a) the marginal *replacement rate*, or (benefits per recipient) divided by (market wage), net of taxes;
(b) the *coverage* rate, the share of unemployed persons who are eligible;
(c) the *take-up rate*, the share of eligible persons who apply for benefits;
(d) the *duration* of coverage (one month, three months, one year, etc.); and
(e) the *elasticity* of the labor supply curve.

Unfortunately, past studies measuring unemployment compensation have been content to measure the replacement rate and the elasticity of labor supply alone, missing the three other key components of the overall effect of unemployment compensation. One of the present authors has incorporated

Panel A. Core EU Countries

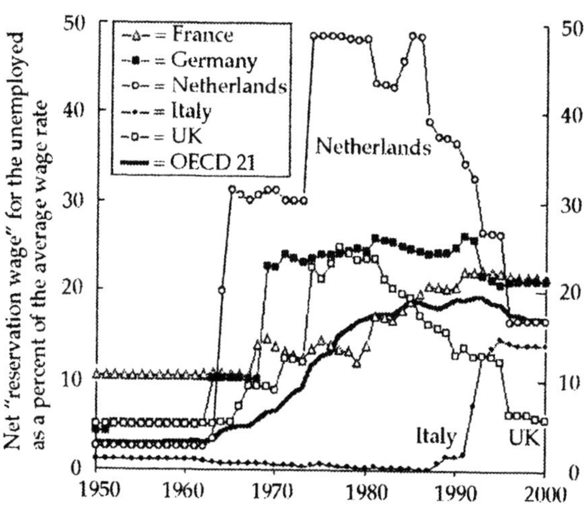

Panel B. The Outer World

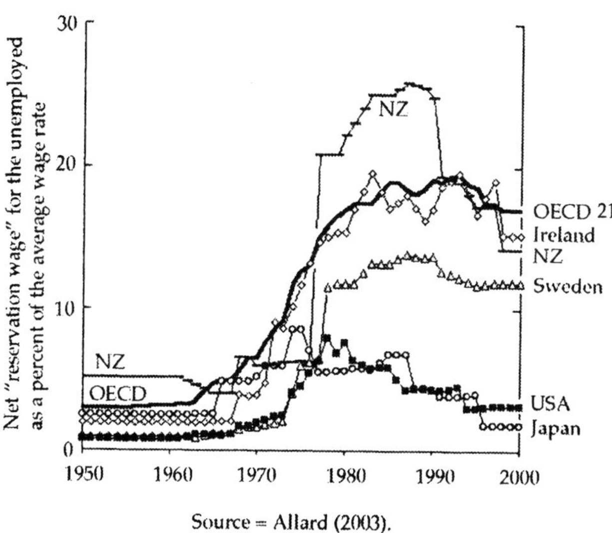

Source = Allard (2003).

FIGURE 19.2. Unemployment compensation 1950–2000.

the first four components, (a) through (d), into a single measure of the *net reservation wage*, the expected value of unemployment compensation as a percentage of the median market wage, both measured after taxes.[3]

The history of the unemployment insurance systems began to become markedly more generous in the 1960s, even though jobless rates were still low. As Figure 19.2 shows, the OECD-average net reservation wage, our measure of the generosity of the unemployment compensation system, hovered around 3 percent through the 1950s and until 1963. Yet by the early 1980s the average dole had reached 18 or 19 percent of an average wage rate. By the century's end it was still about 17 percent. Note that these rates are all lower than the previously publicized replacement ratios, which failed to allow for the fractional rates of coverage, take-up, and duration of benefits.

With the dole as with the unemployment rate, national rates diverged sharply after the late 1960s. Dutch workers got almost half their would-be average earnings between 1973 and 1986, partly through the excessive disability benefits described in earlier chapters. Other above-average benefit rates in the 1970s and 1980s were those offered by governments in New Zealand, Germany, and pre-Thatcher Britain.

The job impact of unemployment compensation cannot be determined until we have sorted out the roles of several determinants of employment and unemployment. This calls for regression analysis. The analysis must endogenize policies and institutions before trying to estimate their separate job impacts. We should also explore equations for both the employment ratio and the unemployment rate. The employment ratio has the advantage of revealing impacts on the number of jobs actually held. Any impact of, say, unemployment compensation on the employment ratio is a true impact on jobs and not an influence on the number of people who say they are looking for a job. The unemployment rate has the potential drawback of reflecting mere labor-force status rather than actual job-holding, but it usefully dramatizes movements in jobholding among those who say they really seek jobs.

The national determinants of employment and unemployment can be shown with either of two kinds of samples from recent history. Here it is more convenient to use the 1978–1995 sample of triennial averages that has been used elsewhere in this volume. Similar job impacts have also been estimated with a larger unbalanced panel of annual observations for 1980–1998. The latter has the advantage of exploiting more information, but with more difficult serial correlation issues and less comparability to the results of other chapters in this volume.

The job impacts of some key policies and institutions are summarized in Table 19.1, which includes results from an equation for labor productivity, to be discussed later. In each case the underlying equation controls for educational attainment, the age distribution of the population, and global shocks in aggregate demand and aggregate supply. Each equation also allows for nonlinearities suggested by theory. The effects of the net reservation wage are allowed to be cubic in form to allow for the complexities of aggregating labor supply functions of unknown form. Employment protection laws enter the equation both via their current index level and via their level lagged by three years, since they should (and do) have a more negative effect after a few years than when the laws are first tightened. All policy variables are, to repeat, endogenous values predicted by a first-stage equation.

TABLE 19.1. *Institutional Impacts on Employment, Unemployment And Productivity, 1978/80–1993/95*

	Eq. (1) log (Employment/pop.)		Eq. (2) Unemployment Rate		Eq. (3) log (GDP/ Employment) = Labor Productivity	
	Coeff.	|t|	Coeff.	|t|	Coeff.	|t|
Effect of raising the unemployment compensation support ratio (net reservation wage)						
From 5% to 20%	−0.023	(1.48)	0.011	(1.79)[b]	0.016	(0.64)
From 5% to 40%	−0.053	(1.97)*	0.020	(1.90)[a]	0.059	(1.46)
Effect of a permanent tightening of EPLs by 1 index point:	−0.032	(3.40)**	0.0086	(2.41)*	−0.034	(2.52)
Effect of raising spending on ALMPs by 1% of GDP	−0.028	(2.27)*	0.018	(3.16)**	0.039	(1.91)[a]
Effect of raising collective wage negotiations ("corporatism") by one index point	0.029	(2.25)*	−0.017	(3.37)**	−0.020	(0.92)

Notes to Table 19.1:

(** = significant at the 1% level, two-tail; * = significant at the 5% level; [a]significant at the 7% level; [b]significant at the 10% level.)
For fuller versions of the regression equations, see Appendix Table F.6.

The 1978–1995 results confirm that more generous unemployment compensation cuts jobs and raises the unemployment rate, as shown in the first two columns of Table 19.1. Raising the net reservation wage from 5 percent of a median wage, which is one of the lowest percentages observed in the sample, to a sample-average 20 percent cuts employment by about 2.6 percent, or raises unemployment by about 1.3 percent of the labor force.[4] Raising the net reservation wage from that same 5 percent to 40 percent, one of the highest ratios in the sample, raises the job effects further. In this case, the effect is proportional, and allowing for a possible nonlinearity made no difference. The job effects are also conventional, in that the current results resemble those found in the earlier literature. That is, raising the percentage of a wage offered to the unemployed cuts jobholding significantly, though only by a small fraction of the percentage increase in the generosity of compensation.

Employee Protection Laws

When we think about the sources of unemployment, we think first of people losing their jobs by being laid off. Our usual thinking receives some startling news from the international differences in layoffs. In the 1970s and 1980s, we would have expected that high-unemployment Europe would have been losing more jobs to layoffs than lower-unemployment America. Yet that did not happen, as pointed out by Robert Flanagan and others.[5] The first column of numbers in Table 19.2 relays their news. In the European Community, heavily afflicted with unemployment, workers hardly ever lost their jobs. Layoffs were much more frequent in the United States, even though unemployment was not.

The other columns of Table 19.2 show how so many job-seekers could stay out of work in the European Community, when so few were losing jobs. Once a worker in the EC was unemployed, he or she tended to stay there

TABLE 19.2. *In and Out of Unemployment: A Curious Trans-Atlantic Contrast*

	Inflows into Unemployment (e.g. Layoffs) (% of Whole Labor Force, per Year)	Outflows from Unemployment (Get Job or Give up) (% of the Unemployed, per Year)	Share of Unemployment That is Long-Term (>1 Year) (% of the Unemployed)
EC			
1979	0.3	9.8	29
1988	0.3	5.0	55
US			
1979	2.1	43.5	4
1988	2.0	45.7	7

Source for Table 19.2: Bean (1994).

longer than in the United States. In other words, there were fewer entrants into unemployment and far fewer successful exits from unemployment in the European Community each year.

Very few traditional sources of unemployment can explain this pattern, especially the low layoff rates in high-unemployment countries. Slumps in aggregate demand could not do it, since they would have predicted more layoffs in the countries where the slumps created extra unemployment. Differences in subsidies to the unemployed also could not explain why so few people got laid off in those countries where those subsidies were more generous. Nor could many other factors.

The real explanation must lie in an insider–outsider problem in high-unemployment contexts like the European Community in Table 19.2. Something must be protecting the steadily employed insiders against job competition from outsiders, who must wait a long time before getting hired. As Flanagan has put it, high rates of unemployment in much of Western Europe reflect a hiring problem, not a firing problem. The insiders must get that power from the collective organized strength of labor unions or from special laws protecting insiders' jobs, or both. We favor emphasizing the laws, since these seem to correlate better with job losses than does union strength measured by membership as a share of the workforce.

To understand the role of such employee protection laws (EPLs) in the latter half of the twentieth century, one must first read their history and then codify it into an index of the strictness of workers' protection against layoffs. This huge task has been completed elsewhere, for a couple dozen countries from 1950 to 2000.[6] Employee protection laws were neither fixed over time nor the same across countries. Figure 19.3 illustrates the historical movements of the EPL indexes for several countries. Most countries entered the postwar period with relatively deregulated labor markets, as portrayed by EPL indices near zero for the 1950s in Figure 19.3.

In the 1960s, most OECD countries stepped up their job protection laws. The rising indices in Figure 19.3 reflect the passage of specific laws in a host of countries. At the beginning of the decade, Italy regulated individual dismissals and set severance payments of up to fourteen months' pay (1962) and the Netherlands began requiring not only severance payments, but also government authorization for dismissals (1960). Belgium legislated on collective dismissals in 1960 and on individual dismissals in 1966; Austria followed suit in 1969;[7] and Finland in 1966 passed a law requiring valid reasons for layoffs,[8] and setting priorities for dismissals, followed by another in 1968 that mandated six-month notice periods. Ireland's Redundancy Payments Act in 1967 also guaranteed economic compensation for workers dismissed for economic reasons,[9] and Japan required authorization for collective dismissals starting in 1966 (severance payments were voluntary). Germany's redundancy law of 1969 declared null and void all dismissals that were not socially justified, with the burden of proof on the employer;

Growing Public

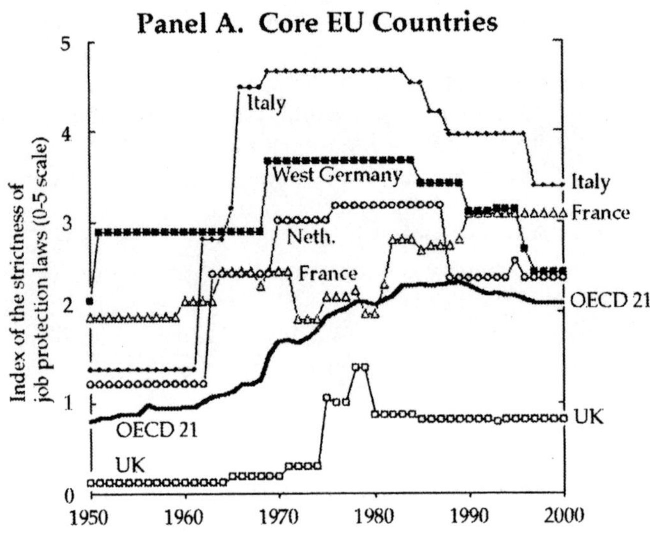

Panel A. Core EU Countries

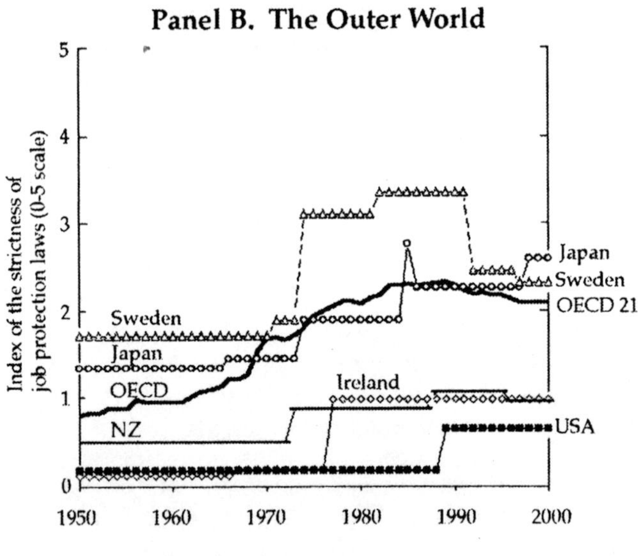

Panel B. The Outer World

Source = Allard (2003).

FIGURE 19.3. Employment protection laws 1950–2000.

and it opened the door for court-mandated severance payments of up to twelve times the monthly wage (eighteen times for older workers). In the same year, France set up a strict regulation of layoffs, buttressed by a July 1973 law restricting layoffs to those for "real and serious reasons." In Britain the Heath government passed a law in 1971 prohibiting dismissals for union activities, and worker rights were further supplemented in the 1975 Employment Protection Act.

Thus by the early 1970s, with unemployment still below 3 percent in Europe, momentum continued to gather for both companies and the government to provide more security to workers. Fueled by the worker unrest of the late 1960s, the movement for worker protection reached its height in the first half of the 1970s, with nearly every country extending worker rights to greater job security. However, legislation took on a less strident tone as the decade progressed and especially after the 1973–1974 oil price shock, as concern over steadily rising unemployment rates began to seep into policymaking and eventually emerged as governments' primary focus.

One surprising development in the 1980s was the move toward stricter EPLs by the main outlier, the United States, which had no employment-protection legislation and which led to the deregulation wave of the 1980s. Congress in 1989 passed the Worker Adjustment, Retraining and Notification Act (WARN), which required sixty days advance written notice (to workers and government) of plant closures or mass layoffs that affected 100 workers or more.[10] In Australia, another example of the decentralized, common-law approach to job security, a landmark federal tribunal case in 1984 approved levels of protection in an industry award that became the established minima for all industries. With these two exceptions, Figure 19.3's average EPL index for the whole OECD shows a timing like those for average unemployment and for the average dole: stabilization in the 1980s, with hints of reversal late in the decade.

For the 1990s, Figure 19.3's slight decline in the overall OECD average EPL index is a rough net result of countercurrents in different countries. The countries where labor markets were partially deregulated were Finland, Germany, Italy, New Zealand, Spain, and Sweden, yet other countries tightened up, leaving only a slight average deregulation within the 1990s.

Through the whole half-century, there was a fairly consistent geography. The English-speaking countries remained relatively deregulated, while in Southern Europe the political outcomes bred strict job protection laws.

What effect did the employee protection laws have on jobholding and joblessness? As already noted, we need to allow for the effect to change over time. When the laws are first tightened in favor of employee rights, they could either raise or lower employment. On the one hand, restricting layoffs keeps employment higher. On the other, it makes firms reluctant to hire new employees. Initially, either effect could outweigh the other. With time, however, the negative hiring effect would theoretically dominate since the protected employees are a stagnant group and the prevented hires would rise with economic growth. And that is what the regression results show in Table 19.1. Once the strictness of EPLs has been elevated by 1 or more index unit for three or more years, it cuts employment by over 3 percent and raises unemployment by 0.8 percent of the labor force. Thus stricter EPLs have significant job costs, even though by themselves they cannot explain more than a four-point difference in any two countries' unemployment rates.[11]

Our estimates of the overall average job effects of employee protection laws might misrepresent them in cases where the actual workings of the laws differ from what the codes themselves have revealed. A clear example emerges from the contrast between Spain and Portugal. Both countries passed laws that read similarly in principle, causing their EPL indices to look similar. Yet Spain has had unemployment rates soar over 20 percent, while Portugal has kept unemployment below the OECD average since the mid-1980s. The contrast resulted from a large, but hard-to-measure, difference in legal enforcement. In lawsuits filed in the wake of employee dismissals, the laid off workers tend to win their cases in Spain, but not in Portugal. With enforcement proclivities so different, some of the true differences in the effects of EPLs are hidden.[12]

The job costs of employee protection laws have not been equally shared among demographic groups. Knowing that stricter job protections were legislated in response to lobbying by organized labor, we would not be surprised to find that EPLs raise the employment of already senior insiders at the expense of groups outside the gates. That is apparently the case. Where EPLs protect more rigidly, youths and women suffer even higher unemployment rates, relative to senior male employees, than in countries with deregulated labor markets. The gaps in unemployment rates between youths and senior men, or between women and senior men, apparently widened more between 1970 and 1995 in countries where EPLs tightened up more. EPL seems designed to protect prime male breadwinners' jobs.[13] It slows down job-market entry by denying new jobs. The pattern of EPLs fits the cynical view that senior males were a powerful lobby promoting and designing the legislation. This suspicion gains support from the fact that EPLs are highly correlated with the share of elderly in the adult population. Another support for the cynical view is how differently policy in the high-EPL countries has treated elderly male employees. They have been bought out generously with golden handshakes and disability policy. Youths and women have not been bought out of their jobs. Instead they have been shut out by EPLs and do not qualify for generous unemployment compensation because of their shorter work histories.

Active Labor Market Policies[14]

Active labor market policies, or ALMP, have become increasingly popular in several OECD countries during the postwar period, and their popularity appears to coincide with the rise and persistence of unemployment. ALMP generally refers to spending on (a) government placement services to make the matching process between vacancies and job seekers more efficient; (b) labor market training to upgrade and adapt the skills of the labor force;

and (c) direct job creation, in the form of either public-sector employment or subsidization of private-sector work. ALMP has been touted as a better remedy for unemployment than passive labor market policies such as unemployment benefits, because it aims at giving unemployed workers the skills, experience, and contacts that should enable them to return to the job market.

Proponents of ALMP have been able to point to some signs of job success. Open unemployment has been significantly reduced in some countries with higher ALMP – particularly in the Nordic ones, where spending is greatest and schemes such as the Restart scheme in the United Kingdom, which involved intensified counseling for the long-term unemployed, have been credited with reducing joblessness.

On the other hand, large-scale wage subsidy programs, expected to reduce unemployment sharply in countries where they were implemented, may have had strong substitution effects, which would reduce their effectiveness. In some countries such as Finland, income maintenance of the unemployed has been a stronger objective of ALMP spending than getting the jobless back to work, as countries have used ALMP as a way for the unemployed to requalify for unemployment benefits after a short government course or public-sector job. Some time-series studies have found that ALMP also increases aggregate wage pressure, and hence may squeeze out regular employment.

Fortunately, measurement of ALMP is straightforward: The OECD has statistics on spending as a percentage of GDP for most member countries from the early 1980s and scattered figures before that. As a share of GDP it leveled off at 0.7 percent between 1985 and 1990, rose to 0.9 percent for 1994, and fell to 0.8 percent for 1997. On the OECD average, active (work-targeted, or workfare) policies have stayed steady at about a third of all labor-market-related spending over this whole period. The Nordic countries are upper outliers and the United States spends the least.

What effects do active labor market policies have on job creation and on unemployment? Our tests yield generally negative results on the employment front, as typified by the regression coefficients for ALMP in Table 19.1, even though the spending on these policies has been endogenized to minimize simultaneity bias.[15] When both public employment and ALMP spending were included in the same regression, both tended to show negative job impacts. The generally negative employment result matches the drift of the earlier econometric literature. Around this negative overall tendency, there were variations, of course. The most consistently positive results relate to adult women. This may be due to a difference in self-selection. Adult women's being unemployed and eligible for ALMP participation is less related to any negative attitude toward schooling and training than it is characteristic for male school dropouts, who had the worst job-getting results as ALMP participants. Among the forms of ALMP, job search assistance had better effects than training or providing public sector employment.[16]

Why would programs designed to secure jobs seem to have an even negative effect overall, even after correcting for simultaneity bias? The most likely culprit is misspecification of the dynamics of ALMP. With a lag, ALMP may create jobs and enhance productivity, even though little of this success would show up in the same year or, in these regressions, the same three-year period. We should no more expect a fully contemporaneous payoff to ALMP than we should expect the payoff to extra educational expenditures to show up in each same year. Another redemptive theme will be heard when we turn to the apparent positive productivity effects of ALMP.

Reinterpreting the Role of Corporatism

Another labor market institution has received a lot of attention from scholars without ever being defined very carefully. In a number of OECD countries, wages are set as part of a collective bargain between organized business and organized labor, with or without the participation of government. As one might suspect, the sustainability of this institution depends on the whole complex diplomacy between business and labor and also on the ability of each encompassing national organization to control the behavior of its own members.[17] It is not a stable institution. Since the 1970s it has retreated in Australia, Sweden, and Britain. By contrast, it gained new strength in Italy in the early 1990s.

While it lasts, corporatist wage bargaining seems to preserve jobs and reduce unemployment. So said the regression results in Table 19.1. The positive job effect is not surprising, since in many cases the bargaining involves an exchange of wage restraint for job protection.

HOW THE SAME FORCES AFFECTED PRODUCTIVITY

Having confirmed that the rise and fall of unemployment compensation did affect the number of jobs, we are ready for that showdown between this firm finding and the finding that neither unemployment compensation nor total social transfers has a significantly negative effect on GDP per capita. One could play down the contradiction a bit just by noting that the announced insignificance of the effect on GDP per capita may just hide a negative effect behind a fat confidence interval. That is, the literature's inability to find significant growth costs may mean only that we really can't tell whether the true cost is zero because our estimates are so rough. However, there is something else bringing the GDP cost of transfers close to zero, something that has more economic meaning.

More generous transfers to the unemployed seem to raise the productivity of those still at work. The final column in Table 19.1 hinted as much, both for outright transfers to the unemployed and for expenditures on active labor market policies.

There are two basic mechanisms that could create the positive productivity effect, one operating in ordinary private job markets and one caused by government policy. In an ordinary market, the principle of diminishing marginal returns means that removing some labor will raise the average and marginal product of the remaining labor. Even in the absence of government policy, private labor markets leave low-skilled workers less employed on the average over the business cycle.

Government policy could also create a positive productivity effect, by making the dole and early retirement policies remove from work a set of workers that tended to be less productive even while at work. Indeed public unemployment compensation policies tend to give relief that is a higher percentage of the would-be wage to workers who had been earning less. As Chapter 10 suggested in crude shorthand, it is likely that the dole harvests lemons.

An outstanding case of this bias toward leaving the more productive at work and paying the less productive to stay away has arisen in the form of early retirement policies. As Chapter 10 already documented to some extent, government subsidies to early retirement also tend to cull out the less productive workers. We can underline this tendency here by taking a closer look at just how strongly government policies in several countries are biased toward removing low-skilled, low-paid senior workers from the ranks of the employed. What the government offers each person leaving employment depends not only on its current-year support but also on how the retirement annuities depend on each extra year of work. An extremely generous golden handshake is one that offers the retiree as much as, or even more than, his or her current rate of pay at work. Such a retirement package puts a huge tax on continuing to work. At the other extreme, a retirement package that offers only a small share of the salary as a retirement annuity hardly taxes work at all, especially if the retirement annuity would grow considerably with each extra year of staying at work.

Where the productivity bias enters retirement policy is in the government's decisions about how golden a handshake to offer to workers with high, versus low, productivity as reflected in their rate of earnings at work. Table 19.3 shows us the productivity bias, measured by the difference between two implicit tax rates on men's continuing to work after age fifty-five. Each number in Table 19.3 is the difference between the tax on extra work faced by men who earn only in the tenth percentile of earnings and the tax on more work by men up in the ninetieth percentile of earnings. For many countries, the differences are substantial, especially after the sixtieth birthday. One extreme case is Spain, where low-earning men over sixty face a work tax that is 72 percent above the positive work tax paid by high-earning men. Even more extreme is Italy's differential, albeit for a wider gap in percentiles. In Italy before the partial reform of 1995, the difference between the work taxes faced by low and high earners was nearly 80 percent for the fifty-five

TABLE 19.3. *Marginal Tax Rates on Continuing to Work: High-Pay vs. Low-Pay Senior Men in 1985–1995*

Percentage-Point *Difference* in the Tax Rate Implicit in the Tax and Pension Codes, 10th Percentile Worker Versus 90th Percentile in Terms of Earnings

	Age 55–59	Age 60–64
Countries inviting low earners to retire early		
Canada	6.8	13.3
France	5.1	30.8
Japan	5.1	16.4
Netherlands	22.7	22.6
Spain	37.0	72.0
Sweden	10.9	14.8
Italy (5th vs. 95th)	77.9	89.8 (pre-1995 rates)
Countries giving neither high nor low earners much reason to retire early		
U.K.	−3.5	−3.0
U.S.	−4.3	−5.6

Source and note for Table 19.3:
The source is Gruber and Wise (1999). The tax rates are those that would be experienced by a man born in 1930 when he reached the 55–64 age range in 1985–1995.

to fifty-nine age range, and nearly 100 percent after the sixtieth birthday. A high-paid Italian worker should keep working to sixty-five or older, while a low-paid Italian worker could hardly afford to keep working. The same is not true in Britain or the United States, where both low- and high-paid workers are given an incentive to keep working well into their sixties. Here, then, is an extreme case of the productivity bias in the dole – a policy clearly designed to get the less productive employees out of work, while retaining the more productive.

But in what sense could the marginal product of those removed workers truly be zero, so that the policy completely shields GDP from the work loss? Probably not in the individual sense. The marginal workers presumably do produce something individually, albeit less than the average working person of their age group, but their being at work may have further negative effects on others at work. The presence of the marginal workers in the workplace may force others to take time away from other tasks to help them, monitor them, discipline them, and prepare to get rid of them. Their presence in the workplace may also lower the implicit standards expected of other workers. Such effects might make the true marginal product of those extra workers – their effect on the collective productivity of whole work units – very close to zero. Still, in the end, we continue to believe that more generous unemployment compensation does reduce GDP, even if the cost is hard to distinguish

TABLE 19.4. *The Effects of Labor-Market Institutions on GDP, as Implied by Their Effects on Employment and Labor Productivity, OECD Countries in 1978–1995*

	Percentage Effects		
	On Employment	On Labor Productivity	Implied Effect on GDP
Effect of raising the unemployment compensation support ratio (net reservation wage)			
From 5% to 20%	−2.3	+1.6	−0.7
From 5% to 40%	−5.1	+6.1	+0.7
Effect of a permanent tightening of EPLs by 1 index point	−3.1	−3.3	−6.3
Effect of raising spending on ALMPs by 1% of GDP	−2.8	+4.0	+1.1
Effect of raising collective wage negotiations ("corporatism") by one index point	+2.9	−2.0	+0.9

Note to Table 19.4:
The implied GDP effects are not direct sums of the percentage effects on employment and productivity shown here. Rather they are the direct sums in logarithms in Table 19.1, separately converted to percentages.

from zero statistically. It's just that the cost is so small that the positive effects of social transfers other than the dole easily cancel any clear net cost of the overall social transfer package.

Do all policies that reduce work also raise productivity? To confirm that the tendency shows up in various, but not all, policy dimensions, let us look at the implied GDP effects of all the labor market policies featured in this chapter. Converting the logarithmic effects of Table 19.1 into percentage changes, Table 19.4 shows us how the effects on jobs per capita and on GDP per job imply different impacts on GDP per capita, based on the 1978–1995 experience of OECD countries.

Social transfers to the unemployed do not seem to reduce GDP. Raising their net reservation wage has a small GDP effect that falls on one or the other side of zero. It looks slightly negative if we contemplate a shift from a 5-percent to a 20-percent net reservation wage, which is the shift from low U.S. levels to something near the OECD average for those years. Yet it looks slightly positive over the bigger jump from the U.S. 5-percent level to a top-dole country. The true value of either effect on GDP could be zero. The other social transfer policy, spending on ALMP, actually has a positive estimated effect on GDP, despite the negative job effect we pondered earlier. The implied reason is that keeping some people unemployed and in training raises the productivity of those at work, whether because the ALMP beneficiaries are a low-productivity group or because previous

ALMP spending has raised productivity when beneficiaries have returned to work.

More direct interference with the functioning of labor markets probably has a more negative impact on productivity and GDP than do social transfers. As we saw, tightening the laws protecting insiders' jobs eventually lowered employment, while interfering in labor markets with corporatist collective wage setting tended to preserve jobs. Yet both kinds of interference ended up lowering labor productivity. The net result is that employee protection laws stand out as a negative influence on GDP, while corporatist wage setting might have had a positive effect.

SUMMARY: INSTITUTIONS, JOBS, AND GROWTH

We now have a clearer view of how labor market policies affect employment, unemployment, productivity and GDP.

Jobs are indeed lost when the government offers more generous unemployment compensation. They are also lost, eventually, after each tightening of the laws that protect senior workers against firing. Even spending on active labor market policies – retraining workers and matching them with new jobs – seems to have a negative concurrent effect on the number of jobs held, despite its goal of putting people back to work in better jobs. Of the labor market policies considered here, only corporatist wage-bargaining between organized labor and organized business seemed to create or preserve jobs.

The negative impact of unemployment compensation on jobs is consistent with its lack of impact on GDP. The reconciliation involves the fact that making unemployment compensation more generous removes lower-productivity labor, raising the average productivity of those who continue to work. By itself, this offsetting productivity response probably does not push the overall effect on GDP to zero. Rather, it probably pushes it close enough to zero to be offset or even reversed by any growth-enhancing force correlated with the provision of safety nets for the unemployed. One possibly positive correlate is even suggested by the tests shown here. Spending on active labor market policies may even have sufficiently positive effects on productivity to raise GDP despite their holding more people temporarily in the unemployment bin.

The results also suggest, in a preliminary way, that the social transfer side of government interventions in labor markets is better for productivity and GDP than some other interventions. Of the labor market policies featured here, the one that has a clearly negative effect on GDP is employee protection legislation, not social transfers.

Reconciling the job consequences with the lack of GDP consequences makes it easier to understand the persistence of a striking difference in labor market outcomes between Britain and the United States on the one hand and Continental Western Europe on the other. As Richard Freeman and others have often observed, the European drift toward higher unemployment can be coupled with the Anglo-American drift toward wage inequality since the late 1970s.[18] The difference has often been portrayed as a conscious policy choice, and rightly so. The Anglo-American strategy since the late 1970s has been to push people into low-wage employment. The Continental strategy has been to push them out of it, protecting wages while holding people temporarily in the unemployment bin. As we have seen, the Anglo-American message to many workers, especially women and young adults, has been delivered in the form of high job turnover, low minimum wages, "workfare" reforms, and tax credits for the lowest levels of earnings, such as Earned Income Tax Credit (EITC) or Working Family Tax Credit (WFTC). The Continental alternative has divided the same groups into those getting better bottom salaries and those still waiting. What we can now see is that the persistence of this policy difference for a quarter century is sustainable in at least one respect: It does not entail any clear difference in GDP growth, aside from those costs of employee protection laws.

Appendix A

Time Series on School Enrollments and Teachers, 1830–1930

APPENDIX TABLE A1. *Student Enrollment Rates in Primary Schools, Selected Countries, 1830–1930*

	1830	1840	1850	1860	1870	1880	1890	1900	1910	1920	1930
A. Total primary school students enrolled (thousands)											
Austria, pub + priv	1,244	1,313	1,426	1,637	1,821	2,591	3,220	3,742	4,757	988	944
Austria, pub only					1,761	2,506	3,114	3,612	4,341	868	793
Belgium, pub + priv	293	453	487	506	593	609	616	794	931	961	835
Belgium, pub only					424	433	442	480	511	961	835
Bulgaria, pub + priv							197	318	454	560	656
Denmark						190	335	376	406	437	446
Finland, pub + priv									183	272	425
Finland, public						29	55	110	173	272	425
France, pub + priv	2,280	3,164	3,322	4,336	4,723	5,341	5,556	5,550	5,682	4,518	4,710
France, public enr.		2,457	2,369	2,726	2,716	3,568	3,901	4,040	5,623	3,627	3,834
France, pub. subsid.	651	2,215	2,263	3,059	3,300	5,109	5,346	5,295	5,631	4,472	4,672
Germany, pub only				5,545		6,998	8,120	8,966	10,310	8,894	7,590
Prussia, pub only	1,898	2,253	2,525	2,916	3,912	4,468	5,019	5,806	6,766		
Prussia, pub + priv	1,921	2,278	2,553	3,005	3,991	4,517	5,072	5,844	6,828		
Greece					86	117	164	190	260	726	772
Hungary			900	935	1,156	1,698	2,118/2,030	2,315	2,471	857	967
Italy, pub + priv	106		545	1,109	1,605	1,976	2,334	2,655	3,309	4,166	4,550
Italy, public only				983	1,459	1,851	2,146	2,470	3,059	3,988	4,382
Netherlands, pub + priv			369	410	474	541	643	740	904	1,032	1,244

122

Netherlands, public			284	323	364	408	455	508	563	1,032	1,244
Norway, pub + priv					257		299				
Norway, pub only	178	180	193	215	237	247	287	339	377	386	404
Portugal, pub only			42		125	236	238	231	264	317	423
Romania, pub only						108	191	352	587	834/1,516	2,111
Russia							4,372				
Serbia					23.3	36.3	65.7	102	146		
Spain					1,380	1,769	1,882	1,930	2,045	2,625	3,617
Sweden, public				462	576	638	691	742	792	744	834
Switzerland, pub only	271				412	434	468	473	544	536	472
U.K., mostly public			2,652	3,305	4,006	4,411	5,558	6,265	6,605	6,315	5,945
Eng-Wales, pub + priv	892	1,315	1,995	2,617	3,124	3,302	4,349	5,063	5,382	5,206	4,930
Scotland, priv + pub			390	441	542	663	746	735	732	627	595
Scotland, public only			376	425	523	640	720	724	727	627	595
Ireland, pub + priv			377	355	484	548	537	478	496	482	421
Ireland, public only			280	263	359	469	489	478	496	482	420
N. Ireland										153	172
Canada, pub w/sec					767	849	936	1,080	1,355	1,817	2,080
Canada, pub, elem only					759	841	927	1,069	1,310	1,739	2,009
USA, pub only	1,930		4,175		7,481	9,757	12,520	14,984	16,899	18,897	20,556
USA, pub + priv						10,101	14,182	16,041	18,250	20,290	22,703
Mexico						493	558	600	658	887	1,300
Australia, elem + sec		8.6	21	102	260	497	552	777	787	994	1,156
Australia, elem only				102	259	492	544	761	767	963	1,116
New Zealand, pub + priv					54	95	134	149	180	225	253
New Zealand, public					46	82	118	131	156	198	219
Argentina						98	228	387	694	1,121	1,445
Bolivia						10	24	34.5		81	80

(*continued*)

	1830	1840	1850	1860	1870	1880	1890	1900	1910	1920	1930
Brazil					138	209	259	475	638	1,251	2,085
Chile						63	119	157	317	401	559
Colombia							93	137	240	334	470
Costa Rica						13	9	19	27	35	49
Cuba, w/sec, pub only to '22								172	153	358/386	484
Ecuador							58	68	94	103	147
El Salvador							28	30	32	49	44
Guatemala						41	65	47	54	77	88
Honduras										36	42
Jamaica, w/sec to 1895					33	56	84	99	97	100	134
Nicaragua							12	18	18	30	
Paraguay							19	25	52	71	108
Peru							53	105	146	196	342
Trinidad & Tobago				3.7	4.1	9.1	20	30	49	55	64
Uruguay					17	25	39	52	95	124	178
Venezuela										89	114
China										4,805	9,745
Egypt								16	216	343	622
India (British)					273	659	2,394	3,002	3,434	4,851	6,435	9,363
Indonesia, pub + priv							85	117	172	366	863	1,801
Iran										27	112
Japan						1,326	2,349	3,097	4,684	6,338	7,728	8,788
Philippines, pub only									150	607	924	1,144
Sri Lanka, w/sec	14	16	18	29	41	90	146	209	336	397	579
Thailand									115	169	657
Turkey										336	489

B. Primary-school students per 1000 children of ages 5–14

Austria, pub + priv		367	389	417	426	562	633	670	746	917	839	
Austria, pub only					412	543	612	647	680	805	704	*
Belgium, pub + priv	346	526	549	557	597	522	434	592	618	757	701	
Belgium, public only					500	437	364	496	518	757	701	*
Bulgaria, pub + priv							238	332	412	444	472	
Denmark						462	701	717	687	648	674	*
Finland, pub + priv									274	400	582	
Finland, public						68	105	188	260	400	582	*
France, pub + priv	388	513	515	665	737	816	832	859	857	704	803	
France, public enr.		398	367	418	424	545	584	625	848	565	653	
France, pub subsid.		359	351	469	515	780	800	820	850	697	796	*
Germany, pub only				719		711	742	732	720	758	699	
Prussia, pub only	687	736	722	698	717	741	747	763	757			
Prussia, pub + priv	695	744	730	719	732	749	755	768	764			
Greece					253	293	312	324	408	589	617	*
Hungary					334	457	513	542	526	484	495	
Italy, pub + priv	28		124	247	286	346	370	382	446	506	594	
Italy, public only				219	260	324	350	362	422	479	563	*
Netherlands, pub + priv			541	591	639	628	647	663	703	706	780	
Netherlands, public			417	466	491	473	458	456	438	706	780	*
Norway, pub + priv					657		662					
Norway, pub only	685	671	640	616	606	596	637	674	685	694	717	*
Portugal, pub only			52		132	178	220	194	200	219	300	*
Romania, pub only								256	354	293	588	
Russia							99	149				
Serbia												
Spain				285	401	517	506	475	473	566	717	*

(continued)

	1830	1840	1850	1860	1870	1880	1890	1900	1910	1920	1930	
Sweden, public					589	705	683	689	699	640	779	*
Switzerland, pub only					759	753	789	727	707	710	701	
U.K., mostly public				521	559	549	646	720	729	701	745	*
Eng-Wales, pub + priv	274	351	498	588	609	555	657	742	748	725	755	
Scotland, priv + pub			592	643	697	776	802	765	729	648	675	
Scotland, public only			572	620	673	749	774	748	724	648	675	
Ireland, pub + priv				294	384	443	508	525	574	559	751	
Ireland, public only				218	285	379	462	525	574	559	751	
N. Ireland (these seem low)									272	316		
Canada, pub w/sec					835	808	831	901	917	992	1,000	*
Canada, pub, elem only					827	800	822	892	886	949	966	*
USA, pub only	546		681		779	800	857	884	896	857	835	*
USA, pub + priv						906	971	939	975	924	921	
Mexico						187	181	185	186	231	374	*
Australia, elem + sec				453	601	891	762	872	892	883	923	*
Australia, elem only				453	598	882	751	855	870	856	890	*
New Zealand, pub + priv					923	756	803	879	912	887	962	
New Zealand, public					775	654	706	769	793	778	835	*
Argentina						143	266	324	409	548	613	*
Bolivia								136				
Brazil					61	70	69	102	123	147	215	*
Chile						111	192	245	431	422	556	
Colombia										250		
Costa Rica						271	142	259	306	329	405	
Cuba, w/sec, pub only to '22								373	354	414	516	
El Salvador											119	

Guatemala			453			218		
Jamaica, w/sec to 1895		381	509	506	449	442	554	
Nicaragua						174		
Trinidad & Tobago			444	517	690	663	688	
Uruguay				207	292			
Egypt				7	74	108	178	
India (British)		42	44	47	65	80	113	
Japan	182	306	370	507	599	602	609	*
Philippines, pub only							364	
Sri Lanka, w/sec						352		
Thailand					59	78	242	
Turkey							135	

Notes to Appendix Table A1:

w/sec = primary plus secondary enrollments together.

pub only = just public (government-run) schools.

pub + pr = public plus private schools together.

(blank after country name) = secondary source does not state whether the estimates include private schools.

italics = Interpolations or extrapolations using population shares, age-groups shares, or public/private ratios.

*Series used in the 1880–1930 sample.

Austria: Flora et al. (1983, 556–557). Cisleithania (excluding the Italian provinces) to 1914, and the Republic of Austria subsequently. The following years' enrollments data were used in place of their respective nearest benchmark years listed at the top of the table: 1861, 1881, 1891, 1901, and 1911. The figures include the postprimary schools from 1911 on.

Belgium: Flora et al. (1983, 562). The benchmark-year substitutions are as follows: 1850 is really 1851, 1870 is really 1869, the 1882 figure is an interpolation because the "battle of the schools" in 1881 disrupted reporting, 1920 is 1919, and 1930 is 1929. Flora et al. list the 1830 and 1840 enrollments as public, but their magnitudes suggest that they refer to all schools. The Primary Education Act of 1914 entitled all schools, public or private, to state subsidies. Accordingly, I have counted all of the reported enrollments as public in the tax-effort sense. Enrollments in the so-labeled public schools in 1919 and 1929 are estimated at 514,000 and 430,000, respectively. A similar procedure is adopted for the Netherlands below, because of similar legislation in 1920.

Bulgaria: Mitchell (1998b). The 1890 figure is for state schools only.

Denmark: Mitchell (1998b). Before 1905, only lycees were classed as secondary schools and all others were classed as primary schools. The entry for 1890 is from 1893. The entry for 1900 is from 1902. (Public, or public plus private?) The 1882 figure is based on Banks' (1971) rate of primary students per capita.

(continued)

(*cont.*) *Notes to Appendix Table* A1:

Finland: Flora et al. (1983, 573) and Mitchell (1998b). Figures prior to and including 1890 include night schools. The nonpublic enrollments for 1910–1930 include postprimary schools. The 1919 constitutional law made all primary (but not secondary) schools free, whether or not they were in the public school system. Accordingly, I have counted all officially reported enrollments for 1920 and 1930 as public in the tax-effort sense. Enrollments in the so-labeled public schools in 1920 and 1930 are 259,058 and 371,086, respectively.

France: Flora et al. (1983, 578). The actual years are 1830, 1843, 1850, 1863, 1872, 1881, 1891, 1901, 1911, 1920, and 1930. Alsace and Lorraine are excluded, 1871–1918. The public-school enrollment (public enr.) category consists of *ecoles laiques*. Some of these were private, yet many other private schools received government money. To derive a public-subsidy-equivalent (pub. sibsid.), I multiplied total enrollments in all primary schools by a public-money share of all expenditures on education, from Carry (1999). The figures for 1921 and 1930 from Flora et al. (1983) include the *ecoles primaires supérieures publiques*. They do not explain their high 1910 figure.

Germany: Mitchell (1998b). Only public primary schools are included. In 1910 there were 26,000 pupils in private primary schools, and in 1921 there were 36,000 pupils in private primary schools. The entry for 1920 is from 1921. The figures for **Prussia** are based on Lundgreen and Thirlwall (1976), and refer to 1828, 1837, 1846, 1864, 1873, 1882, 1891, 1901, and 1911. In Prussia the public-school share of these public plus private enrollments remained above 97 percent. The middle-school enrollments were split between primary (girls) and secondary (boys).

Greece: Mitchell (1992). Hellenic schools were counted as primary until 1929 and subsequently divided between primary and secondary. The entry for 1900 is from 1901. The entry for 1920 is from 1926. Banks reports lower rates for 1910–1930. Mitchell does not say whether these rates include private-school students.

Hungary: Mitchell (1998b). Transleithania (excluding Croatia-Slavonia) to 1917, and subsequently the territory established by the Treaty of Trianon. After 1890, an element of double-counting was eliminated. Figures prior to 1903 are of all Volksschulen. Subsequently only elementary schools are covered. The entries for 1850 and 1860 include Croatia-Slavonia. The entry for 1850 is from 1854. The entry for 1860 is from 1859.

Italy: Flora et al. (1983, 599–600).

Netherlands: Flora et al. (1983, 604). For 1920 and 1930, I counted all officially reported students as public. The Elementary Education Act of 1920 made all public and private schools equally eligible for state aid. In response, many students shifted to private religious schools across the 1920s. But state funds dominated over fees, and children from poor families were schooled completely at taxpayer expense. The officially public school enrollments in 1920 and 1930 were only 501,000 and 474,000, respectively. See the Netherlands *Jaarcijfers* yearbook, and de Kwaasteniet (1990, 73–111).

New Zealand: Bloomfield (1984, 13).

Norway: Public-school series are from Norway, Statistisk Sentralbyrån (1978, 619–622). The 1830 entry refers to 1837. The source implies (p. 613) that the pre-1867 figures exclude the towns. The private enrollments are from Rust (1989, 135).

Portugal: Mitchell (1998b). State schools only until 1939. The entry for 1850 is from 1849. The entry for 1870 is from 1872. The entry for 1882 is from 1883. The entry for 1890 is from 1888. The entry for 1900 is from 1899. The entry for 1920 is from 1925.

Romania: Mitchell (1998b). State schools only. After 1920, including the newly acquired territories. The entry for 1882 is from 1880. A longer series of enrollment rates is reported by Banks (1971) from unknown sources.

Russia: Banks (1971) and the 1897 census of the Russian Empire.

Serbia: Mitchell (1998b). Mitchell does not say whether private schools are included.

Spain: The estimates in this case are from Banks (1971), since the Mitchell estimates have unexplained gaps and dips around the turn of the century.

Sweden: Instead of Flora et al. (1983, 614) or Mitchell, (1998b), I have relied on Sweden, Statistisk Tidskrift (1873, 1913, 1932). The source explicitly identifies the drop in enrollments across World War I as a drop in total schooling.

Switzerland: Mitchell (1992). State schools only, 1850 on. The 1830 figure is based on a Mulhall guess of unknown origin. The entry for 1882 is for 1881.

United Kingdom as a whole: The numbers and rates are those implied by the detail for the separate UK countries.

UK-England & Wales: The official-inspections estimates reported in Mitchell are known to involve serious underreporting of enrollments before 1891. The present estimates are a compromise between the scholars ages 5–15 (used for the 1851–1871 estimates) and the total enrollments for other dates implied by David Mitch's dissertation, summarized in Mitch (1992). See Appendix B.

UK-Scotland: Here again, as with England and Wales, the inspections data used by Mitchell yield serious underestimates in the nineteenth century. Instead we have used census counts of the numbers of scholars in 1851, 1871–1891, and have accepted the Mitchell series from 1910 (1911) on. The 1860–1861 and 1900–1901 figures are interpolations based on the rate per child 5–14. As for the public component of schooling, Scotland's school returns of 1888 and 1897 show that public school-board and state-aided schools accounted for 96.5% of attendance in 1888 and 98.5% in 1897. Using the 96.5% figure for the nineteenth-century benchmarks, and interpolating to 100% public-aided schools in 1920 yields the public-only estimates. For 1890 and 1900, what Mitchell calls the state school enrollments would appear to be total enrollments.

UK-Ireland: For public plus private, Mitchell (1988). For public alone, Flora et al. (1983, 594). The figures represent attendance, since the only enrollments data are the highly inflated numbers of children on the rolls. The figures for 1920 refer to Southern Ireland, the same area as the Republic in the 1930 figures.

Canada: Mitchell (1998c). Canada, Dominion Bureau of Statistics (1921) breaks public enrollments into elementary and secondary for 1901, 1910, and 1919. Using the 1901 and 1919 ratios of (public elementary/public elementary plus secondary) for other dates yields the full time series on elementary vs. secondary.

USA: For 1871 on, U.S. Census Bureau, *Historical Statistics of the United States* (1976), as repeated in the Millennial Edition of *Historical Statistics* (forthcoming) and in Mitchell (1998c). The figures from 1890 on are adjusted to exclude kindergarten. The figures for 1830 and 1850 are early guesses repeated in many sources.

Mexico: Mitchell (1998c). All schools, both primary and secondary, are included through 1895. The entry for 1890 is from 1895. The entry for 1910 is from 1907. The entry for 1920 is from 1927. The U.S. Commissioner of Education's *Report* for 1900–1901 (p. 2481) gives 684,563 students enrolled and 474,622 attending for 1899.

Australia: Mitchell (1998a). An alternative, but similar, series is given in Banks (1971). All Mitchell entries include both primary and secondary school. To estimate the share for primary school alone, I drew first on the 86.8% share reported in U.S. Commissioner of Education's *Report* for 1903. To estimate the share for primary school alone, I used a sliding scale for the elementary share, from 100% for 1861 down to 96.5% for 1931, guided by numbers in Browne (1927) and Barcan (1980), and the descriptive history in Austin (1976).

(continued)

(*cont.*) *Notes to Appendix Table* A1:

New Zealand: Bloomfield (1984, 113).

Argentina: Mitchell (1998c). The entries for 1880 and 1890 refer to 1882 and 1892, respectively.

Brazil: Mitchell (1998). The entry for 1870 is from 1871. The entry for 1890 is from 1889. The entry for 1910 is from 1906.

Chile: Mitchell (1998c).

Colombia: Mitchell (1998c). State schools only for 1897. The entry for 1882 is from 1887. The entry for 1890 is from 1889. The entry for 1900 is from 1897. The entry for 1930 is from 1928.

Costa Rica: Mitchell (1998c). All schools, primary and secondary, through 1890. State schools only to 1954. The entry for 1882 is from 1885.

Cuba: Mitchell (1998c). State schools only from 1902 to 1922. The 1920 entry is from 1922.

Ecuador: Mitchell (1998c). The entry for 1890 is from 1891. The entry for 1900 is from 1904. The entry for 1910 is from 1909.

Guatemala: Mitchell (1998c). Mitchell conjectures that the unexplained drop in 1899 is a switch from enrollments to attendance, and the unexplained rise in 1921 is a switch back to enrollments.

Honduras: Mitchell (1998c). Including preprimary schools until 1950. Statistics from 1918 to 1929 are of attendance rather than enrollment. The entry for 1930 is from 1929.

Jamaica: Mitchell (1998c). The years are years ending in 1, from 1861 through 1931. Exceptions: The enrollments for 1901 and 1911 are actually from 1899 and 1915, respectively.

Nicaragua: Mitchell (1998c). The entry for 1890 is from 1887. The entry for 1910 is from 1913. The entry for 1920 is from 1922.

Paraguay: Mitchell (1998c). The entry for 1890 is from 1891. The entry for 1900 is from 1902.

Peru: Mitchell (1998c). The entry for 1890 is from 1889. The entry for 1900 is from 1902.

Trinidad and Tobago: Mitchell (1998c). The figures before 1900 refer to Trinidad alone. Each year is the census year ending in 1: 1861, …, 1931.

Uruguay: Mitchell (1998c). The entry for 1870 is from 1876. In 1904 the switch from the old series to the new is from 50,000 to 73,000.

Venezuela: Mitchell (1998c). The entry for 1920 is from 1926. The entry for 1930 is from 1931.

China: Banks (1971).

India: Mitchell (1998a). The statistics to 1871 cover all students in government and government-aided schools in Bengal, Bombay, and Madras to 1855 and in British India (excluding Burma) from 1856 on.

Iran: Banks (1971). All entries include both primary and secondary enrollment.

Japan: Mitchell (1995, p. 957) agrees with the enrollment figures of Bank of Japan (1966, 12, 368).

Sri Lanka: Mitchell (1998a). With the exception of 1850, the other population census years end in 1 (1861 through 1931). The 1830 figure is actually 1834.

Thailand: Banks (1971). All entries include both primary and secondary enrollment.

Turkey: Mitchell (1998a).

	1830	1840	1850	1860	1870	1880	1890	1900	1910	1920	1930
A. Total primary teachers (thousands)											
Austria, pub + priv		27.3	28.4	27.6	35.3	52.3	63.2	79.9	110.0	31.4	22.2
Austria, public only					32.7	48.4	58.2	75.7	104.3	29.8	21.0
Belgium, pub + priv			5.6	5.9	7.1	8.2	11.8	16.6	21.3	25.9	32.0
Belgium, pub only			3.6	4.2	5.8	8.2	8.6	10.2	12.1	25.9	32.0
Bulgaria							4.3	7.8	10.4	13.6	17.4
Denmark								10.9	11.5	15.3	16.3
Finland, pub + priv									5.2	7.7	12.2
Finland, public					0.5	0.8	1.5	3.1	5.1	7.7	12.2
France, pub + priv		76		109	110	125	147	159	158		
France, public only		59		62	63	78	99	109	157	119	133
Germany, public								147.0	187.0	196.0	190.0
Greece								4.1	4.6	13.9	14.6
Hungary			20.6	20.8	18.5	22.4	25.5	29.1	33.0	17.6	19.3
Italy				28.2	41.0	51.8	59.0	65.0	72.8	105.0	105.0
Netherlands, pub + priv			6.4	8.4	10.7	15.9	18.1	24.7	30.1	35.3	39.4
Netherlands, public only					6.9	10.2	11.6	15.9	19.3	35.3	39.4
Norway, public only	2.1	2.2	2.5	3.0	3.7	4.4	5.1	7.3	8.6	11.1	11.2
Portugal			1.2			3.6	4.1			8.5	9.3
Romania						3.0	4.4	5.9	7.9	13.6/25.8	37.8
Serbia					0.6	0.9	1.3	1.9	2.5		
Spain									37.0		49.2
Sweden					7.8	12.6	13.5	16.6	21.5	27.1	30.7
Switzerland, pub only						8.8	9.3	10.5	12.5	13.5	13.4

(continued)

APPENDIX TABLE A2 (*continued*)

	1830	1840	1850	1860	1870	1880	1890	1900	1910	1920	1930
United Kingdom				15.5	25.6	70.1	97.7	144.8	196.8	189.1	193.8
England-Wales			2.0	7.6	14.4	52.7	77.0	119.0	164.0	167.0	169.0
Scotland				1.9	2.4	6.9	9.6	13.9	20.0	17.9	19.5
Ireland, public			4.6	6.0	8.8	10.5	11.1	11.9	12.8	13.3	13.6
N. Ireland										4.2	5.3
Canada, public w/sec							21.0	28.0	38.0	56.0	70.0
Canada, public, elem only					12.3	13.6	20.8	27.7	36.7	53.6	67.6
USA, public elem					199.0	281.3	353.1	406.1	491.3	562.4	619.2
USA, total elem									533.1	608.7	687.1
USA, pub elem + sec					201.0	287.0	364.0	423.0	523.0	680.0	854.0
Mexico, prim + sec									40.0		
Argentina						3.3	8.0	11.0	20.0	36.0	57.0
Bolivia, w/sec							0.8	1.2	1.4	2.9	3.2
Brazil								16.0		47.0	53.0
Chile							2.0	2.7	4.8	8.6	9.6
Colombia										5.7	12.0
Costa Rica							0.5	0.9	1.0	1.3	1.9
Cuba, w/sec, pub only to '22								3.6	3.9	6.1/7.6	9.2
Ecuador										2.5	5.3
El Salvador										1.5	
Guatemala											4.1
Honduras										1.1	2.0
Nicaragua											0.1
Paraguay											2.5
Peru									2.8	5.1	6.5
Uruguay					0.3	0.5	0.8	1.1	2.3	3.2	4.8

B. Primary-school teachers per 1000 children 5–14

Austria, pub + priv		7.7	7.0	8.3	11.3	12.4	14.3	17.2	29.1	19.7
Austria, pub only				7.6	10.5	11.4	13.6	16.3	27.6	18.7
Belgium, pub + priv		6.3	6.5	7.2	7.0	8.3	12.4	14.1	20.4	26.8
Belgium, public only		4.0	4.6	5.8	7.0	6.1	7.6	8.0	20.4	26.8
Bulgaria						5.2	8.1	9.4	10.8	12.5
Denmark							20.8	19.5	22.7	24.6
Finland, pub + priv								7.8	11.4	16.7
Finland, public				1.3	1.9	2.8	5.3	7.6	11.4	16.7
France, pub + priv	12.2		16.7	17.2	19.1	22.0	24.6	23.9		
France, public only	9.5		9.5	9.9	11.9	14.8	16.9	23.7	18.6	22.6
Germany							12.0	13.1	16.7	17.5
Greece							6.9	7.3	11.3	11.7
Hungary				5.3	6.0	6.4	6.8	7.0	9.9	9.9
Italy			6.3	7.3	9.1	9.4	9.4	9.8	12.8	13.7
Netherlands, pub + priv		9.4	12.1	14.4	18.4	18.2	22.1	23.4	24.1	24.7
Netherlands, public				9.3	11.8	11.7	14.2	15.0	24.1	24.7
Norway, public only		7.8	9.5	9.5	10.5	11.4	14.5	15.6	19.9	19.8
Portugal						3.8			6.2	6.6
Romania							4.1	4.6		10.5
Serbia										
Spain								8.6		9.8
Sweden				8.0	13.9	13.4	15.4	19.0	23.3	28.7
Switzerland, pub only					15.3	15.7	16.1	16.3	17.9	19.9
United Kingdom			2.4	3.6	8.7	11.4	16.6	21.7	23.2	26.2
England-Wales		0.5	1.7	2.8	8.9	11.6	17.4	22.8	23.3	25.9
Scotland			2.8	3.1	8.1	10.3	14.5	19.9	18.5	22.1
Ireland, public			5.0	7.0	8.5	10.5	13.1	14.8	15.4	23.9

(continued)

APPENDIX TABLE A2 (*continued*)

	1830	1840	1850	1860	1870	1880	1890	1900	1910	1920	1930
N. Ireland										7.0	9.5
Canada, public w/sec							18.3	23.3	25.6	28.5	31.7
Canada, public, elem only					12.4	12.7	18.1	23.1	24.7	27.3	30.6
USA, public					20.7	23.1	24.2	24.0	26.5	25.8	25.4
USA, total									28.7	27.9	28.1
USA, elem + sec public					20.9	23.5	24.9	24.9	28.2	31.2	35.0
Mexico											
Argentina							9.3		11.8		24.2
Bolivia								4.5			
Brazil								3.4		5.5	5.5
Chile								4.2	6.5	9.1	9.6
Costa Rica							7.9				
Cuba, w/sec, pub only to '22							11.5	9.6	9.3	7.6	
Ecuador											
El Salvador										4.6	
Guatemala											7.2
Honduras											9.0
Uruguay								4.4	7.1		

Notes to Appendix Table A2:

Austria: Mitchell (1998b). Cisleithania (excluding the Italian provinces) to 1914, and the Republic of Austria subsequently. From 1879 to 1905 the number of private primary school teachers is not known, except in 1889 (5,000) and in 1879 and 1905. Public share = 92.7% in 1889/90. The entry from 1840 is from 1842. Flora (1983, 556) gives similar figures.

Belgium: Flora et al. (1983, 562). The benchmark-year substitutions are as follows: 1850 is really 1851, 1870 is really 1869, the 1882 figure is 1881, 1920 is 1919, and 1930 is 1929. As in the table on primary enrollments, I interpret Belgium's Primary Education Act of 1914 as making all schools, and all teachers, public in the tax-effort sense for the 1920 and 1930 benchmarks. The numbers of teachers in schools labeled public were 14,165 in 1919 and 17,404 in 1929.

Bulgaria: Mitchell (1998b).

Denmark: Mitchell (1998b). All entries are for teachers in all schools (primary and secondary). The entry for 1900 is from 1905.

Finland: Flora et al. (1983, 573) and Mitchell (1998b). Figures prior to and including 1890 include night schools. As in the primary-enrollments table, I note that the 1919 constitutional law made all primary (but not secondary) education free, whether or not they were in the public school system. Accordingly, I have counted all primary-school teachers in 1920 and 1930 as public in the tax-effort sense. Teachers in so-labeled public schools in 1920 and 1930 numbered 7,574 and 12,006, respectively.

France: Mitchell (1998b). Figures after 1850 have a more complete coverage of private schools. Auxilary teachers temporarily in charge of classes are included after 1889. The entry for 1850 is from 1852. Alsace-Lorraine is excluded from 1871 to 1922. From 1914 to 1920 the invaded departments are excluded.

Germany: Mitchell (1998b). Public primary schools only. In 1921 there were 1.8 thousand teachers in private primary schools. The entry from 1920 is from 1921.

Greece: Mitchell (1998b). Hellenic schools were counted as primary until 1929/1930, and subsequently divided into primary and secondary. The entry for 1900 is from 1901. The enry for 1920 is from 1926.

Hungary: Mitchell (1998b). Transleithania (excluding Croatia-Slavonia) 1917, and subsequently the territory established by the Treaty of Trianon. The entries for 1850 and 1860 include Croatia-Slavonia. Before 1903, figures are of all Volksschulen. Subsequently only elementary schools are covered. The entry for 1850 is from 1854. The entry for 1860 is from 1859. The entry from 1890 is from 1891.

Italy: Mitchell (1998b). The source says that exact comparisons over time are impossible owing to the different meanings for the term elementary, but that this series is an attempt to provide as consistent a series as possible. A number of the figures are estimated–viz. 1864, 1868, 1876, 1880, 1896, 1901, 1902–1906, and 1908–1925. The entry for 1860 is from 1861. Mitchell does not say whether these include private-school teachers.

Netherlands: Flora et al. (1983, 604). For 1920 and 1930, I counted all teachers as public. Legislation in 1920 made all public and private schools equally eligible for state aid. Accordingly, many students shifted to private religious schools across the 1920s. But state funds dominated over fees, and children from poor families were schooled completely at taxpayer expense. Teachers in the officially public schools were approximately 22,700 in 1920 and 25,300 in 1930.

Norway: Public-school series are from Norway, Statistisk Sentralbyrån (1978, 619–622). The 1830 entry refers to 1837. The source implies (p. 613) that the pre-1867 figures exclude the towns.

Portugal: Mitchell (1998b). All entries after 1870 include only state schools. The entry for 1850 is from 1849. The entry for 1882 is from 1883. The entry for 1890 is from 1888. The entry for 1920 is from 1925.

Romania: Mitchell (1998b). All entries include only state schools. After 1920, the newly acquired territories are included. The entry for 1882 is from 1880.

Spain: Mitchell (1998b). The entry for 1910 is from 1914. The entry for 1930 is from 1932.

Sweden: Mitchell (1998b). The entry for 1882 is from 1886.

Switzerland: Mitchell (1998b). All entries include only state schools. The entry for 1882 is from 1884.

England–Wales: Mitchell (1998b). The entry for 1850 is from 1852.

Scotland: Mitchell (1998b). The entry for 1860 is from 1864.

(continued)

(*cont.*) *Notes to Appendix Table* A2:
<u>Ireland</u>: Mitchell (1988). The entry for 1850 is from 1851. The entry for 1920 is from 1919. The figures for 1920 refers to Southern Ireland, the same area as the Republic in the 1930 figures.
<u>N. Ireland</u>: Mitchell (1988). The entry for 1920 is from 1922.
<u>Canada</u>: Mitchell (1998c). For 1890–1930 the public-school ratios of students to teachers were assumed to be the same for elementary as for secondary schools. The 1882 figure is the total for Canada (then still excluding Saskatchewan and Alberta) from the U.S. Commissioner of Education *Report* for 1884–85. The 1870 figure is extrapolated from the 1882 figure assuming no change in the pupil/teacher ratio.
<u>USA</u>: Mitchell (1998c). The figures represent numbers employed rather than number of posts. Librarian, guidance, and some other nonsupervisory posts are included, but school principals are not. The elementary shares of public teachers are extrapolated back to 1870 by assuming that the shares of primary teachers in (primary + secondary) was 98% for 1870, 97% for 1880, and 96% for 1900.
<u>Mexico</u>: Mitchell (1998c). Entry is for primary and secondary schools together.
<u>Argentina</u>: Mitchell (1998c). The entry for 1890 is from 1894. The population totals are interpolated between the censuses of 1869, 1895, 1914, and 1930.
<u>Brazil</u>: Mitchell (1998c). The entry for 1900 is from 1906. The entry for 1920 is from 1928.
<u>Chile</u>: Mitchell (1998c). (See his comments 29 & 24). The entry for 1930 is from 1934.
<u>Colombia</u>: Mitchell (1998c). The entry for 1920 is from 1916. The entry for 1930 is from 1934.
<u>Costa Rica</u>: Mitchell (1998c). All entries are state schools only. The entry for 1890 is from 1892.
<u>Cuba</u>: Mitchell (1998c). Between 1902 and 1922, all entries include only state schools. All entries include preprimary schools and secondary schools as well as primary. The entry for 1920 is from 1922.
<u>Ecuador</u>: Mitchell (1998c). The entry for 1920 is from 1921. The entry for 1930 is from 1938.
<u>Honduras</u>: Mitchell (1998c). All entries include preprimary schools. The entry for 1920 is from 1922. The entry for 1930 is from 1929.
<u>Paraguay</u>: Mitchell (1998c).
<u>Peru</u>: Mitchell (1998c).
<u>Uruguay</u>: Mitchell (1998c). The entry for 1870 is from 1876. In 1904 the switch from the old series to the new is from 1.2 (thousand) to 2.0.

APPENDIX TABLE A3. *Student Enrollment Rates in Secondary Schools, Selected Countries, 1830–1930*

	1830	1840	1850	1860	1870	1880	1890	1900	1910	1920	1930
A. Total secondary school students enrolled (thousands)											
Austria, pub + priv		25	26	38	50	66	73	106	163	39	54
Austria, pub only					41	54	60	87	134	32	44
Belgium, pub + priv				19.8	22.6	29.1	34.4	37.2	41.6	56.7	64.5
Belgium, pub only				11.1	12.7	16.4	19.4	20.9	23.4	31.9	36.3
Bulgaria								34.0	71.0	122.0	168.0
Denmark						4.1	5.9	7.0	25.6	38.9	51.5
Finland, pub + priv						8.0	10.2	14.4	24.4	32.5	49.6
Finland, public						3.8	4.8	6.8	8.3	10.5	20.8
France, pub + priv										153.9	185.5
France, public only	42.2	41.9	47.9	55.9	74.4	77.6	74.5	68.7	90.4	105.7	111.8
Germany									1,016.0	1,081.0	1,016.0
Prussia, pub + priv	22.5	32.3	39.6	68.4	151.2	186.0	214.6	301.4	390.2		
Greece										66.0	68.7
Hungary		26.6	18.3	30.0	33.0	38.6	42.1	64.2	77.6	56.9	64.2
Italy, pub + priv						59	80	84	84	126	145
Italy, pub only				12	17	39	53	66	78	118	134
Netherlands, pub + priv		1.3	1.7	1.8	4.2	6.8	9.4	13.4	18.9	35.0	45.2
Netherlands, pub only					3.2	5.1	7.0	10.1	14.2	26.2	27.4
Norway, pub + priv					16.1	17.8	20.7	22.5	25.5	39.0	29.9
Portugal, pub only							3.5	5.2	10.6	11.7	18.5
Romania, pub only								17.8	17.2	27.4	
Serbia					1.8	4.1	6.8	4.5	7.1		
Spain			17.6	21.5	28.7				48.8	52.3	76.1

(continued)

	1830	1840	1850	1860	1870	1880	1890	1900	1910	1920	1930
Sweden							14.0	18.0	24.0	34.0	42.0
Switzerland, pub only							36.6	49.2	73.2	81.7	76.5
U.K., mostly public					16.9	23.3	28.9	71.1	212.8	387.1	464.1
England-Wales, state								36.0	171.3	336.8	411.3
Scotland, pub + priv							23.0	17.7	20.5	23.8	23.8
Scotland, public only						4.6	5.4	5.0	13.1	23.8	23.8
Ireland, pub + priv					16.9	18.7	23.5	30.2	28.3	26.4	29.0
N. Ireland										11.2	12.3
Canada, pub only					7.8	8.7	9.5	11.1	45.0	78.1	70.7
USA, pub only					80	110	203	519	915	2,200	4,399
USA, pub + priv						184	298	630	1,032	2,414	4,740
Mexico							2.8		5.8		17.0
Australia, pub only					3.0	8.9	11.4	17.4	22.3	27.4	32.3
New Zealand, priv + pub						1.6	2.3	3.8	9.1	15.4	31.0
New Zealand, pub						1.6	2.1	3.4	8.3	14.0	27.2
Argentina						2.3	3.2	5.8	13.9	28.0	45.0
Bolivia							2.1	2.5	1.6	4.1	4.2
Brazil									30.0	52.0	73.0
Chile						3.1	2.0	4.7	8.7	53.0	52.0
Colombia, pub only							5.1	6.0	26.0	33.0	31.0
Costa Rica									0.4	1.2	1.1
El Salvador							1.3			2.3	
Honduras								0.6	0.3	0.2	
Nicaragua										0.4	
Paraguay								0.4	0.7	0.7	1.3
Peru								2.2	3.8	6.9	12.0

Uruguay									1.9	6.0	9.7
Egypt										169	269
India (British)						239	532	622	879	1,264	2,286
Indonesia, pub + priv						0.5	0.5	1.1	3	5.8	17
Japan					1.8	19	23	121	786	1,386	2,383
Philippines, pub only									3	19	79
Thailand									7.8	12	19
Turkey										7	33
B. Secondary school students per 1,000 children ages 5–14											
Austria, pub + priv		7	7	10	12	14	14	19	25	37	48
Austria, pub only					10	12	12	16	21	30	39
Belgium, pub + priv				22	23	25	24	28	28	45	54
Belgium, public only				12	13	14	14	16	16	25	30
Bulgaria								35	64	97	121
Denmark					10	10	12	13	43	58	78
Finland, pub + priv						19	19	25	37	48	68
Finland, public						9	9	12	13	15	28
France, pub + priv										24	32
France, public only	7	7	7	9	12	12	11	11	14	16	19
Germany pub only									71	92	94
Prussia, pub + priv	8	11	11	16	28	31	32	40	44		
Greece										54	55
Hungary					10	10	11	15	17	32	33
Italy, pub + priv						10	13	12	11	15	19
Italy, pub only				3	3		8	10	11	14	17
Netherlands, pub + priv			3	3	6	8	9	12	15	24	28
Netherlands, pub only					4	6	7	9	11	18	17

(continued)

	1830	1840	1850	1860	1870	1880	1890	1900	1910	1920	1930
Norway, pub + priv					41	43	46	45	46	70	53
Portugal, pub only							3	4	8	9	13
Romania, pub only								12	10		
Spain				6	8				11	11	15
Sweden							14	17	21	29	39
Switzerland, pub only							62	76	95	108	114
U.K., mostly public					2	3	3	7	21	44	58
England-Wales state sec								5	24	47	63
Scotland, pub + priv							25	18	20	25	27
Scotland, public only							6	5	13	25	27
Ireland, pub + priv					13	15	22	33	33	31	51
N. Ireland (these seem low)										20	23
Canada, pub only					9	8	8	9	30	43	34
USA, pub only					8	9	14	31	48	100	179
USA, pub + priv						13	20	37	55	110	193
Mexico							1		2		5
Australia, pub only					7	16	16	20	25	24	26
New Zealand, pub + priv						13	14	22	46	61	118
New Zealand, pub						13	13	20	42	55	104
Argentina						3	4	5	8	14	19
Bolivia								10			
Brazil								0	5	6	8
Chile						5	3	7	12	56	52
Colombia, pub only										25	
Costa Rica, w/sec									5	11	9
El Salvador										7.0	

Honduras							
Nicaragua						23.2	
Egypt						53	77
India (British)		4	8	9	12	16	28
Japan	0.2	2	3	13	74	108	165
Thailand					4	6	7
Turkey							9

Notes to Appendix Tables A3 and A4 (see also notes to App. Table A1):

w/sec = primary plus secondary enrollments together.

pub only = just public (government-run) schools.

pub + priv = public plus private schools together.

(blank after country name) = secondary source does not state whether the estimates include private schools.

italics = Interpolations or extrapolations using population shares, age-groups shares, or public/private ratios.

Austria: Flora et al. (1983, 556–557). Cisleithania (excluding the Italian provinces) to 1914, and the Republic of Austria subsequently. The following years' enrollments data were used in place of their respective nearest benchmark years listed at the top of the table: 1841, 1851, . . . , 1911. The figure include the lower-secondary schools up through 1911. The share of public in total students was fixed at .823, its value in the 1928–1932 period.

Belgium: Flora et al. (1983, 563). In 1875, the share of higher-secondary school enrollments that was public was .563. This ratio was applied to both lower- and higher–secondary totals to derive estimates of public and total enrollments. This procedure was applied to the given series on total lower-secondary and on public higher-secondary enrollments.

Bulgaria: Mitchell, (1998b). The secondary enrollment rates seem too high. Was some type of primary school miscounted as secondary?

Denmark: Mitchell, (1998b). Before 1905, only lycees were classed as secondary schools and all others were classed as primary schools. The entry for 1890 is from 1893. The entry for 1900 is from 1902. The estimate for 1882 is an extrapolation based on Banks' (1971) estimate of total primary enrollments and the assumption that the 1882 ratio of secondary to primary students was only slightly below the 1893 ratio.

Finland: The public-plus-private totals are from Mitchell (1998b). Flora et al. (1983, 574) give similar totals, and seem to confirm that the Mitchell totals include both lower-secondary and higher-secondary schools. Flora et al. (1983) also give public-only enrollment totals for higher-secondary schools for 1900–1930. To estimate the public-school totals, I assumed the same share of public in total enrollments applied to both levels of secondary schooling and that the share for 1900 prevailed in 1880 and 1890 as well. I did not consider all secondary schools public in 1920 and 1930 because secondary schools, unlike primary, were fee-based.

(continued)

(cont.) Notes to Appendix Tables A3 and A4 (see also notes to App. Table A1):

<u>France</u>: Flora et al. (1983, 580–581) which details the types of schools covered. Alsace-Lorraine is excluded from 1871 to 1922.

<u>Germany</u>: Mitchell (1998b). Only public primary schools are included. In 1910 there were 26,000 pupils in private primary schools, and in 1921 there were 36,000 pupils in private primary schools. The entry for 1920 is from 1921. The figures for Prussia are based on Lundgreen and Thirwall (1976) and refer to 1828, 1837, 1846, 1864, 1873, 1882, 1891, 1901, and 1911. In Prussia the public-school share of these public plus private enrollments remained above 97%. The middle-school enrollments were split between primary and secondary.

<u>Greece</u>: Mitchell (1998b). Hellenic schools were counted as primary until 1929 and subsequently divided between primary and secondary. The entry for 1900 is from 1901. The entry for 1920 is from 1926. Banks reports lower rates for 1910–1930.

<u>Hungary</u>: Mitchell (1998b). Transleithania (excluding Croatia-Slavonia) to 1917, and subsequently the territory established by the Treaty of Trianon. After 1890, an element of double-counting was eliminated. Figures prior to 1903 are of all Volksschulen. Subsequently only elementary schools are covered. The entries for 1850 and 1860 include Croatia-Slavonia. The entry for 1850 is from 1854. The entry for 1860 is from 1859.

<u>Italy</u>: Flora et al. (1983, 599–600). The secondary schools include lower secondary schools (private and public *ginnasi*), general higher secondary schools, and (for 1930 only) *istituti commerciali*. The public share of enrollments in lower secondary schools was assumed to equal its (always high) share of general higher secondary school enrollments.

<u>Netherlands</u>: Flora et al. (1983, 605). For the years 1870–1920, I assumed that public enrollments were the same .749 share of total enrollments as they were in 1920.

<u>Norway</u>: Public-school series are from Norway, Statistisk Sentralbyrån (1978, 621–622). The 1870 figure refers to 1875/76. The totals include folk high schools *(folkehøgskoler)*, *realskoler*, county schools, and private continuation schools.

<u>Portugal</u>: Mitchell (1998b). State schools only until 1939. The entry for 1850 is from 1849. The entry for 1870 is from 1872. The entry for 1882 is from 1883. The entry for 1890 is from 1888. The entry for 1900 is from 1899. The entry for 1920 is from 1925.

<u>Romania</u>: Mitchell (1998b). State schools only. After 1920, including the newly acquired territories would give an enrollment of 173,000 for 1930. The entry for 1882 is from 1880.

<u>Spain</u>: Mitchell (1998b). The entry for 1850 is from 1855. The entry for 1882 is from 1880. The entry for 1910 is from 1908. The entry for 1920 is from 1926. The entry for 1930 is from 1932.

<u>Sweden</u>: Mitchell (1998b). The entry for 1860 is from 1865. The entry for 1882 is from 1886.

<u>Switzerland</u>: Mitchell (1998b). State schools only. The entry for 1882 is from 1881.

<u>United Kingdom</u> as a whole: The numbers and rates are those implied by the detail for the separate countries.

<u>UK-England & Wales</u>: Mitchell (1988). State-supported secondary education emerged only after 1895.

<u>UK-Scotland</u>: Here again, as with England and Wales, the inspections data used by Mitchell yield serious underestimates in the nineteenth century. Instead we have used census counts of the numbers of scholars in 1851, 1871–1891, and have accepted the Mitchell series from 1910 (1911) on. For 1890 and 1900,

142

what Mitchell calls the state school enrollments would appear to be total enrollments. Scotland's school surveys of 1888 and 1897 show that public secondary schools accounted for 23.7% and 28.2% of secondary-school enrollments, respectively. To construct the public-only series for secondary-school enrollments, these shares were interpolated up to 100% in 1918, when the Education (Scotland) Act of 1918 offered free secondary education to all Scottish schools.

UK-Ireland: Flora et al. (1983, 595). The figures for 1920 refers to Southern Ireland, the same area as the Republic in the 1930 figures.

Canada: Mitchell (1998c), as inferred from Table A1.

USA: For 1871 on, U.S. Census Bureau (1975), as repeated in the Millennial Edition of Historical Statistics (forthcoming).

Mexico: Mitchell (1998b). All schools, both primary and secondary, are included through 1895. The entry for 1890 is from 1895. The entry for 1910 is from 1907. The entry for 1920 is from 1927. The U.S. Commissioner of Education's Report for 1900–1901 (p. 2481) gives 684,563 students enrolled and 474,622 attending for 1899.

Australia: See notes to Appendix Table A1.

New Zealand: Bloomfield (1984, 113).

Argentina: Mitchell (1998c). The entry for 1890 is from 1892, and the entry for 1930 refers to 1929. The figures for 1900, 1910, and 1920 were interpolated by assuming that the ratio of secondary to primary pupils advanced from 0.015 in 1900, .020 in 1910, and .025 in 1920.

Brazil: Mitchell (1998c). The entry for 1870 is from 1871. The entry for 1890 is from 1889. The entry for 1910 is from 1906.

Chile: Mitchell (1998c).

Colombia: Mitchell (1998c). State schools only for 1897. The entry for 1882 is from 1887. The entry for 1890 is from 1889. The entry for 1900 is from 1897. The entry for 1930 is from 1928.

Costa Rica: Mitchell (1998c). All schools, primary and secondary, through 1890. State schools only to 1954. The entry for 1882 is from 1885.

Cuba: Mitchell (1998c). State schools only from 1902 to 1922. The entry for 1920 is from 1922.

Guatemala: Mitchell (1998c). No break is indicated by Mitchell's source at 1899, but it is likely there is one, and the probable cause is a change from enrollment to attendance. The entry for 1890 is from 1891. The entry for 1900 is from 1899. The entry for 1930 is from 1932.

Honduras: Mitchell (1998c). Including preprimary schools until 1950. Statistics from 1918 to 1929 are of attendance rather than enrollment. The entry for 1930 is from 1929.

Nicaragua: Mitchell (1998c). The entry for 1890 is from 1887. The entry for 1910 is from 1913. The entry for 1920 is from 1922.

Paraguay: Mitchell (1998c). The entry for 1890 is from 1891. The entry for 1900 is from 1902.

Peru: Mitchell (1998c). The entry for 1890 is from 1889. The entry for 1900 is from 1902.

Uruguay: Mitchell (1998c). The entry for 1870 is from 1876.

Venezuela: Mitchell (1998c). The entry for 1920 is from 1926. The entry for 1930 is from 1931.

Japan: Mitchell (1995, p. 957) agrees with the enrollment figures of Bank of Japan (Tokyo, 1966, pp. 12, 368).

Thailand: Banks (1971). All entries include both primary and secondary enrollment.

Turkey: Mitchell (1998a).

APPENDIX TABLE A4. *Secondary Teachers in Selected Countries, 1830–1930*

	1830	1840	1850	1860	1870	1880	1890	1900	1910	1920	1930
A. Total secondary teachers in 1,000's											
Austria		0.6	1.3	1.8	2.9	4.7	4.9	6.4	11.7	3.0	4.6
Belgium					1.2 (later years not available)						
Bulgaria								1.5	2.9	5.1	7.7
Denmark	(Included with primary teachers.)										
Finland						0.9	1.2	1.5	1.9	2.4	3.2
France	(n.a.)										
Germany									47.4	49.9	56.4
Greece										2.3	3.4
Hungary		0.8	1.2	1.8	2.0	2.4	2.9	4.2	5.2	3.0	3.0
Italy, pub + priv									20.3	26.0	28.0
Netherlands			0.3	0.3	0.7	1.3	1.3	1.5	2.0	3.8	4.7
Norway, pub + priv					1.2	1.4	1.7	1.7	1.7	2.5	2.0
Portugal, pub only							0.2	0.3	0.5	0.7	0.9
Romania, new territory, pub only											13.9
Serbia					0.1	0.2	0.4	0.3	0.4		
Sweden									1.7	2.2	3.0
Switzerland							2.1	2.4	3.2	4.5	5.1
United Kingdom										26.0	29.0
Eng.-Wales, pub only									9.8	17.7	21.7
Scotland, pub only								0.9	1.1	5.7	6.6
Ireland, pub. Only										2.6	2.6
N. Ireland											0.7
Canada, pub only							0.2	0.3	1.3	2.4	2.4
USA, public									32.9	101.9	213.5
USA, total							7.2	10.2	44.1	119.3	237.9

USA, prim+sec, public			201.0	287.0	364.0	423.0	523.0	680.0	854.0
Brazil						2.3			7.4
Chile							1.1	3.0	2.4
Colombia									2.9
Costa Rica									0.1
Ecuador									0.4
Guatemala									1.1
Peru						0.4	0.3	0.4	0.6
B. Secondary–school teachers per 1,000 children of ages 5–14:									
Austria	0.35	0.46	0.68	1.02	0.96	1.15	1.83	2.78	4.09
Belgium			1.23						
Bulgaria									
Denmark						1.57	2.65	4.05	5.54
Finland				2.02	2.32	2.60	2.88	3.53	4.38
France									
Germany									
Greece									
Hungary			0.58	0.65	0.73	0.98	1.11	1.69	1.53
Italy, pub + priv									
Netherlands	0.37	0.36	1.01	1.45	1.35	1.33	1.58	2.60	2.95
Norway, pub + priv			3.09	3.36	3.80	3.32	3.16	4.52	3.60
Portugal, pub only						0.26	0.38	0.52	0.62
Romania, pub only									
Serbia									
Sweden							1.48	1.89	2.80
Switzerland					3.47	3.76	4.22	5.99	7.52

(continued)

	1830	1840	1850	1860	1870	1880	1890	1900	1910	1920	1930
United Kingdom											
Eng.-Wales, pub only									1.37	2.46	3.32
Scotland, pub only								0.94	1.10	5.89	7.49
Ireland, pub. Only											
N. Ireland											
Canada, pub only							0.19	0.24	0.85	1.22	1.08
USA, public									1.77	4.67	8.75
USA, total							0.49	0.60	2.37	5.47	9.75
USA, prim+sec, public					20.94	23.53	24.92	24.95	28.17	31.21	34.99
Brazil									0.18	0.35	0.25
Chile									1.49	3.16	2.39
Colombia											
Costa Rica											0.67
Ecuador											
Guatemala											
Peru											

Appendix B

Conflicting Data on Elementary School Enrollments within the United Kingdom, 1851–1931[1]

The data on primary-school enrollments before 1914 are as complicated and treacherous for the United Kingdom as for any major country. The government was slow to set up a consistent statistical coverage. There were census questions on children as scholars in the occupational part of the censuses of England and Wales in 1851 and 1871 and similar data for Scotland in 1851, 1871, and 1891. These probably gave household heads an opportunity to take a generous definition of enrollment in school and for this reason might give somewhat higher figures than would other countries' enrollment counts supplied by institutions. On the side of underestimation, what became the eventual reporting series on pupils in inspected schools started out far too modestly in the middle of the nineteenth century. Only by 1891 at the earliest could the coverage of public and private schools have been nearly complete.

We are warned about this by Brian Mitchell:[2]

[The statistics of education are] selected from the much greater amount of badly organised material which is available in the sources, beginning in the middle of the nineteenth century. . . . The nature of what is available may be judged from Sanderson's survey, which concludes that it is not yet possible to draw up a national balance sheet even as to literacy.

It was with some hesitation that even the school statistics for the nineteenth century were included here, because the material is far from easily tractable. The authorities changed the coverage of what they collected, and their methods of collection as well, on numerous occasions, often with little to indicate to the user what changes had taken place. These applied equally to the Irish statistics. . . . Moreover, the figures [on inspected schools in the nineteenth century] do not include privately financed schools. . . . The statistics up to 1900, therefore, must be taken only as rough indicators of the growth of public education. Coverage after 1900 was greatly improved, and changes have been more clearly indicated, even though [some? just the uninspected?] private schools continued to be excluded from the statistics until after the Second World War.

He proceeds to display only data on officially inspected schools, omitting any census data on the number of scholars.

Faced with this warning, I have taken four approaches to minimizing the deception about trends and international differences in primary schooling:

(a) In order to bias against the conclusion about Britain's lagging behind other countries in the nineteenth century, I accept the higher censuses' estimates of primary school participation for 1851–1871. These may be too high.
(b) For the twentieth century I have used the enrollments in inspected schools.
(c) For Ireland, I have used the data on attendance, since the numbers of students listed as on the books are too high to represent true participation.
(d) Chapter 5's expenditure data and its support ratios avoid using enrollments data altogether, using the whole child-age population rather than enrollments in the denominator when calculating support ratios.

PRIMARY-SCHOOL ENROLLMENTS IN ENGLAND AND WALES

We begin with the official returns from inspected schools, as reported by Brian Mitchell in his *British Historical Statistics*.[3] Contrary to the impression one might get from the passage quoted above, private schools were not generally omitted. His inspected school series adds enrollments in four kinds of voluntary schools (Anglican, Roman Catholic, Wesleyan, and British and non-denominational) to the enrollments of public Board schools (compare his totals to the separate subtotals in Sutherland and in the U.S. Commissioner of Education *Reports*. While other kinds of private schools are still omitted, some are included.[4]

Many have pointed out that this official series underestimates enrollments increasingly the further one moves back in time from 1890. So let us turn to alternative sources. For 1851–1871 the census generated schooling participation rates as by-products of a larger census of occupations. A child attending school was anybody returned as a scholar who was under the age of twenty. The census allows us to break the under-twenty population down further into five-year age ranges, so that we can take the five to fourteen age group as a fair approximation of the elementary-school population that other countries were recording. This inference seems plausible for England and Wales in the nineteenth century, since other data show that the scholar shares jump at the fifth and sixth birthdays and start dropping off at the thirteenth, and especially at the fourteenth, birthday.

The enrollment rates from the 1851–1871 censuses are far above the rates for inspected schools alone. The truth for 1851–1871 probably lies closer to the census values than to the lower numbers returned from inspected schools. It seems clear from the time-path of the Board inspections that they were still missing a large share of schools in 1871. As noted at the start of this appendix, the census questions seemed to allow the recording of children as scholars who were not necessarily enrolled. But the prima facie case against the census returns is weaker than the case against the totals from the Board inspections before 1891.

Switching from the high-ish estimates of the 1851–1871 censuses to the Board inspection returns for 1881 would create an implausible drop in the enrollment rate from 609 in 1871 to 543 in 1881. A plausible way to estimate the amount of understatement in the inspection returns for 1881 is to follow the number of schools or departments being inspected and their average size. There is no clear trend in average size, and the number inspected seems to reach a stable level by either the 1891 benchmark or the 1901 benchmark. This tendency suggests three possible interpolations for 1881, each assuming that the true enrollment rate progressed from the high census return of 1871 to a fairly full reporting by the inspections system in either 1891 or 1901 in steps that were proportional to the progress of the number of inspected schools:

(a) First guess at adjusting for the underestimation in 1881 (academic year 1880–1881) = (pupils in 1881 × schools 1891/schools 1881) = 3,206,798 elementary-school pupils in England and Wales in 1881. This yields an enrollment rate of 1393 per 10,000 of total population, or 608 per 1,000 children ages five to fourteen.

(b) Alternatively, assume that the change in inspected schools all the way to 1901 was due only to more complete coverage, not to a true rise in the number of schools. The formula (pupils in 1881 × schools 1901/schools 1881) yields 3,397,362 pupils, which is 1476 per 10,000 of total population or 645 per 1,000 children ages five to fourteen.

(c) Taking the median of these two guesstimated adjustments yields 3,302,080 pupils, or 1,435 per 10,000 of total population or 626 per 1,000 children ages five to fourteen.

My reading of Sutherland in particular suggests that the Fees Act of 1891 should have caused a considerable acceleration of true school enrollment after some inaction in the 1880s. That seemed to happen, and the sudden renewed rise in subsidies would lead one to expect an acceleration after 1891. So I prefer the first set of estimates for 1881, the rates in (a) above, based on assuming that inspection coverage had peaked by 1891.

PRIMARY-SCHOOL ENROLLMENTS IN SCOTLAND

For Scotland we have the same split between early census returns and an initially deficient, but eventually satisfactory, series on enrollments in inspected schools. For Scotland I accept the census figures for 1891, making the switch from the census to the inspections data come two decades later than for England and Wales. While a further interpolation could be made for 1901, the inspections-based enrollment data for 1901 are accepted here.

ELEMENTARY-SCHOOL ENROLLMENTS IN IRELAND

Flora et al.[5] and Mitchell appear to use the same series on Irish students attending public school (before 1900 in the Flora version) and the numbers of students on the rolls (after 1900 in the Flora version). Flora adds the 1871, 1881, and 1891 benchmark estimates of Irish pupils attending private schools. Flora also gives totals of public plus private attendance for 1871, 1881, and 1891. He then reverts to numbers on the public-school rolls thereafter, since the private-school numbers stop.

For Ireland, the choice between enrollments data and attendance data must differ from the choice for other countries. For other countries, one chooses enrollments data because they are available for more countries. Yet in Ireland the enrollment figure is a particularly inflated figure for all students on the rolls. Typically actual attendance was only half this number, a lower attendance rate than the rate for pupils enrolled in other countries. The analysis in this study will make use only of the numbers attending.

ELEMENTARY-SCHOOL ENROLLMENTS FOR THE UNITED KINGDOM, 1851–1931

Aggregating the figures just presented, and following the change in Irish geography, yields the overall United Kingdom estimates shown in Tables B1 and B2. The former shows the results for inspected schools, while the latter reflects the preferred estimates for all schools, as best one can capture private schools in any of the available data. These estimates were used for the United Kingdom in Table 5.1, Appendix Table A1, and Appendix Table A2.

REVISED PRIMARY PLUS SECONDARY ENROLLMENTS FOR THE UNITED KINGDOM, 1881–1931

For the purposes of the statistical regressions on the pooled international sample for 1880–1930, the revisions just suggested for elementary education need to be carried through to the estimates of primary (elementary) plus secondary education. The database for the primary-plus-secondary education regressions in Appendix D and the database used in the working paper version of my "Rise of Social Spending" (1994) article are therefore revised to use the enrollment rates derived in Table B2.

APPENDIX TABLE B1. *An Alternative Set of Estimates for Elementary Enrollments in the United Kingdom, 1851–1931*

School Year Ending in	Elementary Pupils (1,000s)	Census-Year Total Pop. (1,000s)	Pupils Per 10,000 Pop.	Share (%) 5–14s in Total Pop.	1,000s of Persons Ages 5–14	Pupils Per 1,000 5–14s
1851	2,763	27,369	1,009	22.03	6,029	458
1861		28,927		21.93	6,345	
1871	4,150	31,484	1,318	22.77	7,170	579
1881	4,415	34,885	1,266	23.05	8,041	549
1891	5,034	37,734	1,334	22.81	8,607	585
1901	5,865	41,459	1,415	20.98	8,700	738
1911	6,610	45,221	1,462	20.05	9,065	790
1921	6,091	44,026	1,384	19.04	8,383	757
1931	5,797	46,062	1,259	16.60	7,647	789

Notes to Table B1:

These estimates are based on the educational censuses for England and Wales, 1851–1871; the Scotland educational censuses for 1851 and 1871–1891; the inspections data for Great Britain at later dates; Irish attendance rates in private and public schools to 1891; and Irish public-school attendance from 1901 on.

APPENDIX TABLE B2. *Revising the Estimates for Primary Plus Secondary Enrollments in the United Kingdom, 1881–1931 (For the Purpose of Revising the 1880–1930 Regression Data Base)*

Academic Year Ending in	Elementary Primary Pupils (from Table B1)	Secondary Pupils on 31 January (in 1,000s, from Mitchell (1988) and Flora et al. (1983))			Known Secondary Pupils in U.K. (1,000s)	Primary Plus Secondary (k)	1,000s of Persons Ages 5–14	Primary Plus Secondary Pupils Per 1,000 5–14s
		Eng-Wales	Scotland	Ireland/N.Ire.				
1881	4,415				0	4,415	7,292	605
1891	5,034			19	19	5,052	7,931	637
1901	5,865	36	18	23	77	5,942	7,948	748
1911	6,610	171	21	30	222	6,832	8,372	816
1921	6,091	337	154	9	500	6,591	8,050	819
1931	5,797	411	154	12	578	6,375	7,343	868

Notes to Table B2:
Eng-Wales secondary, 1901 = the 1905 number of pupils for general secondary education (94,698) plus pupils in postprimary schools (9,371), this sum multiplied by the ratio of 1901 to 1905 pupils in post-primary schools (3.240/9.371).
Northern Ireland secondary, 1921 = number in 1925.

Appendix C

Public and Total Educational Expenditures as Percentages of National Product, since 1850

APPENDIX TABLE C1. *Public Primary School Expenditures Only, 1850–1910 (Percentages of GDP in Current Prices)*

	1850	1860	1870	1880	1890	1900	1910	Notes and Sources (See Notes to Table C5)
United States	0.32	0.46	0.70	0.68	1.00			Exp. based on f to 1870 (see notes), then s; GNP = b, g
				0.75	0.97			Expenditures = u; GNP = b, g
United Kingdom	0.03	0.10	0.10	0.21	0.27	0.49		h
England-Wales				0.50		0.50	1.15	
France	0.18	0.19	0.23	0.50	0.65	0.60	0.65	ac
Germany		0.48	0.60	0.92	0.89	1.11	1.46	Exp. = i, NNP = a. See endnotes.
Belgium	0.25		0.45	0.69			0.88	Exp. = m; on NNP series, see endnotes.
Denmark					0.66			Exp. for 1892 = ag, GNP = ai
Italy				0.49				Exp. = z, GNP = d. Includes some normal-school exp.
Netherlands		0.28	0.39	0.66	0.81	1.05	1.39	Exp. = n, GNP = o
Norway				0.44	0.47	0.65	0.66	Exp. = q, GNP = d
Spain					0.32			Exp = lv, GDP = ah, both for 1886/7
Sweden			0.39	0.71	0.90	1.03	1.26	Exp. = ad, GNP = ab, 1870 is 1868
Switzerland			0.37	0.63	0.80			Exp. = ag, NNP: notes below. Years 1871, 1881, 1887
Finland (Russia)				0.01		0.05	0.03	Exp = z, ae, GNP = af, 1900 is 1896
Japan				0.07	0.58			Exp= z, national income = r, 1880 is 1883

APPENDIX TABLE C2. *Public Primary Plus Secondary School Expenditures Only, 1850–1910*
(Percentages of GDP in Current Prices)

	1850	1860	1870	1880	1890	1900	1910	Notes and Sources (See Notes to Table C5)
Canada			1.31	1.80	1.68	1.54	1.72	aj
United States	0.32	0.46	0.71	0.71	1.05	1.16	1.36	Exp = s; GNP = b, g. See endnotes below
				0.77	1.01			Exp. = u; GNP = b, g
United Kingdom							0.63	h
France	0.26	0.26	0.30	0.63	0.81	0.75	0.80	ac
Germany		0.56	0.67	1.03	1.01	1.26	1.64	Exp. = i, NNP = a. See endnotes
Belgium	0.33		0.59	1.07	0.85	0.98	1.06	Exp. = m; on NNP series, see endnotes
Netherlands		0.39	0.50	0.77	0.92	1.26	1.63	Exp. = n; GNP = o; see endnotes
				0.89				Exp. = z; GNP = o
Norway				0.50	0.53	0.70	0.71	Exp. = q, GNP = d
Japan				0.10	0.61			Exp= z, national income = r, 1880 is 1883

APPENDIX TABLE C3. *Public Expenditures, All Levels of Education, 1850–1910 (Percentages of GDP in Current Prices)*

	1850	1860	1870	1880	1890	1900	1910	Notes and Sources (See Notes to Table C5)
United States	0.33	0.48	0.73	0.74	1.10	1.24	1.42	Expenditures = f to 1870, then s; GNP = b, g
				0.80	1.05			Expenditures = u; GNP = b, g
United Kingdom	0.07	0.18	0.17	0.29	0.37	0.59	0.74	Expenditures = c, GNP = d
							0.75	h
England-Wales				0.28	0.38	0.66	1.50	Expenditures = c, GNP = d, e (1861, 1891, 1901)
			0.23	0.28	0.37	0.61	1.45	Expenditures = p, GNP = d, e (1861 ... 1911)
France	0.33	0.33	0.37	0.77	0.98	0.92	0.99	ac
Germany		0.82	0.96	1.47	1.42	1.80	2.27	Exp. = i, NNP = d. See endnotes
			0.78	1.16	1.16	1.42	1.81	Exp. = i, NNP = d. See endnotes
Belgium	0.38		0.62	1.10				Exp. = m; on NNP series, see endnotes
Italy		0.17	0.15	0.26	0.37	0.36	0.52	Exp. = p; GNP = d; 1860 is 1862
		0.16	0.17	0.26				z and d; actual years are 1861, 1871, 1880
			0.41	0.50	0.69			Exp. = j, GNP = d
Netherlands				1.12		1.37	1.77	1880 = 1881, z and o; 1900 and 1910 = n and o
	0.29	0.41	0.69	1.14	1.30	1.64	2.13	Exp. = w, GNP = o
Norway				0.56	0.58	0.77	0.79	Exp. = q, GNP = d
Japan				0.22	0.69			Exp= z, national income = r, 1880 is 1883
Australia						1.09	0.95	ak
New Zealand					1.42	1.77		ak

APPENDIX TABLE C4. *Public Plus Private Expenditures, All Levels of Education, 1850–1910*
(Percentages of GDP in Current Prices)

	1850	1860	1870	1880	1890	1900	1910	Notes and Sources (See Endnotes to Table C5)
United States	0.70	0.83	1.13	0.96	1.39	1.56	1.82	Exp. = f thru 1900, t for 1900 and 1910; GNP = b, g
				1.19	1.66			Expenditures = u; GNP = b, g
United Kingdom				0.90		1.30		f
France	0.42	0.43	0.48	0.87	1.03	0.97	1.02	ac
Germany		1.00		1.60		1.90		f
		1.03	1.11	1.66	1.59	1.98	2.49	i, and the endnote on Germany below
			0.93	1.35	1.33	1.60	2.04	i, and the endnote on Germany below
Italy				0.98	1.11	1.39		k, and z plus d for 1889
Japan					0.72			Exp= z, national income = r

APPENDIX TABLE C5. *Implied Private Expenditures, All Levels of Education, 1850–1910*
(Percentages of GDP in Current Prices)

	1850	1860	1870	1880	1890	1900	1910	Notes and Sources (See Below)
United States	0.37	0.35	0.40	0.23	0.30	0.32	0.40	
United Kingdom				0.61		0.71		
France	0.09	0.10	0.12	0.10	0.05	0.05	0.03	
Germany		0.21	0.15	0.19	0.17	0.18	0.23	Private tuitions in public institutions only
Italy				0.72	0.74	1.03		

Sources and endnotes to Appendix Tables C1–C5.

a. Mitchell (1990).

b. Balke and Gordon (1989, Table 10).

c. Mitchell (1988).

d. Mitchell (1975, 1992).

e. Using 1867 ratios of income per capita, England-Wales vs. U.K., from Baxter (1868).

f. Fishlow (1966b).

g. Gallman (1966, p. 26).

h. Schremmer (1989).

i. Lundgreen and Thirwall (1976). The higher estimates use Hoffman expenditure totals. I have subtracted Lundgreen's data on private tuitions from his and Hoffman's total expenditures. The lower estimates use only those higher-education expenditures that are separately identified for Prussia on Lundgreen's p. 38, magnified to Germany.

j. Italy, *Annuario Statistico*, various years.

k. West (1975).

m. Pirard (1985) and Belgium, *Annuaire Statistique*.

n. Netherlands: *Jaarcijfers*, various years.

o. Smits, Horlings, and van Zanden (1997), production-side estimates.

p. Flora et al. (1983).

q. Norway Central Bureau of Statistics (1978).

(cont.) Sources and endnotes to Appendix Tables C1–C5

   r. Yamada's national income series, in Bank of Japan (1966, p. 30).

   s. U.S. Census Bureau (1976).

   t. Schultz (1960). (The Schultz and Fishlow figures in Panel C match for 1900.)

   u. Solmon (1975). Here we use only Solmon's direct costs, omitting his opportunity costs of earnings foregone by students.

   v. Mitchell (1995).

   w. Van der Voort (1994, pp. 243–245).

   z. Report to the U.S. Commissioner of Education, various issues, especially 1899–1902; converted from dollars at exchange rates.

aa. Norway: *Statistik Aarborg*, various issues.

ab. Krantz and Nilsson (1975).

ac. Carry (1999) for expenditures and Toutain (1987) for GNP.

ad. Sweden, *Statistik Tidskrift*, 1913 and earlier years.

ae. 1910 expenditures from Finland (1912).

af. Hjerppe (1989).

ag. Levasseur (1897).

ah. Prados de Escosura (1995, Appendix Table D1).

ai. Svend Aage Hansen (1977, Table 3).

aj. Urquhart (1993, Tables 1.3, 1.6).

ak. Browne (1927, 426) for expenditures and Mitchell, *Africa, Asia, and Oceania* (1998) for GNP.

Each panel's share for a given country and year can be used as a low estimate on the broader measures in later panels.

USA: U.S. primary-education expenditures were .97 of primary and secondary (public) expenditures in 1880 and .957 of the corresponding total in 1890, according to Solmon (1975, p. 49). Extrapolating from this, Panel A assumes that public primary expenditures were .98 of the Panel B figure in 1870, and .99 for earlier dates.

The ratio of (public primary + secondary) to all public expenditures was .957 for 1880, according to Solmon (1975, p. 49). That is, higher public education (normal schools) was .043 of the total public budget. Extrapolating to earlier dates, the former ratio was assumed to be .97 for 1870, .98 for 1860, and .99 for earlier dates. The extrapolations imply that these shares of national product were spent on education in earlier 1840 (using Fishlow 1966a, 1966b): 0.23% of GNP in Panel A, 0.24% in Panels B and C, and 0.36% in Panel D.

France: Carry's (1999) series continue earlier, giving these percentage shares: Panel A = 0.02 for 1830 and 0.15 for 1840, Panel B = 0.07 and 0.20 for the same respective dates, Panel C = 0.12 and 0.28, and Panel D = 0.19 and 0.36.

(cont.) Sources and endnotes to Appendix Tables C1–C5:

Germany, public primary education: These expenditure figures are based on the all-level totals, assuming that the shares of primary and secondary in total spending were the same as for Prussia, which constituted 65–77 percent of all German expenditures. The years for the Prussian data used in this assumption are 1864, 1891, 1901, and 1911.

In the calculations here, I have grouped "public middle and girls high schools" with elementary schools, rather than with (boys') secondary. This seems the better choice, since this category is dominated by middle schools, which corresponded to upper primary-school levels in other countries.

To estimate all public expenditures in Prussia or Germany, it was necessary to subtract Lundgreen's data on private tuitions from his and Hoffman's total expenditures. For some years this involved interpolations to allocate parts of the known total for all levels of education into its parts (primary, secondary, all other).

For Germany, the "1860" figures refer to 1861.

Also for Germany, the national-product denominator is NNP, not GDP, slightly raising the educational shares.

Belgian NNP: This is based on Mitchell's 1913 nominal NNP (6.5 bill. fr.), Maddison's real GDP series 1850–1913, and a geometric average of Mitchell's wholesale and consumer price indices as a proxy for the NNP deflator.

The odd peak for the 1880 share is due mainly to the data series on primary-school expenditures, not to NNP movements. Netherlands public elementary and secondary from Jaarcijfers through 1890: These are midpoints between the shares of public elementary ed. alone and public elementary plus the 0.21% of GNP spent on secondary in 1900.

Switzerland: The estimates of nominal NNP start from Maddison's estimate of 3,695 m. fr. For 1913.

This figure is projected back to an earlier using an interpolation of Maddison's (1995) estimates of real GDP times the wholesale price index relative to 1913.

Appendix D

Regressions Predicting Schooling, Growth, Social Transfers, and Direct Taxes, 1880–1930

The sample: For most equations, the number of observations = 6 years times 21 countries = 126. The benchmark years covered are 1880, 1890, 1900, 1910, 1920, and 1930. In some cases data from adjacent years had to be substituted. The widest departures from benchmark dates are these: The 1920 dependent variables for Sweden are actually spending ratios from 1917, while those for Austria and Belgium are ratios from 1922.

The twenty-one countries of the main 1880–1930 panel are Argentina, Australia, Austria (without the rest of the Austro-Hungarian Empire), Belgium, Brazil, Canada, Denmark, Finland, France, Greece, Italy, Japan, Mexico, Netherlands, New Zealand, Norway, Portugal, Spain, Sweden, United Kingdom, and United States. All are viewed as sovereign nations, despite limitations on the sovereignty of Australia, Finland, and New Zealand before the turn of the century.

For the equation explaining the number of public primary-school teachers per 1000 children of ages five to fourteen, only eleven of these countries supplied usable teacher counts on all six dates: Austria (without the rest of the Austro-Hungarian Empire), Belgium, Canada, Finland, France, Italy, Netherlands, Norway, Sweden, United Kingdom, and United States.

For the equations explaining the revenues from income tax and inheritance tax as percentages of GNP, the nineteen-country sample consists of the twenty-one-country sample minus Spain and Argentina.

Regression techniques: The regressions were run on SHAZAM for the Macintosh. The regressions used the TOBIT and the generalized-least-squares POOL commands without special restrictions. Predicted values from the first stage in the POOL regressions were calculated ("backed out") by reversing the derivations in Kmenta (1986, 618–622).

Given that the dependent variable is often zero and is limited to nonnegative values, tobit regressions were run for university enrollments and for the social-spending shares.

To deal with the simultaneity of the relationship between growth and social transfers, I combined each equation with a growth equation. The growth rate of real national product per capita is an instrumental variable for each enrollment or social-transfer equation. Conversely, the predicted value of lagged total social spending was used as the growth equation. For the simultaneous estimation of a tobit and a pooled equation, I used a two-step method proposed by Nelson and Olsen. This method, and the lingering uncertainties about simultaneity and serial correlation with tobit, are described in Lindert (1994, notes to Table 2).

Each coefficient in a tobit equation is the unnormalized tobit coefficient, which equals the normalized coefficient times the standard error of estimate. The tobit-approximated absolute *t*-statistics are in parentheses. The elasticities in the first equation are evaluated using the expected value of the dependent variable. The R^2 is the squared correlation between observed and expected values of the dependent variable.

Variables:

Enrollments and primary-school teachers per 1,000 children ages five to fourteen are from Appendix A. Means: Primary = 547.13 enrollees, secondary = 22.27 enrollees, and primary-school teachers = 16.685 (for the eleven-country sample).

Total social transfers = poor relief, unemployment compensation, public pensions, public health expenditures, and public housing, all as a percentage of GNP. The source is Lindert (1994, Table 1). Mean = 0.553 percent.

Poor relief and unemployment compensation is mostly poor relief. The source, again, is Lindert (1994, Table 1). Some of its shares of GNP in the year 1880 differ from those shown for 1880 in Lindert (1998). Different series had to be used depending on whether one wanted a series consistent with the date for later years (Lindert 1994, and here) or a series consistent with earlier years (Lindert 1998). Mean here = 0.253 percent.

Public pensions are noncontributory pensions as a share of GNP, again from Lindert (1994, Table 1). Mean = 0.122 percent.

Income tax as a percentage of GNP and *Inheritance tax as a percentage of GNP* = these for the central government only, from the Brian Mitchell volumes of international statistics plus Flora et al. (1983). Spain and Argentina had to be omitted, because their data were difficult to interpret. Means for the nineteen-country sample: Income tax share = 1.11 percent of GNP, inheritance tax share = 0.11 percent of GNP.

Growth rate of GDP per capita, last 10 years is the annual rate of growth in real GDP (or GNP or national income) per capita from ten years earlier to the year of observation. The natural log *ln (GDP/capita), 10-year lag* is the corresponding level of product per capita ten years earlier. Both variables are based on published estimates of real product, converted into 1980 international dollars. Starting from the Heston-Summers estimates for 1950, I followed either national-source estimates of product per capita or (lacking national-source estimates from the Brian Mitchell volumes) Maddison's estimates back to benchmark years between 1880 and 1930. In a few cases it was necessary to use Colin Clark's estimates of real product per capita, spliced onto the estimates in 1980 international dollars. The sample mean growth rate = 0.012, ln (GDP/capita), lagged = 7.200.

Agriculture share is agriculture's share of employment or the economically active population, either from the Mitchell volumes or from Paul Bairoch *et al.* (1968). Mean = 0.453.

This was a democracy = 1 if the country was a democracy in that year. The country was *not* a democracy in that year if, in the codes of Segment 1 of Arthur S. Bank's *Cross-Polity Time-Series Data* (1971),

either J = 3, which means the chief executive officer is not elected or chosen by any other popular mandate (Banks puts many monarchies in this category);

or [*J* = 1, which means direct election;

and (*K* = 1, there is no parliamentary responsibility *and/or O* = 0, 1 (ineffective legislature) and/or *P* = 0, 1 (legislature nonexistent or selected on the basis of heredity or ascription))]. Mean for democracy = 0.548 (69 cases out of 126).

As noted in the text, this yields some questionable decisions in marginal cases, such as prewar Belgium and Italy.

Women voted = 1 if a majority of women were enfranchised in the previous election, according to Mackie and Rose. Mean = 0.198 overall, or 0.362 for the sixty-nine democracy cases.

Voter turnout = the ratio of voters to population over the age of twenty in the enfranchised genders, as of the election just prior to this date (in a few cases, the next election after this date). The voter counts are from Thomas T. Mackie and Richard Rose (1991 edition). The adult-population denominators are from the sources used for age distributions (below). Mean = 0.286 overall (ignoring the votes in some nondemocracies) or 0.523 for the sixty-nine democracy cases.

Executive turnover is the number of times the chief executive post (president, prime minister, functioning emporer) was relinquished to someone not dependent on the incumbent, over the previous decade (1870–1879 for 1880 observations, etc.). The preferred source was Banks (1971, Segment 1, Field (*n*)), supplemented for 1915–1918 by all changes of incumbent as reported by Bienen and Van De Walle (1991, Appendix). Mean = 2.70 per decade.

Young (20–39/20+) is the ratio of persons twenty to thirty-nine to all persons over the age of twenty.

Old (65+/20+) is the ratio of persons over sixty-five to persons over twenty. The source-preference sequence for estimates ran from the Mitchell volumes, to the United Nations *Aging of Populations* volume (1956), to *Annuaire Statistique de la France* for the 1930s, to Keyfitz-Flieger. For Japan before 1920, I used Irene Taeuber's estimates based on regional returns. In a few cases, interpolations were necessary. Mean = 9.179.

Catholic share and *Protestant share* are very rough shares of those persons declaring any religion who declared themselves Roman Catholic or Protestant. Most data are from *Annuaire Statistique de la France* for the 1930s. Those from France, the United Kingdom, and a few other countries are from encyclopedias, in some cases for postwar years. Means: Catholic = 0.496, Protestant = 0.388.

Catholic majority = maximum of 0 or Catholic share −.50.

Protestant dominance = Lutheran share −.50 for Denmark, Norway, Sweden; and =.16 for declared Anglicans in the United Kingdom before the separation of southern Ireland and .10 after.

To make a generous allowance for econometric fixed effects in these pooled data sets, each equation contained both fixed-time dummies and fixed-country dummies. The five fixed-time dummies are those for the sample years 1880, 1890, 1910, 1920, and 1930, so that 1900 is the base year for comparisons. The fixed-country dummies correspond to each country other than the United Kingdom, the base country for comparisons. These fixed-effect variables are present in all final equations, but their coefficients are not reported here.

APPENDIX TABLE D1. *Regression Equations for School Enrollment Rates per 1,000 Children Ages 5–14, 21 Countries in 1880–1930*

| | Public-School Enrollments per 1,000 Children 5–14 | | | | | |
| | (1) Primary Only | | (2) Primary + Sec. | | (3) Secondary | |
Dependent Variables	Coeff.	$|t|$	Coeff.	$|t|$	Coeff.	$|t|$
Same enrollments/5–14s, 10 years earlier	0.35	(4.43)**	0.32	(4.08)**	1.36	(17.63)**
Predicted log-growth in GDP/capita	513.50	(1.95)[a]	376.01	(1.51)	13.29	(0.70)
ln (GDP/capita), 10 years earlier	50.20	(1.42)	49.31	(1.44)	−1.39	(0.33)
Age distribution						
School-age (5–14) children per adult	−0.01	(0.01)	−1.28	(1.10)	−0.39	(2.10)*
Electoral democracy variables (see also "Effects" below)						
Was this a democracy? (1 = yes)	199.46	(2.81)**	163.57	(2.23)*	−9.67	(1.53)
Voters as a share of population over 20	−821.06	(2.00)*	−356.45	(0.82)	91.32	(1.97)[a]
Voter share, squared	1,896.30	(2.10)*	625.05	(0.66)	−282.23	(2.40)*
Voter share, cubed	−1,055.7	(1.72)[b]	−166.50	(0.27)	214.77	(2.52)*
Did women have the legal right to vote?	−41.17	(3.28)**	−25.90	(1.91)[a]	2.60	(0.98)
Turnover of chief executive, last 10 years	−0.74	(0.31)	0.12	(0.05)	−0.37	(1.93)[a]
Religion						
Catholic majority	185.77	(0.86)	−17.83	(0.08)	−29.51	(1.12)
Protestant dominance	1,984.40	(3.10)**	1,429.30	(2.44)*	−9.56	(0.12)

(Each regression also included 5 fixed-time dummies, 20 fixed-country dummies, and a dummy for Austria after World War I. U.K. 1900 was the base case.)

Constant term	−361.0	(1.28)	−197.83	(0.71)	34.17	(1.02)
R sq., equation F-statistic	.996	531.35	.992	284.82	.965	63.15
Mean of the dep. var., std. error of estim.	546.0	1.18	569.2	1.17	23.167	1.01
Effects of selected shifts toward more electoral democracy						
(a) From nondemocracy to 40% voting	106.8	(3.21)**	110.3	(3.35)**	−4.55	(1.51)
(b) From nondemocracy to 55% voting	145.9	(4.15)**	128.9	(3.84)**	−9.08	(2.57)**
(c) From nondemocracy to 70% voting	191.8	(5.50)**	163.2	(4.86)**	−10.37	(2.82)**
(d) From 40% voting to 70% voting	84.9	(5.54)**	52.9	(2.87)**	−5.82	(2.34)*
(e) From 70% voting to 85% voting	31.5	(1.58)	46.7	(2.55)*	6.30	(2.06)*
Type of equation	pooled GLS		pooled GLS		pooled GLS	

** = significant at the 1% level, two-tail; * = significant at the 5% level; [a]significant at the 7% level; [b]significant at the 10% level.

APPENDIX TABLE D2. *Regression Equations for Primary Teachers, University Enrollment Rates, and Growth of GDP per Adult, 1880–1930*

	(4) Public Primary Teachers/ 1,000 Children 5–14 (Only 11 Countries)		(5) University Enrollment/15–24s 1,000 x		(6) Growth of GNP per Capita, Last 10 Years	
	Coeff.	$|t|$	Coeff.	$|t|$	Coeff.	$|t|$
Teachers/1,000 child. 5–14, 10 years earlier	0.352	(3.86)**				
Prim. enrollments/5–14s, 10 years earlier			0.005	(1.20)		
Prim. + sec. enrollments/5–14s, 10 years earlier					.000016	(4.62)**
Predicted total transfers					−.00601	(2.08)*
Predicted total transfers, squared					.00368	(3.53)**
Predicted log-growth in GDP/capita	21.527	(1.17)	20.131	(1.23)		
ln (GDP/capita), 10 years earlier	−0.052	(0.02)	0.010	(3.47)**		
Shortfall in GDP/capita 10 years earlier					0.0041	(1.89)[a]
Agriculture's empl. share, 10 years earlier					0.007	(1.23)
Age distribution						
School-age (5–14) children per adult	−0.558	(5.20)**	−0.402	(3.46)**		
Share of over-20 population over 65					−0.0002	(0.77)
Electoral democracy variables (see also "Effects" below)						
Was this a democracy? (1 = yes)	1.409	(0.66)	−4.198	(1.05)		
Voters as a share of population over 20	−8.381	(0.59)	52.949	(1.94)[a]		

Voter share, squared	34.040	(0.99)	−185.23	(2.92)**	
Voter share, cubed	−18.268	(0.72)	141.640	(3.23)**	
Did women have the legal right to vote?	0.762	(1.12)	7.465	(6.11)**	
Turnover of chief executive, last 10 years	0.24473	(1.96)[a]	−0.008	(0.05)	
Religion					
Catholic majority among relig. declarants	226.100	(3.70)**	27.579	(1.67)[b]	
Protestant dominance	80.121	(4.49)**	0.040	(0.86)	
Constant term	14.509	(0.75)	−23.644	(2.90)	.00235 (0.69)
R sq., equation F-statistic	.983	82.12	0.5193		0.410 10.92
Mean of the dep. variable, std. error of estim.	16.555	1.26	0.0062	0.005	0.012 0.97
Effects of selected shifts toward more electoral democracy					
(a) From nondemocracy to 40% voting	2.333	(1.78)[b]	−0.102	(0.05)	
(b) From nondemocracy to 55% voting	4.057	(2.96)**	−1.354	(0.66)	
(c) From nondemocracy to 70% voting	5.956	(4.86)**	−2.101	(0.96)	
(d) From 40% voting to 70% voting	3.622	(5.16)**	−1.999	(1.00)	
(e) From 70% voting to 85% voting	1.705	(1.44)	0.439	(0.20)	
Type of equation	pooled GLS		tobit		pooled GLS

Note: *Equation (5) also included 5 fixed-time dummies, 20 fixed-country dummies, and a dummy for Austria after World War I. Equation (4) had only 10 country dummies. Equation (6) had only two time-dummies, for 1920 and 1930.*

APPENDIX TABLE D3. *Regression Equations for Social Transfers as Percentages of GNP, 21 Countries in 1880–1930*

	(7) Total Social Transfers		(8) Poor Relief & Unemploy't Comp.		(9) Public Pension Benefits	
	Coeff.	$|t|$	Coeff.	$|t|$	Coeff.	$|t|$
Predicted total transfers, 10 years earlier	0.151	(1.12)	−0.021	(0.27)	0.062	(0.85)
Predicted log-growth in GDP/capita	5.590	(2.23)*	0.329	(0.25)	−6.740	(2.32)*
ln (GDP/capita), 10 years earlier	0.105	(0.22)	0.081	(0.32)	−0.514	(1.74)[b]
Age distribution						
Share of over-20 population over 65	0.111	(2.56)*	0.056	(1.95)[a]	0.0317	(0.91)
Electoral democracy variables (see also "Effects" below)						
Was this a democracy? (1 = yes)	0.003	(0.01)	0.129	(0.70)	0.269	(1.08)
Voters as a share of population over 20	−4.465	(1.97)[a]	−0.029	(0.02)	−7.706	(4.41)**
Voter share, squared	11.455	(2.16)*	−1.065	(0.36)	18.850	(4.69)**
Voter share, cubed	−7.095	(1.95)[a]	1.463	(0.72)	−12.074	(4.59)**
Did women have the legal right to vote?	0.342	(2.87)**	0.134	(2.02)*	0.003	(0.04)
Turnover of chief executive, last 10 years	0.077	(4.49)**	0.054	(4.99)**	0.017	(1.51)

Religion

Catholic majority among relig. declarants	−208.82	(0.00)	131.400	(0.00)	71.835	(0.00)
Protestant dominance	0.009	(0.00)	−1.997	(0.93)	8.545	(3.48)**
Constant term	−0.741	(0.18)	−0.281	(0.13)	2.852	(1.12)
Squared correlation of observed and predicted	.946		.941		.960	
Mean of the dep. variable, std. error of estim.	0.553	0.224	0.253	0.119	0.122	0.104
(Each regression also included 5 fixed-time dummies, 20 fixed-country dummies, and a dummy for Austria after World War I.)						
Effects of selected shifts toward more electoral democracy:						
(a) From nondemocracy to 40% voting	−1.805	(2.34)*	0.348	(0.39)	−5.487	(3.57)**
(b) From nondemocracy to 55% voting	−0.750	(0.94)	0.296	(0.32)	−2.656	(1.99)a
(c) From nondemocracy to 70% voting	0.254	(0.30)	0.755	(0.84)	−0.288	(0.24)
(d) From 40% voting to 70% voting	2.059	(3.62)**	0.407	(0.70)	5.199	(4.64)**
(e) From 70% voting to 85% voting	0.313	(0.56)	1.220	(1.79)b	−0.446	(0.60)
Type of equation	tobit		tobit		tobit	

Note: ** = significant at the 1% level, two-tail; * = significant at the 5% level; [a]significant at the 7% level; [b]significant at the 10% level.

APPENDIX TABLE D4. *Regression Equations for Income Tax and Inheritance Tax as Percentages of GNP, 19 Countries in 1880–1930*

	(10) Income Tax as a % of GNP		(11) Inheritance Tax as a % of GNP	
	Coeff.	$\lvert t \rvert$	Coeff.	$\lvert t \rvert$
Same tax percentage, 10 years earlier	−0.104	(1.21)	−0.301	(3.22)**
Predicted log-growth in GDP/capita	2.888	(0.36)	−0.380	(0.24)
ln (GDP/capita), 10 years earlier	4.092	(4.41)**	−0.052	(0.39)
Age distribution				
Share of over-20 population over 65	−0.037	(0.23)	0.075	(2.63)*
Electoral democracy variables (see also "Effects" below)				
Was this a democracy? (1 = yes)	−2.610	(1.24)	0.363	(1.20)
Voters as a share of population over 20	7.738	(0.56)	−4.310	(2.05)*
Voter share, squared	−9.085	(0.31)	9.332	(1.88)[a]
Voter share, cubed	6.441	(0.33)	−6.101	(1.74)[b]
Did women have the legal right to vote?	2.011	(3.54)**	0.353	(3.88)**
Turnover of chief executive, last 10 years	−3.415	(2.44)*	2.716	(0.00)

Religion

Catholic majority among relig. declarants	5.036	(0.84)	−6.045	(0.86)
Protestant dominance	16.631	(0.97)	1.776	(0.76)

(Each regression also included 5 fixed-time dummies and 20 fixed-country dummies.)

Constant term	−28.041	(4.17)	−0.801	(0.80)
Squared correlation of observed and predicted	.845		.938	
Mean of the dep. variable, std. error of estim.	1.110	0.974	0.134	0.125

Effects of selected shifts toward more electoral democracy:

(a) From nondemocracy to 40% voting	−0.571	(0.85)	−2.060	(2.00)[a]
(b) From nondemocracy to 55% voting	−0.032	(0.04)	−1.592	(1.37)
(c) From nondemocracy to 70% voting	0.579	(0.76)	−1.388	(1.30)
(d) From 40% voting to 70% voting	1.150	(2.11)*	0.672	(1.09)
(e) From 70% voting to 85% voting	0.816	(1.47)	−1.044	(1.02)
Type of equation	tobit		tobit	

Note: ** = significant at the 1% level, two-tail; * = significant at the 5% level; [a]significant at the 7% level; [b]significant at the 10% level. For Equations (10) and (11), Spain and Argentina had to be omitted, leaving only 114 observations.

Appendix E

Regressions Predicting Social Spending, Growth, and Employment, OECD 1962–1995

Excel files containing the full set of numerical values of all variables used in the regressions can be downloaded from the author's home page (www.econ.ucdavis.edu/faculty/fzlinder) or from www.cup.org/0521821754. This includes the 1880–1930 benchmark data as well as the two postwar samples featured in this appendix (the 1962–1981 sample and the 1978–1995 sample).

Here are the names, definitions, sources, and sample means for the variables cited in the tables of this appendix:

Social expenditures as a percentage of GDP:

For 1961–1981, all social expenditures come from OECD (1985). The categories are public pension expenditures (apparently including contributory public-sector pensions), with a mean value of 6.58 percent of GDP; welfare, with a mean of 3.90 percent; unemployment compensation, with a mean of 0.60 percent; public health, with a mean of 4.32 percent; and public education, with a mean of 5.10 percent.

For 1978–1995, all social transfers were calculated from the detailed OECD *Social Expenditures* database (www.oecd.org) as follows:

Public health expenditures = (occupational injury and disease) + (sickness benefits) + ("health"), with a mean sample value of 6.59 percent of GDP for 1978–1995.

Noncontributory *public pensions* = (old-age cash benefits − old age civil service pensions − veterans' old age pensions) + (disability cash benefits − disabled civil servant pensions − disabled veterans' pensions) + (services for the elderly and disabled people) + (survivors' benefits − civil service survivors' benefits), with a mean of 8.07 percent.

The *public pension support ratio* = (pensions/person over 65)/(GDP per capita). This had an average value of 0.311 in the 1962–1981 sample and 0.598 in the 1978–1995 sample.

Welfare = (family cash benefits) + (family services expenditures) + (active labor market program expenditures), with a mean of 1.61 percent.

Unemployment compensation = unemployment compensation + (early retirement for labor market reasons) + (severance pay), with a mean of 2.44 percent.

Total transfers = the total of these social transfers (thus excluding public housing), with a mean of 18.72 percent of GDP.

Real GDP per capita:

For the 1962–1981 sample, the figures are in 1980 international dollars, from Summers and Heston (1988). The 1962–1981 sample mean is $6,943. The logs of average GDP per capita lagged zero years and ten years were 1.8856 and 1.5356, respectively. The *predicted GDP/capita growth, last 10 years* had a mean value of 0.035.

Those in the 1978–1995 sample are in 1985 international dollars, from Penn World Tables version 5.6, with splicing for figures beyond 1992 from version 6.0 (www.nber.org). Exceptions: West Germany/Germany and Greece were spliced at 1991, and Portugal at 1990. The sample mean value is $12,015. The *predicted GDP/capita growth, last 3 years* had a mean value of 0.0665.

Independent variables in Tables E1 and E3, and in Table 17.2:

The *age-group shares* of total population – those for children ages zero to fourteen, children ages five to fourteen persons over twenty and persons over sixty-five – are from United Nations sources, particularly United Nations (1998). For the 1962–1981 sample, these percentage shares are 25.0, 16.8, 33.0, and 11.48, respectively. For 1978–1995, the corresponding shares are 20.7, 14.1, 27.3, and 13.3.

This is a *democracy* = 1 if the country was a democracy in that year. All countries were democracies in both samples, except that Greece was not, 1967–1973. See Banks (1971) and Mackie and Rose (1991).

Voters as a share of population over 20 = the ratio of voters to population over the age of twenty, as of the general election just prior to this date. The source for the numerator is Mackie and Rose (1991, 1997). Average for 1962–1981 = 0.790 and that for 1978–1995 = 0.768.

Women voted = 1 in all cases except Switzerland before 1972.

Turnover = number of changes of chief executive, last ten years. The source is Bienen and Van de Walle (1991), with updates from Mackie and Rose (1997). The mean value is 2.574 for the 1962–1981 sample and 2.508 for the 1978–1995 sample.

The *Catholic* share and the *Protestant* share are very rough shares of those declaring any religion who declared themselves Roman Catholic or Protestant, respectively. Most data are from *Annuaire Statistique de la France* for the 1930s. Those from France, the United Kingdom, and a few other countries are from encyclopedias, usually postwar. The same religion variables, and sources, were used in Lindert (1994) and Lindert (1996). Average Catholic = .441, and average Protestant = .448 for 1978–1995. For an alternative coverage of religions, see Taylor and Hudson (1972).

APPENDIX TABLE E1. *Regression Equations for Social Spending as Percentages of GDP, 1962/65–1978/81*

Independent Variables	(1) Total Social Transfers		(2) Public Pension Benefits		(3) Public pension Support Ratio[†]	
	Coeff.	|t|	Coeff.	|t|	Coeff.	|t|
A. Without the full set of fixed effects for time and country						
Total transfers, 4 years earlier	0.899	(18.82)**	0.199	(1.50)**	0.017	(4.36)**
Predicted GDP/capita growth, last 10 years	59.174	(4.56)**	4.379	(0.39)	0.715	(0.70)
log of GDP/capita, 10 years earlier	3.533	(6.35)**	1.923	(2.83)**	0.175	(2.94)**
Age distribution (see also "Effects" below)						
Population over 65 as a share of total pop.	1.449	(0.57)	−1.470	(0.53)	0.054	(0.22)
Squared	−0.144	(0.63)	0.142	(0.58)	−0.0047	(0.22)
Cubed	0.0045	(0.66)	−0.0037	(0.51)	0.0001	(0.14)
Electoral democracy variables (see also "Effects" below)						
Voters as a share of population over 20	−100.01	(1.32)	32.063	(0.43)	−3.331	(0.55)
Squared	147.310	(1.34)	−77.976	(0.72)	2.246	(0.26)
Cubed	−69.301	(1.34)	51.772	(1.03)	0.217	(0.05)
Turnover of chief executive, last 10 years	0.144	(2.06)*	0.016	(0.25)	0.003	(0.51)
Religion and ethnic divisions						
Catholic majority among relig. declarants	1.569	(1.97)[a]	1.999	(1.60)	0.178	(1.76)[b]
Ethnic fractionalization index	−2.192	(2.68)**	−2.780	(2.49)*	−0.224	(2.34)*
Competing influences						
Openness to foreign trade	0.033	(4.94)**	−0.012	(1.44)	−0.0013	(1.81)[b]
Military spending	0.156	(1.65)[b]	−0.0002	(0.00)	0.0026	(0.28)
Constant term	10.369	(0.50)	2.556	(0.13)	1.079	(0.65)
R sq., equation F-statistic	.976	232.6	.805	23.618	.689	12.628
Mean of the dependent variable	15.391		6.580		0.558	

Effects of extra population aging:

(a) For a young population	0.006	(0.03)	0.091	(0.38)	−0.005	(0.24)
(b) For a medium-aged populations	−0.085	(0.88)	0.329	(2.77)**	−0.021	(2.05)*
(c) For an old population (e.g., Sweden 1980)	0.153	(0.56)	0.295	(1.00)	−0.031	(1.35)

Effects of selected shifts toward more electoral democracy

(d) From 40% voting to 70% voting	−0.737	(0.68)	−1.669	(1.21)	−0.199	(1.81)[b]
(e) From 70% voting to 85% voting	0.455	(1.52)	0.715	(2.03)*	0.080	(2.69)**

B. With the full set of "fixed effects" for time and country

Total transfers, 4 years earlier	0.699	(10.86)**	0.220	(6.94)**	0.016	(6.68)**
Predicted GDP/capita growth, last 10 years	−30.416	(1.19)	−30.097	(1.95)[a]	−3.277	(2.80)**
log of GDP/capita, 10 years earlier	−0.720	(0.51)	1.659	(1.66)[b]	0.124	(1.64)[b]

Age distribution (see also "Effects" below)

Population over 65 as a share of total pop.	0.150	(0.06)	−3.759	(1.95)[a]	−0.141	(0.85)
Squared	−0.035	(0.16)	0.353	(2.09)*	0.013	(0.90)
Cubed	0.0015	(0.24)	−0.010	(2.11)*	−0.0005	(1.14)

Electoral democracy variables (see also "Effects" below)

Voters as a share of population over 20	−131.00	(1.63)[b]	−33.443	(0.60)	−7.912	(2.00)[a]
Squared	210.23	(1.70)[b]	20.575	(0.24)	9.653	(1.63)[b]
Cubed	−100.68	(1.67)[b]	4.398	(0.11)	−3.520	(1.24)
Turnover of chief executive, last 10 years	0.310	(3.53)**	0.068	(1.32)	0.0069	(1.59)

Competing influences

Openness to foreign trade	−0.0035	(0.13)	0.016	(1.09)	0.00045	(0.37)
Military spending	0.092	(0.45)	−0.1941	(1.70)[b]	−0.018	(2.09)*

Plus 4 fixed-time effects and 18 fixed-country terms, omitted here

Constant term (for U.K. in 1962/65)			24.416	(1.74)	2.7794	(2.67)
Buse *R* sq., equation *F*-statistic	.992	223.45	.987	136.92	.986	120.16
Mean of the dependent variable	15.391		6.580		0.558	

(continued)

APPENDIX TABLE E1 (*continued*)

Independent Variables	(1) Total Social Transfers		(2) Public Pension Benefits		(3) Public Pension Support Ratio[†]	
	Coeff.	|*t*|	Coeff.	|*t*|	Coeff.	|*t*|
Effects of extra population aging						
(a) For a young population	−0.058	(0.05)	−1.428	(1.73)[b]	−0.023	(1.32)
(b) For a medium-aged populations	−0.099	(0.56)	0.222	(1.69)[b]	−0.029	(2.95)**
(c) For an old population (e.g., Sweden 1980)	0.186	(0.49)	−0.346	(1.15)	−0.070	(4.38)**
Effects of selected shifts toward more electoral democracy						
(d) From 40% voting to 70% voting	1.987	(1.29)	−2.016	(1.98)[a]	−0.170	(2.37)*
(e) From 70% voting to 85% voting	1.934	(2.66)**	0.959	(2.06)*	0.103	(3.23)**

Independent Variables	(4) Welfare & Unemploy't Comp.		(5) Public Health Spending		(6) Public Education Expenditures	
	Coeff.	|*t*|	Coeff.	|*t*|	Coeff.	|*t*|
A. Without the full set of fixed effects for time and country						
Total transfers, 4 years earlier	0.196	(4.16)**	0.076	(2.74)**	0.005	(0.23)
Predicted GDP/capita growth, last 10 years	19.510	(1.85)[a]	22.205	(3.00)**	32.296	(4.50)**
log of GDP/capita, 10 years earlier	1.024	(1.85)[a]	2.260	(5.42)**	2.555	(7.25)**
Age distribution (see also "Effects" below)						
Children 5–14 as a % of total population					1.071	(2.05)*
Squared					−0.027	(1.83)[a]
Populat'n over 65 as a share of total pop.	−0.766	(0.36)	0.345	(0.54)		
Squared	0.051	(0.27)	−0.038	(0.55)		
Cubed	−0.001	(0.21)	0.001	(0.62)		

176

Electoral democracy variables (see also "Effects" below)

Voters as a share of population over 20	44.492	(0.72)	−53.273	(1.07)	−47.055	(0.89)
Squared	−0.352	(0.38)	69.795	(0.97)	65.776	(0.87)
Cubed	6.207	(0.14)	−29.099	(0.86)	−28.396	(0.81)
Turnover of chief executive, last 10 years	0.135	(2.52)*	0.062	(1.80)[b]	0.020	(0.61)
Religion and ethnic divisions						
Catholic majority among relig. declarants	0.768	(0.60)	−0.049	(0.06)	0.642	(0.93)
Ethnic fractionalization index	0.647	(0.48)	−2.377	(2.51)*	0.213	(0.23)
Competing influences						
Openness to foreign trade	0.030	(3.10)**	0.006	(0.91)	0.018	(3.55)**
Military spending	0.059	(0.65)	−0.158	(2.37)*	−0.151	(2.08)*
Constant term	−15.251	(1.05)	10.070	(0.75)	−0.696	(0.06)
R sq., equation F-statistic	.606	8.796	.734	15.736	0.693	14.092
Mean of the dependent variable	4.495		4.316		5.098	
Effects of extra population aging					(Effect of rise in	
(a) For a young population	−0.182	(0.94)	0.030	(0.18)	school-age population,	
(b) For a medium-aged populations	−0.068	(0.64)	0.048	(0.59)	at sample mean:)	
(c) For an old population (e.g., Sweden 1980)	−0.041	(0.17)	0.245	(1.14)	−13.890[b]	(1.82)[b]
Effects of selected shifts toward more electoral democracy						
(d) From 40% voting to 70% voting	3.467	(4.02)**	−1.068	(1.21)	−0.333	(0.33)
(e) From 70% voting to 85% voting	0.175	(0.51)	0.348	(1.38)	0.536	(2.42)*

B. With the full set of fixed effects for time and country

Total transfers, 4 years earlier	0.294	(5.44)**	0.119	(4.57)**	0.0091	(0.55)
Predicted GDP/capita growth, last 10 years	−4.526	(0.29)	−0.735	(0.07)	10.409	(1.38)
log of GDP/capita, 10 years earlier	−1.725	(1.87)[a]	0.181	(0.24)	0.179	(0.44)
Age distribution (see also "Effects" below)						
Children 5–14 as a % of total population					−0.116	(0.35)
Squared					0.0085	(0.91)

(continued)

APPENDIX TABLE E1 *(continued)*

Populat'n over 65 as a share of total pop.	2.8238	(1.44)	−0.295	(0.21)		
Squared	−0.272	(1.56)	0.0047	(0.04)		
Cubed	0.0078	(1.53)	0.00017	(0.05)		
Electoral democracy variables (see also "Effects" below)						
Voters as a share of population over 20	52.676	(1.03)	−86.004	(2.43)*	−74.27	(3.01)**
Squared	−40.885	(0.52)	128.110	(2.37)*	105.42	(2.70)**
Cubed	3.229	(0.08)	−59.114	(2.25)*	−46.73	(2.37)*
Turnover of chief executive, last 10 years	0.141	(2.64)**	0.054	(1.55)	0.031	(1.68)[b]
Competing influences						
Openness to foreign trade	−0.0015	(0.09)	−0.0032	(0.27)	0.0036	(0.51)
Military spending	0.262	(1.79)[b]	−0.014	(0.16)	−0.242	(4.04)**
Plus 4 fixed-time effects and 18 fixed-country terms, omitted here						
Constant term (for U.K. in 1962/65)	−25.06	(2.12)	21.535	(2.42)	20.641	(3.71)
Buse *R* sq., equation *F*-statistic	.964	47.089	0.955	37.801	0.980	90.494
Mean of the dependent variable	4.495		4.316		5.098	
Effects of extra population aging					*(Effect of rise in school-*	
(a) For a young population	1.022	(1.25)	−0.250	(0.42)	*age population; at*	
(b) For a medium-aged populations	−0.275	(2.47)**	−0.149	(1.66)[b]	*sample mean:)*	
(c) For an old pop'n (e.g., Sweden 1980)	0.116	(0.34)	−0.011	(0.05)	4.556	(0.95)
Effects of selected shifts toward more electoral democracy						
(d) From 40% voting to 70% voting	3.212	(3.91)**	0.860	(2.72)**	−0.529	(1.18)
(e) From 70% voting to 85% voting	−0.729	(1.57)	−0.250	(0.42)	0.703	(4.13)**

APPENDIX TABLE E2. *Regression Equations for Growth of GDP per capita, 1962/65–1978/81*

Independent Variables	Equation (1)		Equation (2)		Equation (3)	
	Coeff.	|t|	Coeff.	|t|	Coeff.	|t|
Shortfall in GDP/capita 10 years earlier	0.033	(9.58)**	0.032	(9.08)**	0.033	(9.13)**
Capital formation/capita, 1 year earlier	0.017	(7.88)**	0.015	(7.14)**	0.015	(7.28)**
Capital formation/capita, 10 years earlier	−0.011	(5.13)**	−0.010	(4.51)**	−0.010	(4.59)**
Prim. + sec. enrollments/5–14s, 10 years earlier	0.031	(3.29)**	0.029	(3.16)**	0.028	(2.95)**
University enrollments/5–14s, 10 years earlier	0.029	(1.27)	0.039	(1.85)[a]	0.040	(1.87)[a]
Age distribution						
Population under 15 as a share of total pop.	−0.00059	(2.12)*	−.00074	(2.64)**	−0.00070	(2.47)*
Population over 65 as a share of total pop.	−.000050	(0.10)	.000009	(0.02)	.000047	(0.09)
Global demand and supply shocks						
Inflation − unemployment, all OECD	0.0033	(4.67)**	0.0039	(5.39)**	0.0038	(5.25)**
Inflation + unemployment, all OECD	−0.0021	(5.33)**	−0.0024	(5.67)**	−0.0023	(5.41)**
Government policy (see also derived "Effects" below and in Table 18.2)						
Corporatism	0.0022	(1.66)[b]	0.0025	(1.95)[a]	0.0025	(1.93)[a]
Predicted total transfers as % of GDP			0.00020	(0.39)	0.0014	(0.76)
Squared			.000006	(0.42)	.000068	(.061)
Cubed					.000001	(0.66)
Predicted public pensions as % of GDP	0.0020	(2.21)*				
Squared	−.000077	(1.40)				
Predicted welfare and unemp. as % of GDP	0.00014	(0.27)				
Squared	.000018	(0.47)				
Predicted public health exp. as % of GDP	−0.00021	(0.09)				
Squared	.000007	(0.03)				

(continued)

APPENDIX TABLE E2 *(continued)*

Independent Variables	Equation (1)		Equation (2)		Equation (3)	
	Coeff.	$|t|$	Coeff.	$|t|$	Coeff.	$|t|$
Constant term	−0.0041	(0.29)	0.0071	(0.51)	0.00057	(0.04)
R sq., equation F-statistic	.841	31.38	.820	36.05	0.830	35.68
Mean of the dependent variable	0.036		0.036		0.036	
Effects of raising social expenditures by 1% of GDP, starting from 1978–95 average transfer share (18.72%)						
(a) Total social transfers			0.00043	(2.63)**	0.00034	(1.59)
(b) Public pensions	0.00099	(2.96)**				
(c) Welfare and unemployment compens.	0.00030	(1.14)				
(d) Public health spending	−0.00015	(0.25)				

Notes and sources for Appendix Tables E1 and E2:

Dependent variable = log-growth per annum.

(** =significant at the 1% level, two-tail; * =significant at the 5% level;[a] =significant at the 7% level;[b] =significant at the 10% level.)

†The public pension support ratio = (pensions/person over 65)/(GDP per capita).

The slopes of spending with respect to the elderly (over-65) share are evaluated for "young population" = 8% over age 65, around the 8th percentile among the 95 sampled cases; "medium population" = 11.5% over 65, the sample median; and "old population" = 15% over 65, the 94th percentile. (Sweden in 1980 was the oldest in this sample, at 16.2 percent of the population 65 and older.)

The sources are those indicated in Lindert (1996).

The sample consists of these 19 countries: Australia, Austria, Belgium, Canada, Denmark, Finland, France, West Germany, Greece, Ireland, Italy, Japan, Netherlands, New Zealand, Norway, Sweden, Switzerland, the United Kingdom, and the United States of America.

Each equation is generalized least squares, with country-specific variances. The variables called "predicted" are instrumented values from first-stage regressions on all exogenous variables.

Enrollment rates here are per person 5–14, not per 1000 persons 5–14, for the purpose of scaling coefficients.

The full set of fixed effects for 5 time periods and 20 countries was not used in the growth regressions. Including those 25 variables added little insight, and made the whole growth equation less significant.

APPENDIX TABLE E3. *Regression Equations for Social Transfers as Percentages of GDP, 1978/80–1993/95*

Independent Variables	(1) Total Social Transfers		(2) Public Pension Benefits		(3) Public Pension Support Ratio[†]	
	Coeff.	$\lvert t \rvert$	Coeff.	$\lvert t \rvert$	Coeff.	$\lvert t \rvert$
A. Without the full set of fixed effects for time and country						
Total transfers, 3 years earlier	0.933	(26.01)**	0.291	(8.68)**	0.0216	(9.09)**
Predicted GDP/capita growth, last 3 years	−4.512	(1.85)[a]	−1.840	(1.39)	−0.170	(1.73)[b]
log of GDP/capita, 3 years earlier	0.583	(0.98)	1.133	(1.97)*	0.068	(1.61)
Age distribution (see also "Effects" below)						
Population over 65 as a share of total pop.	−0.807	(0.16)	−4.496	(1.23)	−0.159	(0.60)
Squared	0.069	(0.18)	0.384	(1.37)	0.0156	(0.79)
Cubed	−0.0017	(0.17)	−0.010	(1.39)	−0.0005	(1.02)
Electoral democracy variables (see also "Effects" below)						
Voters as a share of population over 20	−139.5	(1.63)	−115.08	(2.09)*	−9.84	(2.39)*
Squared	214.1	(1.70)[b]	168.80	(2.13)*	14.33	(2.41)*
Cubed	−105.5	(1.76)[b]	−78.93	(2.11)*	−6.66	(2.37)*
Turnover of chief executive, last 10 years	−0.015	(0.21)	0.044	(0.72)	0.0022	(0.47)
Religion and ethnic divisions						
Catholic majority among relig. declarants	1.047	(1.50)	3.216	(4.34)**	0.220	(4.18)**
Ethnic fractionalization index	0.020	(0.30)	−1.414	(2.18)*	−0.098	(1.94)[a]
Competing influences						
Openness to foreign trade	−0.0043	(0.93)	−0.012	(2.45)*	−0.0010	(2.55)*
Military spending	−0.027	(0.32)	0.162	(1.93)[a]	0.010	(1.56)
Constant term (for the U.K. in 1993/95)	28.367	(1.10)	32.211	(1.65)	2.264	(1.54)
Buse R sq., equation F-statistic	.962	224.650	.826	42.738	.721	23.228

(continued)

APPENDIX TABLE E3 *(continued)*

Independent Variables	(1) Total Social Transfers		(2) Public Pension Benefits		(3) Public Pension Support Ratio[†]	
	Coeff.	$\|t\|$	Coeff.	$\|t\|$	Coeff.	$\|t\|$
Mean of the dependent variable	18.519		8.046		0.596	
Effects of extra population aging						
(a) For a young population (e.g., Japan 1980)	0.023	(0.05)	0.0061	(0.02)	0.00009	(0.00)
(b) For a medium-aged population	0.134	(1.15)	0.458	(4.22)**	−0.007	(0.84)
(c) For an old population (e.g., Sweden 1985)	0.047	(0.07)	−0.317	(0.63)	−0.083	(2.84)**
Effects of selected shifts toward more electoral democracy						
(d) From 40% voting to 70% voting	−0.640	(0.54)	−0.844	(0.91)	−0.080	(1.20)
(e) From 70% voting to 85% voting	0.244	(1.07)	0.585	(2.77)**	0.051	(3.13)**
B. With the full set of fixed effects for time and country						
Total transfers, 3 years earlier	0.499	(6.95)**	0.204	(4.16)**	0.013	(3.90)**
Predicted GDP/capita growth, last 3 years	−3.014	(1.12)	−1.858	(1.00)	−0.179	(1.45)
log of GDP/capita, 3 years earlier	4.746	(2.66)**	3.799	(3.10)**	0.416	(4.91)**
Age distribution (see also "Effects" below)						
Population over 65 as a share of total pop.	−12.481	(3.28)**	−7.285	(2.51)*	−0.404	(2.11)*
Squared	0.977	(3.32)**	0.530	(2.27)*	0.027	(1.77)[b]
Cubed	−0.025	(3.28)**	−0.012	(1.92)[a]	−0.0006	(1.53)
Electoral democracy variables (see also "Effects" below)						
Voters as a share of population over 20	−158.39	(1.37)	21.39	(0.36)	1.431	(0.38)
Squared	218.66	(1.39)	−16.54	(0.20)	−1.710	(0.33)
Cubed	−98.80	(1.38)	3.62	(0.99)	0.779	(0.34)
Turnover of chief executive, last 10 years	0.231	(2.56)*	0.175	(3.05)**	0.015	(3.69)**

Independent Variables	(4) Welfare, or Basic Assistance		(5) Unemployment Compensation		(6) Public Health Spending	
	Coeff.	|t|	Coeff.	|t|	Coeff.	|t|
Competing influences						
Openness to foreign trade	−0.037	(2.39)*	−0.0077	(0.70)	−0.0005	(0.62)
Military spending	0.564	(2.70)**	0.368	(2.73)**	0.023	(2.61)**
Plus 5 fixed-time effects and 20 fixed-country terms, omitted here						
Constant term (for the U.K. in 1993/95)	47.124	(1.34)	−11.754	(0.55)	−2.313	(1.64)
Buse R sq., equation F-statistic	.986	232.45	.973	120.921	.944	38.814
Mean of the dependent variable	18.519		8.046		0.598	
Effects of extra population aging						
(a) For a young population (e.g., Japan 1978)	−0.869	(2.31)*	−0.634	(2.73)**	−0.064	(4.34)**
(b) For a medium-aged populations	0.453	(2.98)**	0.462	(4.07)**	−0.0109	(1.38)
(c.) For an old population (e.g., Sweden 1985)	−1.218	(2.10)*	0.223	(0.40)	−0.0290	(0.80)
Effects of selected shifts toward more electoral democracy						
(d) From 40% voting to 70% voting	−2.927	(1.00)	1.966	(1.25)	0.083	(0.82)
(e) From 70% voting to 85% voting	0.293	(0.80)	0.343	(1.44)	0.029	(1.68)[b]

Independent Variables	(4) Welfare, or Basic Assistance		(5) Unemployment Compensation		(6) Public Health Spending	
	Coeff.	|t|	Coeff.	|t|	Coeff.	|t|
A. Without the full set of fixed effects for time and country						
Total transfers, 3 years earlier	0.140	(7.67)**	0.107	(5.83)**	0.082	(3.67)**
Predicted GDP/capita growth, last 3 years	0.470	(0.71)	−1.647	(2.86)**	−0.300	(0.28)
log of GDP/capita, 3 years earlier	0.902	(2.53)*	0.485	(1.31)	2.708	(5.73)**
Age distribution (see also "Effects" below)						
Population over 65 as a share of total pop.	0.350	(0.14)	−1.057	(0.54)	2.338	(0.65)
Squared	−0.065	(0.34)	0.089	(0.57)	−0.190	(0.66)

(continued)

APPENDIX TABLE E3 *(continued)*

Independent Variables	(4) Welfare, or Basic Assistance		(5) Unemployment Compensation		(6) Public Health Spending	
	Coeff.	$|t|$	Coeff.	$|t|$	Coeff.	$|t|$
Cubed	0.0027	(0.52)	−0.0027	(0.67)	0.005	(0.67)
Electoral democracy variables (see also "Effects" below)						
Voters as a share of population over 20	60.270	(2.05)*	14.09	(0.37)	−116.0	(2.29)*
Squared	−87.948	(2.06)*	−10.50	(0.20)	175.2	(2.39)*
Cubed	41.729	(2.05)*	0.40	(0.02)	−85.5	(2.48)*
Turnover of chief executive, last 10 years	−0.043	(1.36)	−0.029	(0.91)	0.070	(1.47)
Religion and ethnic divisions						
Catholic majority among relig. declarants	0.435	(1.02)	0.374	(0.92)	1.117	(2.05)*
Ethnic fractionalization index	−1.344	(3.23)**	0.711	(1.24)	−0.644	(1.12)
Competing influences						
Openness to foreign trade	0.0087	(3.06)**	0.0084	(2.31)*	0.0081	(2.09)*
Military spending	0.056	(1.03)	0.044	(0.78)	−0.099	(1.27)
Constant term (for the U.K. in 1993/95)	−21.734	(1.81)	−5.711	(0.45)	−5.42	(0.29)
Buse R sq., equation F-statistic	.655	17.090	.548	10.905	.636	15.178
Mean of the dependent variable	2.425		1.498		6.595	
Effects of extra population aging						
(a) For a young population (e.g., Japan 1980)	−0.184	(0.93)	−0.109	(0.63)	0.149	(0.51)
(b) For a medium-aged population	−0.007	(0.01)	−0.107	(1.88)[a]	−0.038	(0.44)
(c) For an old population (e.g., Sweden 1985)	0.573	(1.34)	−0.468	(1.48)	0.409	(0.67)
Effects of selected shifts toward more electoral democracy						
(d) From 40% voting to 70% voting	0.701	(1.40)	0.873	(1.15)	−0.845	(1.02)
(e) From 70% voting to 85% voting	−0.094	(0.84)	−0.220	(1.89)[a]	0.149	(0.89)

B. With the full set of fixed effects for time and country

Total transfers, 3 years earlier	0.094	(4.36)**	0.122	(5.01)**	−0.020	(0.92)
Predicted GDP/capita growth, last 3 years	0.161	(0.23)	−0.294	(0.86)	−1.177	(1.19)
log of GDP/capita, 3 years earlier	0.561	(1.12)	1.360	(2.09)	0.606	(0.69)
Age distribution (see also "Effects" below)						
Population over 65 as a share of total pop.	−0.211	(0.16)	−3.047	(0.34)	−3.703	(1.38)
Squared	−0.014	(0.13)	0.251	(0.66)	0.348	(1.64)
Cubed	0.00084	(0.30)	−0.007	(0.79)	−0.010	(1.80)
Electoral democracy variables (see also "Effects" below)						
Voters as a share of population over 20	70.16	(1.94)[a]	−99.75	(1.05)	−212.5	(3.67)**
Squared	−98.78	(1.97)*	134.60	(1.18)	280.4	(3.62)**
Cubed	44.32	(1.92)[a]	−61.28	(1.25)	−121.9	(3.54)**
Turnover of chief executive, last 10 years	−0.032	(1.20)	0.069	(0.21)	0.138	(3.39)**
Competing influences						
Openness to foreign trade	−0.0016	(0.36)	0.0062	(1.34)	−0.024	(3.34)*
Military spending	0.211	(3.08)**	0.175	(4.10)**	−0.108	(1.07)
Plus 5 fixed-time effects and 20 fixed-country terms, omitted here						
Constant term (for the U.K. in 1993/95)	−19.475	(1.79)	21.589	(1.71)	64.376	(3.33)
Buse R sq., equation F-statistic	.961	81.51	.964	88.26	.909	33.21
Mean of the dependent variable	2.425		1.498		6.595	
Effects of extra population aging						
(a) For a young population (e.g., Japan 1978)	−0.262	(2.14)*	−0.207	(1.59)	0.139	(0.62)
(b) For a medium-aged populations	−0.153	(3.10)**	−0.024	(0.48)	0.290	(3.50)**
(c) For an old population (e.g., Sweden 1985)	0.095	(0.38)	−0.729	(2.64)**	−0.866	(1.97)*
Effects of selected shifts toward more electoral democracy						
(d) From 40% voting to 70% voting	0.817	(0.92)	2.605	(2.73)**	−5.197	(3.34)**
(e) From 70% voting to 85% voting	−0.427	(3.85)**	−0.282	(2.32)*	0.291	(1.77)[b]

APPENDIX TABLE E4. *Regression Equations for Growth of GDP per capita, 1978/80–1993/95*
(Dependent Variable = Log-Growth Over Three Years)

Independent Variables	Equation (1)		Equation (2)		Equation (3)	
	Coeff.	|t|	Coeff.	|t|	Coeff.	|t|
Shortfall in GDP/capita 10 years earlier	−0.0026	(0.10)	0.039	(2.34)[*]	0.035	(2.08)[*]
Capital form./capita, one year earlier/1000	0.0087	(1.96)[a]	0.0033	(0.66)	0.0028	(0.58)
Capital form./capita, 10 years earlier/1000	−0.0098	(1.72)[b]	−.0086	(1.41)	−0.0086	(1.42)
Prim. + sec. enrollments/5–14s, 10 years earlier	.000085	(3.17)[**]	.000044	(1.94)[a]	.000047	(2.10)[*]
University enrollments/5–14s, 10 years earlier	−.000110	(1.41)	−.00003	(0.40)	−.000039	(0.52)
Age distribution						
Population under 15 as a share of total pop.	−0.00014	(0.07)	−.00088	(0.40)	−0.00030	(0.13)
Population over 65 as a share of total pop.	−0.00274	(0.93)	−.00182	(0.72)	−0.00061	(0.21)
Global demand and supply shocks						
Inflation – unemployment, all OECD	0.0086	(5.87)[**]	0.011	(7.11)[**]	0.010	(6.85)[**]
Inflation + unemployment, all OECD	−0.0142	(5.96)[**]	−0.018	(7.94)[**]	−0.018	(7.91)[**]
Government policy (see also derived "Effects" below and in Table 18.3)						
Corporatism	0.000205	(0.09)	0.0019	(1.03)	0.0024	(1.29)
Predicted total transfers as % of GDP	−0.00545	(1.72)[b]	0.0016	(0.46)	−0.0133	(0.86)
Squared	0.00009	(1.17)	−.00006	(0.64)	0.0007	(0.90)
Cubed					−.000013	(0.97)
Predicted personal income tax as % of GDP	0.0023	(1.00)				
Squared	−0.00012	(1.84)[a]				
Predicted corporate inc. tax as % of GDP	0.0349	(1.32)				

186

	Coeff.	$|t|$	Coeff.	$|t|$	Coeff.	$|t|$
Squared	−0.0078	(2.01)*				
Predicted property tax as % of GDP	0.0194	(1.02)				
Squared	−0.0062	(1.36)				
Predicted consumption tax as % of GDP	0.0036	(0.29)				
Squared	0.00012	(0.20)				
Constant term	0.168	(1.67)	0.276	(3.29)	0.340	(3.26)
Buse R sq., equation F-statistic	.605	9.647	.443	8.339	0.449	7.887
Mean of the dependent variable	0.055		0.055		0.055	
Effects of raising social transfer share by 1% of GDP, at sample mean transfer share (18.72%)						
(a) Social transfers, financed by the implicit tax mix			−.00050	(0.63)	0.000027	(0.03)
(b) Social transfers, financed by personal income tax	−0.0024	(1.55)				
(c) Social transfers, financed by corporate income tax	−0.0084	(1.15)				
(d) Social transfers, financed by property tax	−0.00473	(0.70)				
(e) Social transfers, financed by consumption tax	0.0039	(1.82)[a]				

	Equation (4)		Equation (5)		Equation (6)	
Independent variables	Coeff.	$|t|$	Coeff.	$|t|$	Coeff.	$|t|$
Shortfall in GDP/capita 10 years earlier	0.046	(2.60)**	0.033	(1.52)	0.032	(1.47)
Capital form./capita, 1 year earlier/1,000	0.0017	(0.35)	−.00092	(0.19)	−0.0011	(0.23)
Capital form./capita, 10 years earlier/1,000	−0.0042	(0.72)	−.0089	(1.45)	−0.0089	(1.44)
Prim. + sec. enrollments/5–14s, 10 years earlier	0.000045	(1.98)*	.000088	(3.99)**	0.00009	(3.96)**
University enrollments/5–14s, 10 years earlier	−0.000032	(0.42)	−.00012	(1.44)	−0.00012	(1.48)

(*continued*)

Independent Variables	Equation (4)		Equation (5)		Equation (6)	
	Coeff.	|t|	Coeff.	|t|	Coeff.	|t|
Age distribution						
Population under 15 as a share of total pop.	−0.00071	(0.31)	−0.0005	(0.21)	−0.00033	(0.13)
Population over 65 as a share of total pop.	−0.00218	(0.77)	−0.0033	(0.99)	−0.0027	(0.76)
Global demand and supply shocks						
Inflation − unemployment, all OECD	0.010	(7.04)**	0.010	(6.97)**	0.010	(6.81)**
Inflation + unemployment, all OECD	−0.017	(7.78)**	−0.019	(8.48)**	−0.019	(8.42)**
Sweden-Finland macro mistake, 1991–1994	−0.091	(2.90)**				
Government policy (see also derived "Effects" below and in Table 18.3)						
Corporatism	0.0022	(1.18)	0.018	(3.28)**	0.018	(3.22)**
Predicted total transfers as % of GDP	0.013	(0.74)	0.0105	(2.63)**	0.0037	(0.25)
Squared	−0.00076	(0.86)	−.00021	(2.35)*	0.00014	(0.18)
Cubed	.0000141	(0.95)			−.000006	(0.47)
Employee protection laws			0.0091	(1.48)	0.0085	(1.34)
Three years earlier			−0.014	(2.34)*	−0.0134	(2.27)*
Public employment share			−0.097	(1.13)	−0.099	(1.15)
Unemployment compensation support ratio			−0.0023	(2.36)*	−0.0023	(2.33)*
Squared			.000024	(1.27)	0.000024	(1.25)
Constant term	0.206	(1.87)	0.199	(2.07)	0.232	(1.99)
Buse *R* sq., equation *F*-statistic	.473	8.063	.527	8.427	0.525	7.723
Mean of the dependent variable	0.055		0.055		0.055	

Effects of raising social transfer share by 1% of GDP, at sample mean transfer share (18.72%), financed by the implicit tax mix	−0.0011	(1.10)	.00248	(2.05)*	0.00278	(1.96)[a]
Effect of a permanent tightening of employee protection laws, by 1 index point			−0.0047	(1.14)	−0.0040	(1.18)
Effect of raising the unemployment compensation support ratio by 1% (when it is 20%)			−.00135	(3.34)**	−0.00135	(3.30)**

Notes to Appendix Tables E3 and E4:

** =significant at the 1% level, two-tail; * =significant at the 5% level; [a]significant at the 7% level; [b]significant at the 10% level.

[†]The public pension support ratio = (pensions/person over 65)/(GDP per capita).

The slopes of spending with respect to the elderly (over-65) share are evaluated for "young population" = 9% over age 65 (as in Japan in 1980); "medium-aged population" = 13% over age 65; and "old population" = 18% over 65, just above the sample range. (Sweden in 1985–1987 was the oldest, at 17.9% over age 65.)

The sample consists of the 19 countries of the 1962–1981 sample (as in Appendix Tables E1 and E2) plus Portugal and Spain, and 6 three-year time periods from 1978/80 through 1993/95. In the fixed-effect regressions, the omitted case – the comparison base for all time and country coefficients – is the U.K. in 1993/95.

Each equation is generalized least squares, with country-specific variances. The variables called "predicted" are instrumented values from first-stage regressions on all exogenous variables.

Enrollment rates here are per person 5–14, not per 1,000 persons 5–14, for the purpose of scaling coefficients.

The full set of fixed effects for 5 time periods and 20 countries was not used in the growth regressions. Including those 25 variables added little insight, and made the whole growth equation only marginally significant.

APPENDIX TABLE E5. *Cumulative Growth Effects of Raising Social Transfers above Ten Percent of GDP, 1962–1995*

| | Equations from Table E2 | | | |
| | Equation (2) Quadratic | | Equation (3) Cubic | |
In the 1962–1981 Sample	Log Effect	*p*-Value	Log Effect	*p*-Value
Cum. effect from 10% to 15% transfers	0.0018	(.068)[a]	0.0018	(.065)[a]
Cum. effect from 10% to 20% transfers	0.0039	(.016)*	0.0034	(.055)[a]
Cum. effect from 10% to 25% transfers	0.0063	(.007)**	0.0059	(.011)*
Cum. effect from 10% to 33% transfers	0.0108	(.026)*	0.0147	(.062)[a]

| | Equations from Table E4 | | | |
| | Equation (2) Quadratic | | Equation (3) Cubic | |
In the 1978–1995 sample	Log Effect	*p*-Value	Log Effect	*p*-Value
Cum. effect from 10% to 15% transfers	0.0010	(.888)	−0.0079	(.477)
Cum. effect from 10% to 20% transfers	−0.0008	(.943)	−0.0085	(.506)
Cum. effect from 10% to 25% transfers	−0.0054	(.663)	−0.0112	(.395)
Cum. effect from 10% to 33% transfers	−0.0186	(.322)	−0.0434	(.168)

| | Equation (4) from Table E4 cubic, adjusted for Sweden-Finland in the Early 1990s | |
In the 1978–1995 sample, continued	Log Effect	*p*-Value
Cum. effect from 10% to 15% transfers	0.0013	(.906)
Cum. effect from 10% to 20% transfers	−0.0037	(.776)
Cum. effect from 10% to 25% transfers	−0.0045	(.743)
Cum. effect from 10% to 33% transfers	0.0295	(.441)

Notes to Appendix Table E5:
These are the equations graphed in Figure 18.1 of Chapter 18.
** =significant at the 1% level, two-tail; * =significant at the 5% level; [a]significant at the 7% level; [b]significant at the 10% level.

APPENDIX TABLE E6. *Regression Equations for Employment, Unemployment and Productivity, 1978/80–1993/95*

	Equation (1) ln(Employment/Pop.)		Equation (2) Unemployment Rate		Equation (3) ln(GDP/Employ.) (Productivity)	
	Coeff.	|t|	Coeff.	|t|	Coeff.	|t|
Prim. + sec. enrollments/5–14s, 10 years earlier	.000067	(1.34)	−.000001	(0.07)	.00000	(0.38)
University enrollments/5–14s, 10 years earlier	−.00033	(1.77)	.000053	(0.65)	.0016	(6.15)**
Population under 15 as a share of total pop.	.0022	(0.49)	−.0013	(0.67)	−.0259	(3.69)**
Population over 65 as a share of total pop.	.0197	(3.63)**	−.0043	(1.76)[b]	.0028	(0.30)
Inflation – unemployment, all OECD	.0054	(4.33)**	−.0042	(6.72)**	.0068	(2.93)**
Inflation + unemployment, all OECD	−.0066	(3.80)**	.0049	(5.36)**	−.0129	(3.66)**
Corporatism	.0289	(2.25)*	−.0174	(3.37)**	−.0199	(0.92)
Active labor market programs (ALMP)	−.0284	(2.27)*	.0180	(3.16)**	.0391	(1.91)[a]
No data available on ALMP	−.0115	(0.97)	.00080	(0.14)	.0622	(2.76)**
Employee protection laws	−.0040	(0.46)	.00284	(0.73)	−.0005	(0.31)
Three years earlier	−.0278	(3.39)**	.0058	(1.53)	−.0331	(2.30)[b]
Unemployment compensation support ratio	−.0016	(0.93)	.0009	(1.40)	.00030	(0.11)
Squared	.0000016	(0.05)	−.000008	(0.64)	.000031	(0.63)
Constant term	−.6577	(3.70)	.0776	(1.05)	11.154	(40.6)
Buse R sq., equation F-statistic	.475	8.780	.563	12.505	.532	10.999
Mean of the dependent variable	−0.453		0.075		10.521	
Effect of a permanent tightening of employee protection laws, by 1 index point	−0.032	(3.40)**	0.0086	(2.41)*	−0.034	(2.52)*
Effect of raising the unemployment compensation support ratio from 5% to 20%	−0.0231	(1.48)	0.011	(1.79)[b]	0.016	(0.64)
Effect of raising the unemployment compensation support ratio from 5% to 40%	−0.0528	(1.97)*	0.020	(1.90)[a]	0.059	(1.46)
DW	1.141		1.665		1.136	

Notes to Table E6:

** =significant at the 1% level, two-tail; * =significant at the 5% level; [a]significant at the 7% level; [b]significant at the 10% level.

These three equations probably still contain some serial correlation even after the first-order rho adjustment. The second-stage Durbin–Watson statistics are 1.15, 1.52, and 1.13, respectively. This suggests that the confidence intervals may be too optimistic (understated).

These three equations omitted fixed country effects.

Ethnic fractionalization = an index based on tribal, religious, and linguistic groups around 1960, as developed in (USSR, State Geological Committee, 1964). Its average value = .229 in both samples. For alternative indices of ethnic fractionalization, see Taylor and Hudson (1972).

Corporatism is a crude index of national-level institutions negotiating pay, employment, and government fiscal policies among organized representatives of labor, business, and government. Use of indexes from Bruno and Sachs (1985) and Schmitter (1981) suggests that Corporatism = 4.0 for Austria, Netherlands, Norway, and Sweden; 3.0 for Denmark and West Germany; 2.5 for Finland; 2.0 for Belgium and Switzerland; 1.5 for Japan; 0.5 for Italy and New Zealand; and 0.0 for all other countries. Gayle Allard's PhD thesis (2003) has since improved on these measures and made them into time-series.

Military expenditures as a percentage of GDP are from the SIPRI *Yearbooks*. Its average = 3.1 percent for the 1962–1981 sample and 2.7 percent for the 1978–1995 sample.

Openness to foreign trade = (imports + exports) as a percentage of GDP, at current international prices, from Penn World Tables. Average openness = 53.2 for 1962–1981 and 62.5 for 1978–1995.

Independent Variables in the Growth Equations (Tables E2, E4, 18.2, and 18.3):
The *shortfall in GDP/capita 10 years earlier* = the natural log of (U.S. GDP per capita/this country's GDP per capita) in international dollars, lagged ten years. It comes from the Penn World Tables sources cited above. Its mean = 0.539 in the 1962–1981 sample and 0.430 in the 1978–1995 sample.

Capital formation/capita, 1 year earlier = the value, in 1980 or 1985 international dollars, of gross private capital formation one year earlier, divided by the current (not earlier) total population. Its mean value = 1.82 (thousand 1980 international dollars) in the 1962–1981 sample and $3,142 (1985 international dollars) in the 1978–1995 sample.

Capital formation/capita, 10 years earlier = same thing, lagged ten years. Its mean values in the two samples were 1.201 (thousand dollars/capita) and $1,800 per capita.

Primary and secondary enrollments in ratio to the population of the five to fourteen age group, ten years earlier, are taken from OECD publications and a range of the Brian Mitchell volumes on historical statistics. For 1962–1981 this had a mean value of 0.638 enrolled students per child five to fourteen versus 1032 students per 1000 children five to fourteen in 1978–1995.

University enrollments per child of the five to fourteen age group, ten years earlier, comes from the same sources. For 1962–1981 this had a mean value of 0.041 enrolled university students per child five to fourteen versus 77.3 university students per 1000 children five to fourteen in 1978–1995.

Global demand shock = Inflation − unemployment, for all countries in the sample. Inflation averaged 5.7 in 1962–1981 and 6.4 percent in 1978–1995. Unemployment averaged 3.9 in the first period and 7 percent of the labor force in the latter period. Thus the averages for global demand shock were 1.8 and −0.6, respectively.

Global supply shock = Inflation + unemployment, for all countries in the sample. Thus the averages for global supply shock were 9.6 in the first sample period and 13.4 in the second period.

Additional variables based on the Gayle Allard (2003) data set:

- Employment as a share of the total population
- Standardized OECD unemployment rate
- GDP per worker, in 1985 international dollars, from Penn World Tables 5.2 and 6.0 and from the OECD. For Germany 1978–1995, this was estimated as (France's GDP/worker) × (Germany/France ratio of GDP per capita) × (France/Germany ratio of the employment rates)
- Net (of taxes) *replacement rate* for unemployment compensation, as a percentage of the median wage
- *Net reservation wage* = net replacement rate × coverage rate × take-up rate × years of benefits' duration, as a percentage
- *Coordination* in bargaining = an index of the extent that wages and other economic indicators are collectively bargained at the national level. See Allard (2003)
- Employee protection laws = strictness of laws forbidding or inhibiting layoffs (0–5 scale)
- *Public employment* as a share of total employment
- OECD index of *product regulation* in seven sectors (gas, electricity, postal service, telecommunications, air transport, railways, and road freight). An index of 6 = most restrictive and 0 = free competition. The underlying source is Nicoletti et al. (2000).

Appendix F

Social Transfers circa 1990 versus History

APPENDIX TABLE F1. *Pensions and Total Social Transfers as a Percentage of GDP, the Earlier History versus Transition and Developing Countries, 1980s–1990s*

Country	Year	(1985 $ int'l) GDP/Cap	Elderly Share	Total Social Transfers as % of GDP	Pensions as a % of GDP	Nonpension Transfers as a % of GDP
Japan	1880	602	5.6	0.1	0.0	0.1
Japan	1910	955	5.4	0.2	0.0	0.2
Japan	1930	1,356	4.8	0.2	0.0	0.2
Japan	1960	2,954	5.7	4.0	1.4	2.7
Japan	1970	7,307	7.1	5.7	1.2	4.5
Japan	1980	10,072	9.0	8.2	2.9	5.3
Japan	1990	14,331	12.0	9.5	3.9	5.6
Japan	1995	15,099	14.2	12.1	5.3	6.8
Sweden	1880	1,613	5.9	0.7	0.0	0.7
Sweden	1910	2,604	8.4	1.0	0.0	1.0
Sweden	1930	3,440	9.2	2.6	0.6	2.0
Sweden	1960	7,592	12.0	10.8	4.4	6.4
Sweden	1970	10,766	13.7	16.8	6.2	10.5
Sweden	1980	12,456	16.3	28.2	11.2	17.0
Sweden	1990	14,762	17.8	30.9	12.4	18.6

Sweden	1995	15,544	17.3	30.8	14.8	16.0
USA	1880	2,823	3.4	0.3	0.0	0.3
USA	1910	4,394	4.3	0.6	0.0	0.6
USA	1930	5,499	5.4	0.6	0.0	0.6
USA	1960	9,895	9.2	7.3	4.2	3.1
USA	1970	12,963	9.8	10.4	5.3	5.1
USA	1980	15,295	11.2	10.9	5.0	5.9
USA	1990	18,054	12.4	11.3	4.8	6.5
USA	1995	19,474	12.6	13.0	5.2	7.9
Bangladesh	1990	887	3.4		0.0	
China	1990	1,648	5.6		2.6	
India	1990	1,264	4.3	1.9	0.6	1.3
Indonesia	1990	1,974	3.9	0.6	0.1	0.5
Malaysia (central gov't only)	1990	5,124	3.7	2.6	1.6	1.0
Pakistan	1990	1,496	2.9		0.6	
Philippines	1990	1,763	3.3	1.1	0.6	0.5
Singapore	1990	11,710	5.6	1.4	2.2	−0.8
Sri Lanka	1990	2,003	5.2	5.3	2.2	3.1
Thailand	1989	3,580	4.3	11.1	0.0	11.1
Taiwan*	1990	8,063	6.2		0.0	
Argentina	1987	4,706	8.9	6.5	4.6	1.9
Bolivia cent.	1990	1,658	3.6	3.3	1.5	1.8
Brazil	1990	4,042	4.3		2.9	
Chile	1988	4,338	6.1	9.9	5.7	4.2
Colombia	1990	3,300	4.2		0.8	
Costa Rica	1989	3,300	4.2	10.9	3.7	7.2
Ecuador	1990	2,755	4.1	1.9	1.1	0.8
Guatemala (central gov't only)	1989	2,127	3.2	1.8	1.5	0.3

(continued)

APPENDIX TABLE F1 (*continued*)

Country	Year	(1985 $ int'l) GDP/Cap	Elderly Share	Total Social Transfers as % of GDP	Pensions as a % of GDP	Nonpension Transfers as a % of GDP
Mexico (central gov't only)	1990	5,827	4.0	2.7	1.0	1.7
Panama	1990	2,888	5.0	9.8	5.1	4.7
Uruguay	1990	4,602	11.6	14.2	8.8	5.4
Venezuela	1990	6,055	3.6		0.5	
Egypt	1990	2,620	4.0	4.4	3.0	1.4
Israel	1990	9,298	9.1	14.5	4.3	10.2
Jordan	1990	3,829	2.7	7.5	0.3	7.2
Morocco	1990	2,257	3.8	2.4	1.2	1.2
Syria	1990	3,474	2.7	0.9	0.3	0.6
Tunisia	1990	3,363	4.0	7.0	2.5	4.5
Turkey	1990	3,741	4.3	1.0	2.4	−1.4
Armenia	1990	2,113	5.6		3.6	
Azerbaijan	1990	2,240	4.8		5.6	
Bulgaria	1987–1988	4,973	12.1	11.3	7.7	3.6
Bulgaria	1993	3,098	13.9	10.4	9.6	0.8
Czech Rep.	1987–1988	6,840	12.0		8.0	
Czech Rep.	1989	6,597	12.3	17.5		
Czech Rep.	1993	5,692	12.6	19.9	8.0	11.9
Czech Rep.	1995	6,252	12.6	20.5		
Estonia	1987–1988	7,853	11.4	10.8	6.9	3.9
Estonia	1993	8,398	12.4	9.8	5.6	4.2
Georgia	1990	2,088	9.3		11.0	
Hungary	1987–1988	4,973	12.8		9.0	
Hungary	1989	5,019	13.1	19.8		
Hungary	1993	4,572	13.7	32.5	10.4	22.1
Hungary	1995	4,702	14.0	31.8		
Kyrgyz Rep.	1987–1988	2,391	5.1		6.8	

Kyrgyz Rep.	1993	1,754	5.5		7.2	
Poland	1987–1988	4,014	9.7		7.1	
Poland	1989	4,525	10.0	10.0		
Poland	1993	3,770	10.7	24.8	14.8	10.0
Poland	1995	4,079	11.0	25.8		
Romania	1987–1988	3,211	9.9	9.4	3.9	5.5
Romania	1993	2,109	11.2	9.0	6.8	2.2
Russia	1987–1988	6,247	9.8	7.9	6.2	1.7
Russia	1992	4,827	10.8	9.1		
Russia	1993	3,807	11.2	12.0	7.2	4.8
Russia	1994	3,533	11.6	18.1		
Russia	1995	3,386	12.0	15.4		
Slovenia	1987–1988	6,350	10.6	11.1	8.7	2.4
Slovenia	1993	7,320	11.9	16.3	13.0	3.3
Ukraine	1987–1988	4,642	11.7	9.5	7.9	1.6
Ukraine	1993	3,359	13.3	8.2	7.1	1.1
Uzbekistan	1987–1988	2,199	4.2	9.3	5.4	3.9
Uzbekistan	1993	2,333	4.2	12.5	9.2	3.3

Sources and notes to Figures 9.2–9.5 and to Appendix Table F1:

*from Kuo (1999), not the sources cited below.

The GDP per capita figures are based on the Penn World Tables 5.6 values in international dollars of 1985. The 1995 values for Japan, Sweden, and the USA are spliced to this from PWT 6.0 at 1990. The 1880–1930 figures for the same three countries are hooked from Maddison (1995) to PWT 5.6 at 1960. For the republics of the former Soviet Union, a 1992 splice to the USA was used and scaled back to the USA GDP per capita in 1990. The sources for total social transfers in the OECD countries are Lindert (1994) for 1880–1930, OECD (1985) for 1960 and 1970, and OECD (1998) for 1980–1995. For the Third World countries, the source is IMF, *Government Finance Statistical Yearbook*, series on central and local government expenditures on health, social security, and welfare. The estimates for the Czech Republic, Hungary, and Poland are from Kramer (1997, 73), and those for Russia 1992–1995 are from Åslund (1997, 138).The estimates for Bulgaria, Estonia, Kyrgyz Republic, Romania, Ukraine, and Uzbekistan, and for Russia 1987–88, are from Subbarao et al. (1997, 40). This last source disagrees with Kramer and Åslund on the shares for the Czech Republic, Hungary, Poland, and Russia for 1993. Caution: The total transfer shares come from different sources than the pension shares. One should not estimate nonpension social transfers by subtracting pensions from the totals given here. For example, in the cases of Singapore and Turkey, the IMF's *Government Finance Statistics* give less total social transfers than the public pensions recorded in World Bank (1994, 360).

197

Appendix G

Postregression Accounting Formulae

To judge how large or small are the various influences on any dependent variable requires postregression accounting. In the simplest variant, one easily decomposes any difference in the dependent variable into predicted differences and an error term. The predicted differences are sums of individual terms for each causal influence, where each term is a coefficient times the observed difference in that independent variable. The decomposition allows one to explain historical and comparative international stories, with leading roles for some forces and smaller roles for others. I have used this straightforward approach in earlier writings. Chapter 16's treatment of the 1880–1930 period gave results that were not far from this simple approach.[1]

The accounting and storytelling become more complicated when the regression equation involves the lagged dependent variable as an independent variable, with only a short lag. In this case the straightforward approach will typically give the lion's share of the causal credit to that lagged dependent variable. Such a result generates a boring tale: The dependent variable is different between countries this year because it was different last year. To add insight to the tale, one must decompose that short-lagged value of the dependent variable into the earlier forces that determined it. That leads to a plodding algebraic journey into the history of each variable.

The journey into the determinants of earlier behavior sometimes cannot be avoided, and Chapter 17 is such a case. Much as one might want to avoid including a lagged dependent variable in a regression, the historical realities explored in this book require its inclusion, especially in the equations for social transfers from the postwar era. There is a lot of momentum in social spending or in GDP from one period to the next. I have experimented with some simplifying assumptions to clean up the accounting algebra, such as the steady-state assumption that eventually the current and lagged dependent variable will converge to the same rate of change. The assumptions fail to honor the goal of showing what drove what in real history. There is no alternative to using an approach that decomposes the value of any dependent variable – social spending, school enrollments, GDP growth, employment, unemployment, or productivity – into period-specific behavior plus a lagged dependent-variable term that is pushed as far as possible back into the past. This appendix develops the formulae used in Chapters 15–17.

The postregression accounting starts from an already-fitted regression equation with the general form

$$Y_t = a_0 + a_1 Y_{t-1} + a_2 X_t + e_t,$$

where Y is the dependent variable (say, social spending/GDP), X is the whole vector of independent variables other than the lagged dependent variable, the as are regression coefficients, and e is the error term. The subscripts are time periods going backward from the latest time period t.

The reason we cannot just take differences in this regression equation to decompose changes in Y into separate causal roles plus an error term has already been mentioned. In practice, the coefficient a_1 is often so close to one that its term gets most of the explanatory credit. We need to press on, replacing Y_{t-1} with an expression giving the lagged Xs more credit. Substituting for Y_{t-1} yields

$$Y_t = a_0 + \quad a_2 X_t + e_t,$$
$$+ a_1 a_0 + a_1^2 Y_{t-2} + a_1 a_2 X_{t-1} + a_1 e_{t-1}.$$

This first substitution has succeeded in shrinking the less informative lagged-Y term, because a_1 is typically less than one, so that its squared value is smaller still. Yet we need to press on with further substitutions for lagged Ys, to give a still longer history of the X's its due explanatory credit.

Substituting for Y_{t-2} yields

$$Y_t = a_0 + \quad a_2 X_t + e_t,$$
$$+ a_1 a_0 + \quad a_1 a_2 X_{t-1} + a_1 e_{t-1}$$
$$+ a_1^2 a_0 + a_1^3 Y_{t-3} + a_1^2 a_2 X_{t-2} + a_1^2 e_{t-2}.$$

Combining the substitutions for Y_{t-3} and Y_{t-4} yields the formula that accounts for the level of Y in terms of five periods of history $(t, t-1, \ldots, t-4)$ and the long-ago value of the dependent variable Y_{t-5}:

$$Y_t = a_0 \qquad + a_2 X_t \qquad + e_t,$$
$$+ a_1 a_0 \quad + a_1 a_2 X_{t-1} + a_1 e_{t-1}$$
$$+ a_1^2 a_0 \quad + a_1^2 a_2 X_{t-2} + a_1^2 e_{t-2}$$
$$+ a_1^3 a_0 \quad + a_1^3 a_2 X_{t-3} + a_1^3 e_{t-3}$$
$$+ a_1^4 a_0 \quad + a_1^4 a_2 X_{t-4} + a_1^4 e_{t-4} + a_1^5 Y_{t-5}.$$

The central column of terms involving the Xs represents the explanatory power of the history of the independent variables. The less informative lagged term has shrunken in size because a_1^5 is a dwindling fraction. This formula is used for a five-period history. To a longer history one goes on adding the appropriate terms implied by this sequence. While it is tedious to write out the formulae, the task is manageable on a spreadsheet.

To account for the observed international differences in Period t, such as 1930 in Chapter 16 or 1978–1981 in Chapter 17, we first pick a base country. In Chapter 16 that is France, and in Tables 17.2–17.6 of Chapter 17 it is the United States. We can use the formula just given, with two simple substitutions. First, we imagine that each Y or X now has the additional subscript $_{ij}$, representing a difference between country i and country j, where j is the comparison-base country (France or the United States, in these examples). Second, we drop all the terms involving a_0, since these fixed terms drop out.

To account for observed changes over time requires subtracting an equation for earlier levels from the equation just given for Yt. Whether one wants long-run changes or short-run changes depends on the question being asked. If one wanted to look at historical changes in each country's experiences over the five periods from $t-4$ to t, then one could subtract

$$Y_{t-4} = a_0 + a_1\, Y_{t-5} + a_2\, X_{t-4} + e_{t-4}$$

from the long expression above. Again, the result is a decomposition of changes in Y into the effects of the levels of Xs, a lagged Y_{t-5} term, and an error term.

Notes

Chapter 13

1. Olson (2000, 66). Olson's sagely statement comes, however, after he has carica-
turized the Becker and Coase models somewhat in the preceding pages (45–66).
Olson accuses their frameworks of implying that the political process is Pareto
optimal, Panglossian, and Utopian. I do not read either Becker or Coase that
way. The Becker (1983, 1985) and Becker–Mulligan (1998) predictions about
how pressure group competition can cut deadweight costs seem no more as-
sertive about correction mechanisms than Hirschman's *Exit, Voice and Loyalty*
(1970), which similarly described the search for organizational correctives that
work only crudely and partially.

   Perhaps Olson's criticism was sharpened by his desire to turn our attention to
autocracies and other cases where few have voice and the result is economically
inefficient. I too dwell on such cases elsewhere (Chapters 5, 7, and 15–17 of
this book, and Lindert (2003)), but read the Becker model as applying to more
competitive democracies.
2. For examples of top-down modeling with emphasis on autocracy, see McGuire
and Olson (1996), Niskanen (1997), and Olson (2000). For greater emphasis
on pressure-group competition, see Olson (1965), Peltzman (1980), Meltzer and
Richard (1981), Becker (1983, 1985), and Becker and Mulligan (1998). For a
mathematical survey of political economics, see Persson and Tabellini (2000).
3. The modeling in this section draws mainly on the collaboration of Lorenzo
Kristov and Rob McClellend, as published in Kristov et al. (1992, 137–149).
4. Ordeshook (1986, 129).
5. Some of the signs within this expression are given by a side-result ruling out
an activist's spending resources in favor of both sides. See Kristov et al. (1992,
139).
6. Kristov et al. (1992, 142–145).
7. Other things equal, that is. The ability of the poor – or anybody else outside the
political arena – still depends on the self-interests and concerns of those who
remain in the arena. We return to this when discussing the treatment of outsiders
in this chapter. The corresponding point was noted in the early history of poor

relief, where the enfranchised wealthy of England before the 1830s had their own reasons for backing greater taxes to relieve the poor.

8. Becker and Mulligan (1998).
9. Olson (1965).
10. Baldwin and Robert-Nicoud (2002).
11. U.S. Census Bureau (2001, 360–361).
12. Corneo and Grüner (2000, forthcoming), Luttmer (2001), and Alesina et al. (2001).
13. Easterly and Levine (1997); Alesina, Baqir, and Easterly (1999); Alesina et al. (2001).
14. Corneo and Grüner (2000).
15. Kristov et al. (1992). See also Chapter 7's discussion of the intermobility evidence.
16. Ramsey (1927). The Ramsey rule is more specific, and has more applications, than shown here. See Atkinson and Stiglitz (1980, 370–376) and Persson and Tabellini (2000, Part IV).
17. This efficiency of fuller franchise corresponds in some ways to the McGuire–Olson model of the encompassing interest of either a secure autocrat (their "stationary bandit") or their encompassing democracy. See McGuire and Olson (1996).
18. See the NBER Working Paper version of Lindert (2003) for the tests.

Chapter 14

1. Similar patterns were obtained from the modest sample of nineteen countries in the two years 1930 and 1960. These are omitted here because of the small sample size. For what the 1930–1960 results are worth, they confirm the strong positive influences of income and of population aging on all types of social transfers.
2. Though the second OECD data set begins with 1980, it seemed reasonable to fashion a set of three-year averages for 1978–1980, by ratio-splicing each old and new series at the year 1980. I balked at extending this spliced series back to 1962 or 1960, however, since that would put too much strain on the hybrid nature of the combined longer-run series.
3. For a sampling of the rich comparative literature on postwar social spending, see Wilensky (1975, 2000), Pampel and Williamson (1989), Esping-Andersen (1990), Hicks and Misra (1993), Lindert (1996), MacFarlan and Oxley (1996), Commander et al. (1997), Hicks (1999, Ch. 6), and Kuo (1999). See also the survey of the political economy literature on this and related topics by Persson and Tabellini (2000, Parts II and III).
4. Rodrik (1997, 1998) and Kuo (1999). While I did not test the openness effect in the 1880–1930 sample, Michael Huberman and Wayne Lewchuk (2003) have confirmed such an effect with a similar prewar sample.
5. Since the OECD data on the stock of fixed nonhuman capital do not cover five of the countries in this chapter's postwar sample, the capital stock had to be proxied by prior real capital formation per capita of (current) population.
6. Hicks (1999, Ch. 6). Hicks did allow corporatism, a strong correlate of Left government and union power over the long run, to remain as an independent

variable in regressions for social transfers. One can take any of several stands on the endogeneity or exogeneity of corporatism. I prefer to omit the link from corporatism to social transfers since both are often part of the same political bargain. Instead, I use corporatism as an influence on economic growth, as shown on the right side of Figure 14.1, though its presence or absence does not affect any main conclusion of this book.

7. Some have argued that non-Parliamentary governments reflect a history of pop-ular suspicion of big government. Some countries opted for a system of checks and balances that institutionalized veto power over the actions of any branch. It is plausible to expect such countries to adopt smaller government budgets, as shown by evidence in a recent cross-sectional study of countries around the globe (Persson et al. 2000). Unfortunately, part of the price of the higher quality of OECD data is that our OECD samples contain only two non-Parliamentary cases, Switzerland and the United States, making it hard to isolate any effect of non-Parliamentary government on social spending.

8. Fogel (1964).

Chapter 15

1. Easterlin (1981).
2. The three extra countries of the twenty-four-country sample are Germany, Switzerland, and Thailand.
3. The 1880–1930 regressions and the 1881–1937 regressions differ in one respect: The former, in Appendix D, include the lagged dependent variable, namely the enrollment rate or teacher supply per child ten years earlier. While the lagged term was omitted in the 1881–1937 regressions summarized in Table 15.1, its exclusion makes little difference to the qualitative conclusions about the other influences, as should be evident from comparisons with Appendix D.
4. See Lindert (1978, Chapters 6, 7).
5. See Appendix Table D2, Equation (4).
6. The university enrollment data are not specific to public institutions. Private universities and private tuition endowments tended to dominate more before 1930 than in the postwar era.
7. Engerman et al. (1998).
8. The democracy and voting effects featured here were enhanced by the inclusion of fixed-time and fixed-country effects. Without the fixed effects, the democracy effects were smaller but clearly nonzero. The contrast between the strong slope above a 40-percent voting share and the weaker or absent slope in the less democratic range is also independent of the inclusion of fixed effects.

    Unlike the democracy and voting effects, other variables had their coefficients reduced by the inclusion of fixed effects. See Lindert (2001).
9. McGuire and Olson (1996).
10. Psacharapoulos and Woodhall (1990) survey the rate-of-return literature world-wide.
11. In 1998, for example, taxpayers paid for over three-quarters of primary and secondary educational expenditures in every OECD country. The same does not hold for tertiary education, of course. Private funds paid for over half of tertiary

education in Japan, Korea, and the United States and almost a quarter of tertiary funding for the OECD as a whole (OECD, 2001).

12. In defining the school-age population it is important to choose the same age range for all countries, even though the number of years spent in primary school may vary. Choosing almost any age group in the under-twenty range gives the same comparative results if applied consistently.

    Instead of GDP per capita, a more appropriate denominator might be the average income per adult, a measure of society's effort to raise the knowledge of individual children relative to society's ability to pay. But data on conventional GDP per capita are more abundant.

13. Note the difference in denominators: higher education per *pupil*, but primary education per *child of primary-school age*. The intent here is to omit the university-age population not receiving higher education, to better isolate the rates of public subsidy to the truly privileged, while weighing down the support measure for primary education by including those who received none. In this way, we make the ratio a stiffer test of true bias in favor of the privileged.

14. Tan and Mingat (1992); Drèze and Sen (1995); World Bank (1997); PROBE Team (1999); World Bank (2000); Mehrotra and Delamonica, submitted; Mehrotra et al., submitted.

15. Tan and Mingat (1992, 144–5).

16. Macauley did not equivocate about English superiority and the need to concentrate on training rulers, not masses:

> I have no knowledge of either Sanscrit or Arabic. But . . . a single shelf of a good European library [is] worth the whole native literature of India or Arabic. . . . In India, English is the language spoken by the ruling class. . . .
>
>   [I]t is impossible for us, with our limited means, to attempt to educate the body of the people. We must at present do our best to form a class who may be interpreters between us and the millions whom we govern – a class of persons Indian in blood and colour, but English in tastes, in opinions, in morals and in intellect.

(As reprinted in Zastoupil and Moir (1999, 165–6, 169, and 171.)

17. Nurullah and Naik (1964, Chapter 10).

18. Kearney (1987), Weiner (1987, 80).

19. Weiner (1987, 41).

20. Kearney (1987, Table 3.9, on 101); Weiner (1987, 52).

21. Jackman and Miller (forthcoming, Chapter 1).

22. For the most recent measurement of the educational gaps by caste, tribe, gender, income class, and state, see World Bank (1997, 112–141).

Chapter 16

1. The current research project of Jari Eloranta has been gathering the data on military expenditures. The 1920–1938 part of the military expenditure story is detailed in Eloranta (2002, including a CD-Rom giving detailed numbers).

2. See Lindert (1994, 4–5 and 21–22).

3. Huberman and Lewchuk (2003). While I might have included the same openness variable in the analysis here, it was one variable I did not have at hand when performing the tests for this chapter. Given the Huberman–Lewchuk result and

the openness results I report in Chapter 17, I assume that openness was a significant force hiding in the error term in the regressions reported in Table 16.1 and Appendix Table D.3.

4. The twenty-one countries are, again, Argentina, Australia, Austria, Belgium, Brazil, Canada, Denmark, Finland, France, Greece, Italy, Japan, Mexico, Netherlands, New Zealand, Norway, Portugal, Spain, Sweden, the United Kingdom, and the United States.

5. Note that the key parameters b and s are true to the functional form of the equation used in Table 16.1 and in Appendix D. One might have been tempted to use an elasticity of the support ratio with respect to the elderly share, which conventional definitions for elasticities might have set equal to

Elasticity $Es = \partial s / \partial$ (N_{old}/N) divided by $S/(N_{old}/N)$.

This elasticity would translate into $(b - 1)$, and would be negative in all cases. Yet the slope s seems preferable to the elasticity Es, which answers a different question. Here we seek to answer the slope question "How does a rise in the share of the total population that is over sixty-five affect the support ratio?" The elasticity would answer the different question "How does a rise in the elderly share of the population by 100 percent of itself raise affect the ratio of the support ratio to the elderly share of the population?" The latter can be a negative number, but the former question is true to the fitted functional form and to the theoretical specification of Chapter 13.

6. Perhaps regime insecurity leads to more social transfers, without more taxes, and therefore to greater central-government budget deficits. The overall surplus or deficit has not been studied here, however.

7. See Chapter 3 on the limited amounts of church aid given earlier.

8. Wilensky, in Flora and Heidenheimer (1981, 362–8).

9. The one prewar case in which a Catholic country broke out of the low-spending mold was the Irish Free State. Timothy Guinnane (1993) has offered what is probably the correct explanation for the exceptionalism of the Irish Free State. Independent Ireland inherited Britain's pension system, which gave comparable pensions in Ireland and Britain, despite the gap in average incomes. The new government could not resist pressure to maintain such levels of pension support, even though they required a higher share of national product than even in Britain.

10. For a characteristically spirited summary of the McCloskey critique, see McCloskey and Ziliak (1996).

11. Readers can derive additional international contrasts from the data in Table 16.2. First, any two countries can be contrasted for 1930 by subtracting one relative-to-France column from another. Second, one can derive the implicit full set of contrasts for 1880. With B = France and A = any other country, each implicit 1880 contrast $(B_{1880} - A_{1880})$ equals $(A_{1930} - A_{1880}) - (B_{1930} - B_{1880}) + (B_{1930} - A_{1930})$. All three differences on the right-hand side appear in Table 16.2.

Chapter 17

1. Similar patterns were obtained from the modest sample of nineteen countries in the two years 1930 and 1960. These are omitted here because of the small sample

size. For what the 1930–1960 results are worth, they confirm the strong positive influences of income and of population aging on all types of social transfers.

2. Wolfinger and Rosenstone (1980), Teixeira (1987).

3. Age effects took center stage in Wilensky (1975), Pampel and Williamson (1989), Hicks and Misra (1993), Lindert (1996), Hicks (1999, Ch. 6), and Kuo (1999), at least.

4. By contrast, Gayle Allard (2003) finds that an older society offers more generous parameters of unemployment entitlements, even holding constant some worker attributes and the state of the economy.

5. As one can find in Appendices D and E, two different approaches were taken to measuring the lagged share of total social transfers. For the 1880–1930 and the 1962–1981 regressions, the lagged value is a predicted value, to cut the role of serial correlation. In the 1978–1995 sample, the lagged value is just the observed value. The coefficients do differ, whether due to the change in measure or due to the change in sample. In either case, the role of momentum is clear enough.

6. Easterly and Levine (1997); Alesina et al. (1999, 2001).

7. Rodrik (1997a, Ch. 4).

8. Kuo (1999) tests the openness hypothesis using five different measures of openness, in a pooled global sample of fifty-three countries. His results show mixed support for a positive effect of openness on social spending.

9. For easier comparison of coefficients and impacts across equations, I decided to use lagged social transfers (divided by GDP) as the lagged dependent variable in all cases. The usual alternative would have been to use lagged pensions in the pension equation, lagged health care spending in the health care spending equation, and so forth. The qualitative results should come out much the same.

Chapter 18

1. Lucas (2003, 2–3), citing Prescott (2002) and the sources cited in the next footnote. Emphasis in the original.

2. The crucial role of theorizing to get the result is evident enough in the titles of the studies Lucas cited in support of his first result:

    "The Analysis of Macroeconomic Policies in Perfect Foresight Equilibrium" (Brock and Turnovsky 1981); "The Welfare Cost of Capital Income Taxation in a Growing Economy" (Chamley 1981); "Capital Taxation and Accumulation in a Life Cycle Growth Model" (Summers 1981); "The Welfare Cost of Factor Taxation in a Perfect Foresight Model" (Judd 1987); and *Dynamic Fiscal Policy* (Auerbach and Kotlikoff 1987).

    Prescott (2002) used similar material to fashion the second result cited by Lucas.

3. The hung-jury verdict emerges from the summaries by Easterly and Rebelo (1993), Slemrod (1995), Agell et al. (1997, 1999), and Atkinson (1999). For a guilty verdict, arguing that government taxation (and by implication transfers) would cut GDP, see Folster and Henrekson (1999).

4. Furthermore, one of the studies finding a negative effect is based on only thirteen observations, and another shows effects on private output, not counting increases in social-program public outputs, such as public health services.

Another recent study finding a significant effect of taxes on growth is Padovano and Galli (2001), who examined behavior of OECD countries in the 1960s–1980s. Padovano and Galli identify separate overall marginal tax rates for each country, with adjustments for known tax reforms. These marginal rates have negative signs in conventional growth equations. Their procedure is subject to the limitations mentioned in the text. In particular, their handling of the tax–income relationship is hard to interpret. If an exogenous hike in tax revenues affects GDP in the same period, as they seem to imply, this feedback complicates the initial estimation of the marginal tax rate. By the time this possibly biased tax rate has competed with prior GDP itself in an equation determining the growth rate of GDP, the true effect of an exogenous raising of tax revenues or tax rates eludes identification.

5. See Appendix Table D.2, Equation (6).
6. See Kuo (1999).
7. See OECD (1985). These figures did not allow a separation of noncontributory pensions from the contributory pensions of employees in the public sector. I was able to make that separation, however, in the more detailed OECD social expenditure data series for 1980–1996.
8. See OECD (1999).
9. Generating the three-year averages for 1978–1980 required some limited splicing of 1978–1980 behavior from the early OECD sample to the 1980 level in the newer sample. The later sample could not be extended beyond 1995, because OECD estimates for later years were not sufficiently available in time for this study.
10. I had three reasons for wanting to generalize to the cubic function. First, even if theory were correct about the quadratic form of the GDP costs of each tax-transfer distortion, there is no assurance that these aggregate across taxed and subsidized activities in a way that yields a quadratic GDP cost. Second, I had the hunch that there might be special bends at both the low and the high end of the social-transfers spectrum, and the results in the text will confirm that hunch. Finally, the cubic generalization has served well as a way to capture the shape of the voting-rights effects and population-aging effects in earlier chapters.
11. The first stage equations could be estimated using both the Xs and the Zs in both kinds of first-stage equations. Experimenting with the more restricted form shown in the text made no important difference to any of the results.
12. The Xs correspond to the influences on the right side of Figure 14.1 and the Zs correspond to those on the left side.
13. Sala-i-Martin (1997).
14. For a fuller view of these three side-policies, see Appendix Tables E.2 and E.4.
15. For the fuller equations, again see Appendix Tables E.2 and E.4. Each reference to significant effects in this text paragraph refers to the p-values reported for cumulative growth effects in Appendix Table E.5.
16. To follow the contours of the extra strength of the temporary recession in Sweden and Finland, I constructed a special variable that equaled one-half for either country in the 1990–1992 period and one in the 1993–1995 period. See Equation (4) in Appendix Tables E.4 and E.5.

17. A mirage for Sweden, though not a complete mirage for Finland. Sweden's mirage was dispelled by the strong recovery of economic growth and fuller employment after 1995. Finland recovered less fully and still had 10.2 percent of the labor force out of work in 2000. Part of the incompleteness of Finland's recovery was due to the country's clinging to employee protection laws are generous unemployment benefits, which Sweden had been progressively abandoning. See Chapter 19.
18. Crafts (1997, 81).
19. Nordhaus and Tobin (1972, 9–12 and 38–49).

Chapter 19

1. Labor-demand forces such as the oil shocks will return to the stage once they are interacted with institutional supply-side forces later in this chapter. For a more thorough explanation that features interactions between demand shocks and labor market institutions, see Blanchard and Summers (1986), Blanchard and Wolfers (2000), Blanchard and Portugal (2001), and Allard (2003).
2. Layard and Nickell (1985), Broadberry (1994). Similarly, Sneessens and Drèze (1986), using econometrics, find that, of Belgium's 16 percent rate of registered unemployment, structural mismatch between sectors contributed only 4.5 percent.
3. Allard (2003).
4. The two magnitudes do not align perfectly, if we assume that more generous unemployment compensation does not cut the overall rate of labor force participation. Since most of the labor force is employed, the percentage effect on jobs should be closer to -1 times the effect on the unemployment rate. Yet the confidence intervals of the two estimates are wide enough to make them compatible.
5. Job losses from employment protection laws figure prominently in Flanagan (1988), Buechtmann (1993), Bean (1994), OECD (1994), Scarpetta (1996), Siebert (1997), Nickell (1997), Flanagan (1999).
6. See Allard (2003) for the EPL indexes, an explanation of how they were constructed, and a discussion of the history they reveal.
7. Labor Market Promotion Act (Arbeitsmarktförderungsgesetz).
8. Act on Employment, cited in Lilja et al. (1990, 112–113).
9. Malo and Tohario (1999).
10. *OECD Employment Outlook*, June 1999, Paris, p. 52.
11. Not more than 4 percent because the EPL index only ranges from zero to six, and no country had an index above five. Five times the 0.8 coefficient is a maximum explanatory potential of 4 percent of the labor force.
12. Allard (2003, Ch. 6).
13. See Bertola et al. (2001, Table 10).
14. For an overview and appraisal of ALMP, see Martin (2000), the whole issue of *OECD Studies, no. 31* (2000/2), and Allard (2003, Chs. 5, 6).
15. For a fuller set of regression results, see Allard (2003, Ch. 5).
16. Martin (2000, 93–98).

17. For a summary of corporatism and its apparent effects, see Flanagan (1999).
18. See the series of Freeman's writings on the comparative wage inequality theme, such as Freeman (1994, Chs. 1, 2; 1998).

Appendix B

1. For a fuller version of this appendix, see Lindert (2001, WP 105, Appendix B).
2. Mitchell (1988, 774–775).
3. Mitchell (1988, 798–804).
4. See Sutherland (1973, 350), and U.S. Commissioner of Education (1903, 247).
5. Flora et al. (1983, 183).

Appendix G

1. See Lindert (1994, 1996). For the 1880–1930 sample, Chapter 16 again stuck with the simpler accounting formula that simply left the lagged dependent variable only one period deep, instead of pushing it back to the beginning of the sample data. This caused little interpretive difficulty because the lagged term intruded less on the causal analysis. Its value for social transfers was low, presumably because the observations were fully a decade apart in the 1880–1930 sample.

   For the 1880–1930 period it was necessary to use a tobit regression technique because the dependent variable was often zero. How my accounting dealt with the nonlinearity of the final tobit equation is described in Lindert (1994, Table 4 and surrounding text).

Bibliography

Agell, Jonas, T. Lindh, and H. Ohlsson. 1997. "Growth and the Public Sector: A Critical Review Essay." *European Journal of Political Economy* 13: 33–52.

1999. "Growth and the Public Sector: A Reply." *European Journal of Political Economy* 15: 359–366.

Alesina, Alberto, Reza Baqir, and William Easterly. 1999. "Public Goods and Ethnic Divisions." *Quarterly Journal of Economics* 114, 4 (November): 1243–1284.

Alesina, Alberto, Edward L. Glaeser, and Bruce Sacerdote. 2001. "Why Doesn't the US Have a European-Style Welfare State?" *Brookings Papers on Economic Activity*, no. 2 of 2001: 187–277.

Allard, Gayle. 2003. "Jobs and Labor Market Institutions in the OECD." Doctoral dissertation, University of California – Davis.

Åslund, Anders. 1997. "Social Problems and Policy in Postcommunist Russia." In Ethan B. Kapstein and Michael Mandelbaum (eds.), *Sustaining the Transition: The Social Safety Net in Postcommunist Europe*. New York: Council on Foreign Relations, 124–146.

Atkinson, A. B. 1999. *The Economic Consequences of Rolling Back the Welfare State*. Cambridge, MA: MIT Press.

Atkinson, A. B. and J. E. Stiglitz. 1980. *Lectures on Public Economics*. New York: McGraw-Hill.

Auerbach, Alan J. and Laurence J. Kotlikoff. 1987. *Dynamic Fiscal Policy*. Cambridge: Cambridge University Press.

Austin, A. G. 1976. *Australian Education 1788–1900*, 3rd edition. Westport: Greenwood Press.

Bairoch, Paul. 1968. *The Growth of Population and Its Structure*. Université Libre de Bruxelles.

Baldwin, Richard E. and Frederic Robert-Nicoud. 2002. "Entry and Asymmetric Lobbying: Why Governments Pick Losers." NBER Working Paper 8756 (February).

Balke, Nathan and Robert J. Gordon. 1989. "The Estimation of Prewar National Product: Methodology and New Evidence." *Journal of Political Economy* 97, 1 (February): 38–92.

Bank of Japan. 1966. *Hundred-Year Statistics of the Japanese Economy*. Tokyo.

Banks, Arthur S. 1971. *Cross-Polity Time-Series Data*. Cambridge, MA: MIT Press.

Barcan, Alan. 1980. *A History of Australian Education*. Melbourne: Oxford University Press.

Baxter, R. Dudley. 1868. *The National Income*. London: Macmillan.

Bean, Charles. 1994. "European Unemployment: A Survey," *Journal of Economic Literature*, 32, 2 (June): 573–619.

Becker, Gary S. 1983. "A Theory of Competition among Pressure Groups for Political Influence." *Quarterly Journal of Economics* 98, 3 (August): 371–400.

   1985. "Public Policies, Pressure Groups, and Dead Weight Costs," *Journal of Public Economics*, 28, 3 (December): 329–48.

Becker, Gary S. and Casey B. Mulligan. 1998. "Deadweight Costs and the Size of Government." *NBER Working Paper* 6789 (November).

Belgium, Statistique Générale. Various years. *Annuaire Statistique*.

Bertola, Giuseppe, Francine D. Blau, and Lawrence M. Kahn. 2001. "Comparative Analysis of Labor Market Outcomes: Lessons for the US from International Long-Run Evidence." NBER Working Paper 8526, October.

Bienen, H. and N. van de Walle. 1991. *Of Time and Power: Leadership Duration in the Modern World*. Stanford: Stanford University Press.

Blanchard, Olivier and Pedro Portugal. 2001. "What Lies Behind an Unemployment Rate: Comparing Portuguese and U.S. Labor Markets." *American Economic Review* 91, 1 (March): 187–207.

Blanchard, Olivier and Lawrence Summers. 1986. "Hysteresis and the European Unemployment Problem." *NBER Macroeconomic Annual*.

Blanchard, Olivier and Justin Wolfers. 2000. "The Role of Shocks and Institutions in the Rise of European Unemployment: The Aggregate Evidence," *Economic Journal* 110, 462 (March): C1–C33; and "Data and Appendix." *http://econ-wp.mit.edu/RePEc/2000/blanchar/harry_data/*. Last accessed November 3, 2003.

Bloomfield, G. S. 1984. *New Zealand: A Handbook of Historical Statistics*. Boston: G. K. Hall.

Broadberry, Stephen. 1994. "Employment and Unemployment." In Roderick Floud and D. N. McCloskey (eds.), *The Economic History of Britain since 1700*. Second edition, *Volume 3: 1939–1992*. Cambridge, UK: Cambridge University Press, 195–220.

Brock, William A. and Stephen J. Turnovsky. 1981. "The Analysis of Macroeconomic Policies in Perfect Foresight Equilibrium." *International Economic Review* 22, 1 (February): 179–209.

Browne, G. S. (ed.) 1927. *Education in Australia: A Comparative Study of . . . the Six Australian States*. London: Macmillan.

Bruno, Michael and Jeffrey Sachs. 1985. *Economics of Worldwide Stagflation*. Cambridge, MA: Harvard University Press.

Buechtmann, Christoph (ed.). 1993. *Employment Security and Labor Market Behavior: . . . International Evidence*. Cornell University: ILR Press.

Canada, Dominion Bureau of Statistics. 1921. *Historical Statistical Survey of Education in Canada*. Ottawa: Thomas Mulvey.

Carry, Alain. 1999. *Le compte satellite rétrospectif de l'éducation en France (1820–1996)*. Économies et sociétés, Cahier de l'ISMÉA, Série AF, no. 25 (Fev.-Mar).

Castle, Francis G. and Steve Dowrick. 1990. "The Impact of government Spending Levels on Medium-term Economic Growth in the OECD, 1960–1985." *Journal of Theoretical Politics* 2: 173–204.

Chamley, Christophe P. 1981. "The Welfare Cost of Capital Income Taxation in a Growing Economy." *Journal of Political Economy* 89, 3 (June): 468–496.

Commander, Simon, Hamid R. Davoodi, and Une J. Lee. 1997. "The Causes of Government and the Consequences for Growth and Well-Being." World Bank Policy Research Working Paper 1785. World Bank (June).

Corneo, Giacomo and Hans Peter Grüner. 2000. "Social Limits to Redistribution." *American Economic Review* 90, 5 (December): 1491–1508.

  Forthcoming. "Individual Preferences for Political Redistribution." *Journal of Public Economics.*

Crafts, N. F. R. 1997. "Economic Growth in East Asia and Western Europe since 1950: Implications for Living Standards." *National Institute Economic Review* 162 (October): 75–84.

de Kwaasteniet, Marjanne. 1990. *Denomination and Primary Education in the Netherlands (1870–1984).* Amsterdam: Instituut voor Sociale Geografie, Universiteit van Amsterdam.

Diebolt, Claude. 1997. "L'évolution de longue période du système éducatif allemand xixe et xxe siécles." Paris: *économies et sociétés: Cahiers de l'ISMÉA, Série Histoire quantitative de l'économie française,* A.F. no. 23 (Février-Mars): 278–279, 338–341.

  2000. *Dépenses d'éducation et cycles économiques en espagne: XIXe et Xxe siécles.* Paris: L'Harmattan.

Drèze, Jean and Amartya Sen. 1995. *India: Economic Development and Social Opportunity.* New Delhi: Oxford University Press.

Easterlin, Richard A. 1981. "Why Isn't the Whole World Developed?" *Journal of Economic History* 41, 1 (March): 1–17

Easterly, William and Ross Levine. 1997. "Africa's Growth Tragedy: Policies and Ethnic Divisions." *Quarterly Journal of Economics* 112, 44 (November): 1203–1250.

Easterly, William and Sergio Rebelo. 1993. "Fiscal Policy and Economic Growth." *Journal of Monetary Economics* 32, 417–458.

Eloranta, Jari. 2002. "The Demand for External Security by Domestic Choices: Military Spending as an Impure Public Good among Eleven European States, 1920–1938." Doctoral thesis, European University Institute, June.

Engerman, Stanley L, Elisa Mariscal, and Kenneth L. Sokoloff. "Schooling, Suffrage, and the Persistence of Inequality in the Americas, 1800–1945." Manuscript, October 1998.

Esping-Andersen, Gøsta. 1990. *The Three Worlds of Welfare Capitalism.* Princeton: Princeton University Press.

Finland. 1912. *Statistisk Arsbok.* Helsinki.

Fishlow, Albert. 1966a. "The Common School Revival: Fact or Fancy?" In Henry Rosovsky (ed.), *Industrialization in Two Systems.* New York: Wiley.

  1966b. "Levels of Nineteenth-Century American Investment in Education." *Journal of Economic History* 26, 4 (December): pp. 418–436.

Flanagan, Robert J. 1988. "Unemployment as a Hiring Problem." *OECD Economic Studies* 11 (Autumn): 123–154.

——— 1999. "Macroeconomic Performance and Collective Bargaining: An International Perspective." *Journal of Economic Literature* 37, 3 (September): 1150–1175.

Flora, Peter and Arnold J. Heidenheimer (eds.). 1981. *The Development of Welfare States in Europe and America*. London: Transaction Books.

Flora, Peter, Jens Albert, Richard Eichenberg, Jürgen Kohl, Franz Kraus, Winifried Pfenning, and Kurt Seebohm. 1983. *State, Economy and Society in Western Europe, 1815–1975*. Frankfurt: Campus Verlag.

Fogel, Robert W. 1964. *Railroads and American Economic Growth: Essays in Econometric History*. Baltimore: Johns Hopkins University Press.

Fölster, S. and M. Henrekson. 1999. "Growth and the Public Sector: A Critique of the Critics." *European Journal of Political Economy* 15 (June): 3337–358.

France, Ministère du Commerce. Various years. *Annuaire Statistique de la France*. Paris.

Franklin, Mark N., Thomas T. Mackie, Henry Valen. 1992. *Electoral Change: Responses to Evolving Social and Attitudinal Structures in Western Countries*. Cambridge, UK: Cambridge University Press.

Freeman, Richard B. 1994. *Working under Different Rules*. New York: Russell Sage Foundation.

——— 1998. "Single-Peaked vs. Diversified Capitalism: The Relation between Economic Institutions and Outcomes." NBER Working Paper 7556.

Gallman, Robert E. 1966. "Gross National Product in the United States, 1834–1909." In William N. Parker (ed.), *Output, Employment, and Productivity in the United States after 1800*. New York; Columbia University Press, 3–90.

Gruber, Jonathan and David Wise (eds.). 1999. *Social Security Programs and Retirement around the World*. Chicago: University of Chicago Press.

Guinnane, Timothy. 1993. "The Poor Law and Pensions in Ireland." *Journal of Interdisciplinary History* 24, 2 (Autumn): 271–291.

Hansen, Svend Aage. 1977. *Økonomisk vækst I Danmark*, Bind II: 1914 [actually 1818]–1975. København: Akademisk Forlag.

Hansson, P. and M. Henrekson. 1994. "A New Framework for Testing the Effects of Government Spending on Growth and Productivity." *Public Choice* 81, 3–4 (December): 381–401.

Hicks, Alexander. 1999. *Social Democracy and Welfare Capitalism: A Century of Income Security Politics*. Ithaca: Cornell University Press.

Hicks, Alexander and Joya Misra. 1993. "Political Resources and the Growth of Welfare in Affluent Capitalist Democracies, 1960–1982," *American Journal of Sociology* 99, 3 (November): 668–710.

Hirschman, Albert O. 1970. *Exit, Voice, and Loyalty: Responses to Decline in Firms, Organizations, and States*. Cambridge, MA: Harvard University Press.

Hjerppe, Riitta. 1989. *The Finnish Economy 1860–1985*. Helsinki: Bank of Finland, Government Printing Center.

Huberman, Michael and Wayne Lewchuk. 2003. "European Economic Integration and the Social Compact, 1850–1913." *European Review of Economic History* 7, 1 (April): 3–42.

International Monetary Fund. Various years. *Government Financial Statistics Yearbook.* Washington, DC: IMF.

Italy, Ministero de Agricoltura, Industria e Commercio. 1881. *Annuario Statistico Italiano, Anno 1881.* Roma: Eredi Botta.

Jackman, Robert W. and Ross A. Miller. Forthcoming. *Culture, Institutions, and Political Behavior.* Ann Arbor: University of Michigan Press.

Judd, Kenneth L. 1987. "The Welfare Cost of Factor Taxation in a Perfect Foresight Model." *Journal of Political Economy* 95, 4 (August): 675–709.

Kearney, Robert N. 1987. "Sri Lanka." In Myron Weiner and Ergun Özbudun (eds.), *Competitive Elections in Developing Countries.* Durham: Duke University Press, 77–111.

Kmenta, Jan. 1986. *Elements of Econometrics.* Second edition. New York: Macmillan.

Korpi, Walter. 1985. "Economic Growth and the Welfare System: Leaky Bucket or Irrigation System?" *European Sociological Review* 1: 97–118.

Kramer, Mark. 1997. "Social Protection Policies and Safety Nets in East-Central Europe: Dilemmas of the Postcommunist Transformation." In Ethan B. Kapstein and Michael Mandelbaum (eds.), *Sustaining the Transition: The Social Safety Net in Postcommunist Europe.*" New York: Council on Foreign Relations, 46–123.

Krantz, Olle and Carl-Axel Nilsson. 1975. *Swedish National Product 1861–1970.* CWK Gleerup.

Kristov, Lorenzo, Peter Lindert, and Robert McClelland. 1992. "Pressure Groups and Redistribution," *Journal of Public Economics* 48, 2 (June): 135–163.

Kuo, Chun Chien. 1999. "The Determinants and Sustainability of Social Insurance Spending: A Cross-Country Examination." Doctoral dissertation in Economics, University of California–Davis.

Landau, Daniel L. 1985. "Government Expenditure and Economic Growth in the Developed Countries." *Public Choice* 47, 3: 459–478.

Layard, Richard, and Stephen J. Nickell. 1985. "The Causes of British Unemployment." *National Institute Economic Review* 111: 62–85.

Levasseur, E. 1897. *L'Enseignement primaire dans les pays civilisés.* Paris: Berger-Levrault.

Lilja, Reija, Tuire Santamaki-Vuori and Guy Standing. 1990. *Unemployment and Labour Market Flexibility: Finland.* Geneva: International Labour Office.

Lindert, P. H. 1978. *Fertility and Scarcity in America.* Princeton: Princeton University Press.

1994. "The Rise of Social Spending, 1880–1930." *Explorations in Economic History* 31, 1 (January): 1–36.

1996. "What Limits Social Spending?" *Explorations in Economic History* 31, 1 (January): 1–36.

1998. "Poor Relief before the Welfare State: Britain versus the Continent, 1780–1880." *European Review of Economic History* 2 (August): 101–140.

2001. "Democracy, Decentralization, and Mass Schooling before 1914." University of California, Agricultural History Center, Working Papers 104 (main text) and 105 (appendices), April.

2003. "Voice and Growth: Was Churchill Right?" *Journal of Economic History* 63, 2 (June): 315–350.

Lucas, Robert E., Jr. 2003. "Macroeconomic Priorities." *American Economic Review* 93, 1 (March): 1–14.

Lundgreen, Peter and A. P. Thirlwall. 1976. "Educational Expansion and Economic Growth in Nineteenth-Century Germany: A Quantitative Study." In Lawrence Stone (ed.), *Schooling and Society: Studies in the History of Education.* Baltimore: Johns Hopkins University Press, pp. 20–66.

Luttmer, Erzo F. P. 2001. "Group Loyalty and the Taste for Redistribution." *Journal of Political Economy* 109, 3 (June): 500–528.

MacFarlan, Maitland and Howard Oxley. 1996. "Social Transfers: Spending Patterns, Institutional Arrangements and Policy Responses." *OECD Economic Studies* 27, 2.

Mackie, Thomas T. and Richard Rose. 1991. *The International Almanac of Electoral History–Fully Revised Third Edition.* London: MacMillan.

1997. *A Decade of Election Results: Updating the International Almanac.* Glasgow: University of Strathclyde, Centre for the Study of Public Policy.

Maddison, Angus. 1995. *Monitoring the World Economy 1820–1992.* Paris: OECD.

2001. *The World Economy: A Millennial Perspective.* Paris: OECD.

Malo, Miguel and Luis Tohario. 1999. "Costes de despido y legislación labor en Europa: ¿Qué podemos aprender de las comparaciones internacionales?" *Cuadernos de información económica*, no. 150.

Martin, John P. 2000. "What Works among Active Labour Market Policies: Evidence from OECD Countries' Experiences." *OECD Economic Studies* 30, 1: 79–113.

McCallum, John and André Blais. 1987. "Government, Special Interest Groups, and Economic Growth." *Public Choice* 54, 1: 3–18.

McCloskey, Dierdre N. and Stephen T. Ziliak. 1996. "The Standard Error of Regressions." *Journal of Economic Literature* 34, 1 (March): 97–114.

McGuire, Martin C. and Mancur Olson, Jr. 1996. "The Economics of Autocracy and Majority Rule: The Invisible Hand and the Use of Force." *Journal of Economic Literature* 34, 1 (March): 72–96.

Mehrotra, Santosh and Enrique Delamonica. Submitted for publication. *Public Spending for the Poor. Basic Services to Enhance Capabilities and Promote Growth.*

Mehrotra, Santosh, P. R. Panchamukhi, Ranjana Srivastava, and Ravi Srivastava. Submitted for publication. *Uncaging the Tiger Economy: Financing Elementary Education in India.*

Meltzer, Allan H. and Richard, Scott F, 1981. "A Rational Theory of the Size of Government," *Journal of Political Economy* 89, 5 (October): 914–27.

Mendoza, Enrique G., Gian Maria Milesi-Ferretti, and Patrick Asca. 1997. "On the Ineffectiveness of Tax Policy in Altering Long-Run Growth: Harberger's Superneutrality Conjecture." *Journal of Public Economics* 66, 1 (October 1997): 99–126.

Mitchell, Brian R. (ed.) 1975. *European Historical Statistics, 1750–1970.* Cambridge: Cambridge University Press.

1988. *British Historical Statistics*. Cambridge: Cambridge University Press.

1990. *International Historical Statistics: The Americas, 1750–1988*. Cambridge: Cambridge University Press.

1992. *International Historical Statistics: Europe 1750–1988*. 3rd edition. Stockton Press.

1995. *International Historical Statistics: Africa, Asia & Oceania, 1750–1988*. Cambridge: Cambridge University Press.

1998a. *International Historical Statistics: Africa, Asia & Oceania, 1750–1993*. Cambridge: Cambridge University Press.

1998b. *International Historical Statistics: Europe 1750–1993*. Cambridge: Cambridge University Press.

1998c. *International Historical Statistics: The Americas 1750–1993*. Cambridge: Cambridge University Press.

Mitch, David F. 1992. *The Rise of Popular Literacy in Victorian England: The Influence of Private Choice and Public Policy*. Philadelphia: University of Pennsylvania Press.

Mitchell, Brian R., and Phyllis Deane (eds.). 1962. *Abstract of British Historical Statistics*. Cambridge University Press.

Netherlands. *Jaarcijfers*. Various years to 1914.

Nickell, Stephen J. 1997. "Unemployment and Labor Market Rigidities: Europe versus North America." *Journal of Economic Perspectives* 11, 3 (summer): 55–74.

Nicoletti, G., S. Scarpetta, and O. Boyland. 2000. "Summary Indicators of Product Market Regulation with an Extension to Employee Protection Legislation." OECD Economics Department Working Paper 226.

Niskanen, William A. 1997. "Autocratic, Democratic, and Optimal Government." *Economic Inquiry* 35, 3 (July): 464–479.

Nordhaus, William and James Tobin. 1972. "Is Growth Obsolete?" In F. Thomas Juster (ed. for the National Bureau of Economic Research), *Economic Growth: Fiftieth Anniversary Colloquium V.* New York: Columbia University Press for the NBER. Issued as a separate paperback volume.

Norway, Central Bureau of Statistics (Statistisk Sentralbyrån). Various years. *Statistik Aarborg*. Olso.

Nurullah, Syed, and J. P. Naik. 1964. *A Students' History of Education in India (1800–1965)*. Calcutta: Macmillan.

Olson, Mancur. 1965. *The Logic of Collective Action*. Cambridge, MA: Harvard University Press.

2000. *Power and Prosperity: Outgrowing Communist and Capitalist Dictatorships*. New York: Basic Books.

Ordeshook, Peter C. 1986. *Game Theory and Political theory: An Introduction*. New York: Cambridge University Press.

Organisation for Economic Cooperation and Development (OECD). 1985. *Social Expenditure 1960–1990*. Paris: OECD.

1992. *Education at a Glance 1992*. Paris: OECD.

1994. *The OECD Jobs Study: Evidence and Explanations*. Two volumes. Paris: OECD.

1999. *Employment Outlook 1999*. Paris: OECD.

1999. *Social Expenditure Database, 1980–1996.* Paris, OECD.

2001. *Education at a Glance 2001.* Paris: OECD.

Padovano, Fabio and Emma Galli. 2001. "Tax Rates and Economic Growth in the OECD Countries (1950–1990)," *Economic Inquiry* 39, 1 (January): 44–57.

Pampel, Fred C. and John B. Williamson. 1989. *Age, Class, Politics and the Welfare State.* Cambridge: Cambridge University Press.

Peltzman, Sam. 1980. "The Growth of Government." *Journal of Law and Economics* 23, 2 (October): 209–288.

Persson, Torsten, Gérard Roland, and Guido Tabellini. 2000. "Comparative Politics and Public Finance." *Journal of Political Economy* 108, 6 (December): 1121–1161.

Persson, Torsten and Guido Tabellini. 1994. "Is Inequality Harmful for Growth?" *American Economic Review* 84, 3 (June): 600–621.

2000. *Political Economics: Explaining Economic Policy.* Cambridge, MA: MIT Press.

Pirard, Joseph. 1985. *Le pouvoir central Belge et ses comptes economiques 1830–1913.* Brussels: Palais des Académies.

Prados de Escosura, Leandro. 1995. "Spain's Gross Domestic Product, 1850–1913: Quantitative Conjectures." Universidad Carlos III de Madrid, Working Paper 95–06.

Prescott, Edward C. 2002. "Richard T. Ely Lecture: Prosperity and Depression." *American Economic Review* 92, 2 (May): 1–15.

PROBE Team. 1999. *Public Report on Basic Education in India.* New Delhi: Oxford University Press.

Psacharapoulos, George and Maureen Woodhall. 1990. *Education for Development: An Analysis of 'Investment' Choices.* Oxford: Oxford University Press.

Ramsey, Frank P. 1927. "A Contribution to the Theory of Taxation." *Economic Journal* 37, 47–61.

Rodrik, Dani. 1997. *Has Globalization Gone too Far?* Washington, DC: Institute for International Economics.

1998. "Why Do More Open Economies Have Bigger Governments?" *Journal of Political Economy* 106, 5 (October): 997–1032.

Rust, Val D. 1989. *The Democratic Tradition and the Evolution of Schooling in Norway.* Westport: Greenwood Press.

Sala-i-Martin, Xavier. 1997. "I Just Ran Two Million Regressions." *American Economic Review* 87, 2 (May): 178–183.

Scarpetta, Stefano. 1996. "Assessing the Role of Labour Market Policies and Institutional Settings on Unemployment: A Cross-Country Study." *OECD Economic Studies* 26, 1: 43–98.

Schmitter, Philippe C. 1981. "Interest Intermediation and Regime Governability in Contemporary Western Europe and North America." In Suzanne Berger (ed.), *Organizing Interests in Western Europe.* Cambridge: Cambridge University Press, 285–327.

Schremmer, D. E. 1989. "Taxation and Public Finance: Britain, France, and Germany." In Peter Mathias and S. Pollard (eds.), *Cambridge Economic History of Europe,* Vol. VIII. Cambridge: Cambridge University Press, 315–349.

Schultz, Theodore W. 1960. "Capital Formation by Education." *Journal of Political Economy* 68, 6 (December): 571–583.

Siebert, Horst. 1997. "Labor Market Rigidities: At the Root of Unemployment in Europe." *Journal of Economic Perspectives* 11, 3 (summer): 37–54.

Slemrod, Joel. 1995. "What Do Cross-Country Studies Teach about Government Involvement, Prosperity, and Economic Growth?" *Brookings Papers in Economic Activity* 2, 373–431.

Smits, J. P., E. Horlings, and J. L. van Zanden. 1997. *The Measurement of Gross National Product and Its Components: The Netherlands, 1800–1913.* N. W. Posthumus Instituut, Utrecht University, Research Memorandum no. 1. February.

Sneessens, Henri R. and Jacques Drèze. 1986. "A Discussion of Belgian Unemployment, Combining Traditional Concepts and Disequilibrium Econometrics." *Economica Supplement,* 53 (210(S)): S89–S119.

Solmon, Lewis. 1975. *Capital Formation by Expenditures on Formal Education 1880 and 1890.* New York: Arno Press.

Subbarao, K., Aniruddha Bonnerjee, Jeanine Braithwaite, Soniya Carvalho, Kene Ezemenari, Carol Graham, and Alan Thompson. 1997. *Safety Net Programs and Poverty Reduction: Lessons from Cross-Country Experience.* Washington, DC: World Bank.

Summers, Lawrence H. 1981. "Capital Taxation and Accumulation in a Life Cycle Growth Model." *American Economic Review* 71, 4 (September): 533–544.

Summers, Robert, and Alan Heston. 1988. "A New Set of International Comparisons of Real Product and Price Levels: Estimates for 130 Countries, 1950–1985." *Review of Income and Wealth* 34, 1 (March): 1–25 and accompanying floppy disks.

Sutherland, Gillian. 1973. *Policy-Making in Elementary Education 1870–1895.* Oxford: Oxford University Press.

Sweden. Various years. *Statistisk Arsbok* and *Statistisk Tidskrift.*

Tan, Jee-Peng and Alain Mingat. 1992. *Education in Asia: A Comparative Study of Cost and Financing.* Washington, DC: The World Bank.

Taylor, Charles Lewis and Michael C. Hudson. 1972. *World Handbook of Political and Social Indicators,* 2nd edition. New Haven: Yale University Press.

Teixeira, Ruy A. 1987. *Why Americans Don't Vote: Turnout Decline in the United States,* New York: Greenwood Press.

Toutain, Jean-Claude. 1987. *Le produit intérieur brut de la France de 1789 a 1982. Economies et Sociétés.* Cahiers de l'I.S.M.E.A., Série Histoire quantitative de l'Économie française, no. 15.

Union of Soviet Socialist Republics, State Geological Committee. 1964. *Atlas Narodov Mira* [Atlas of the Peoples of the World] (Moscow: The N.N. Miklukho-Maklaya Institute).

United Nations, Department of Economic and Social Affairs. 1956. *The Aging of Populations and Its Economic and Social Implications.* New York: UN.

    1998. *World Population Prospects: The 1996 Revision.* New York: UN.

United Nations Educational, Scientific, and Cultural Organization (UNESCO). 1991–1998. *World Education Report.* New York: UNESCO.

United States Census Bureau. 1976. *Historical Statistics of the United States from Colonial Times to 1970.* Two volumes. Washington, DC: GPO.

2001. *Statistical Abstract of the United States: 2001.* Washington, DC: GPO.

United States, Commissioner of Education. 1873–1903. *Reports.* Washington, DC: GPO.

Urquhart, M. C. 1993. *Gross National Product, Canada, 1870–1926: The Derivation of the Estimates.* Kingston: McGill-Queen's University Press.

van der Voort, R. H. 1994. *Overheidsbeleid en overheidsfinanciën in Nederland 1850–1913.* Amsterdam: NEHA.

Weede, Erich. 1991. "The Impact of State Power on Economic Growth Rates in OECD Countries." *Quality and Quantity* 25, 4 (November): 421–438.

Weiner, Myron. 1987. "India." In Myron Weiner and Ergun Özbudun (eds.), *Competitive Elections in Developing Countries.* Durham: Duke University Press, 37–76.

West, E. G. 1975. "Educational Slowdown and Public Intervention in 19th-Century England: A Study in the Economics of Bureaucracy." *Explorations in Economic History* 12, 1 (January): 61–87.

Wilensky, Harold. 1975. *The Welfare State and Equality.* Berkeley: University of California Press.

2002. *Rich Democracies: Political Economy, Public Policy, and Performance.* Berkeley: University of California Press.

Wolfinger, Raymond E. and Steven J. Rosenstone. 1980. *Who Votes?* New Haven: Yale University Press.

World Bank. 1994. *Averting the Old Age Crisis.* New York: Oxford University Press.

1997. *Primary Education in India.* Washington, DC: World Bank.

2000. *India: Reducing Poverty, Accelerating Development.* New Delhi, Oxford University Press.

Zastoupil, Lynn, and Martin Moir. 1999. *The Great Indian Education Debate: Documents Relating to the Orientalist-Anglicist Controversy, 1781–1843.* Richmond, Surrey: Curzon.

Index